Quarter Notes and Bank Notes

The Princeton Economic History of the Western World

Joel Mokyr, *Editor*

Growth in a Traditional Society: The French Countryside, 1450–1815, by Philip T. Hoffman

The Vanishing Irish: Households, Migration, and the Rural Economy in Ireland, 1850–1914, by Timothy W. Guinnane

Black '47 and Beyond: The Great Irish Famine in History, Economy, and Memory, by Cormac Ó Gráda

The Great Divergence: China, Europe, and the Making of the Modern World Economy, by Kenneth Pomeranz

The Big Problem of Small Change, by Thomas J. Sargent and Francois R. Velde

Farm to Factory: A Reinterpretation of the Soviet Industrial Revolution, by Robert C. Allen

Quarter Notes and Bank Notes: The Economics of Music Composition in the Eighteenth and Nineteenth Centuries, by F. M. Scherer

Quarter Notes and Bank Notes

THE ECONOMICS OF MUSIC COMPOSITION

IN THE EIGHTEENTH

AND NINETEENTH CENTURIES

F. M. Scherer

PRINCETON UNIVERSITY PRESS

PRINCETON AND OXFORD

Library of Congress Cataloging-in-Publication Data

Scherer, F. M. (Frederic M.)
Quarter notes and bank notes : the economics of music composition in the eighteenth and
nineteenth centuries / F.M. Scherer.
p. cm. — (The Princeton economic history of the Western world)
Includes bibliographical references (p.) and index.
ISBN 0-691-11621-0
1. Composers — Economic conditions — 18th century.   2. Composers — Economic
conditions — 19th century.   I. Title.   II. Series.
ML3795.S23835 2004
331.7′617813′09033 — dc21   2003053645

British Library Cataloging-in-Publication Data is available

This book has been composed in Postscript Sabon

Printed on acid-free paper. ∞

www.pupress.princeton.edu

Printed in the United States of America

1   3   5   7   9   10   8   6   4   2

CONTENTS

List of Figures and Tables   vii

Foreword   ix

CHAPTER ONE
Introduction   1

CHAPTER TWO
The Political, Social, and Economic Milieu   14

CHAPTER THREE
Music Composition as a Profession   53

CHAPTER FOUR
Composers' Backgrounds, Aspirations, and
Economic Rewards   79

CHAPTER FIVE
The Geography of Composer Supply and Demand   117

CHAPTER SIX
Changes in Transportation and Composers' Mobility   142

CHAPTER SEVEN
The Economics of Music Publishing   155

CHAPTER EIGHT
Conclusion   197

APPENDIX TO CHAPTER ONE
A Currency Conversion Matrix   203

APPENDIX TO CHAPTER FOUR
Consumption Outlays of Robert and
Clara Schumann, 1841   210

Notes   215

References   249

Index   259

FIGURES AND TABLES

FIGURES

1.1	Recorded Music for the 646 Composers by Birth Year	9
2.1	Trends in Population: Seven European National Groups	28
2.2	Trends in Income per Capita: Six European Nations, 1820–1900	29
2.3	Production of New Pianos in the United States, 1850–1939	35
3.1	Percentage of Composer Cohorts with Support from Nobility	69
3.2	Percentage of Composer Cohorts Employed by the Church	70
3.3	Composers Engaging in Significant Freelance Activity	71
3.4	Number of Composers with Fewer Than Two Operas Pursuing Significant Freelance Activity	73
3.5	Number of Composers with Minimal Church or Court Employment Pursuing Significant Freelance Activity	74
3.6	Percent of Composers in Birth Cohort with Other Means of Support	76
4.1	Percent of Half-Century Cohorts with Selected Career Preparation Modes	83
5.1	Number of Composers Born in Nations and National Groups, 1650–1849	120
5.2	Number of Composers Born per Million Population	122
5.3	Composer Births per Million Population, by 50-Year Birth-Date Period	124
5.4	Number of Composers Employed by Nation and National Groups	125
5.5	Number of FTE Composers Employed per Million Population	126
5.6	Employment of Composers, by 50-Year Birth Date Period	127
5.7	Balance of Trade in Composers by Nation	133
5.8	Birth Locations of German Composers	137
5.9	Work Locations of German Composers	138
6.1	Growth of Rail Networks in Major European Nations	146
6.2	Percent of Composers Born in One Nation Who Died in Another	148

6.3   Numbers Equivalents for Nations in Which Composers
      Lived from Age 20   149
7.1   Cost-Volume Relationships for Engraved and Typeset
      Sheet Music   162
7.2   Distribution of Breitkopf & Härtel Inventory by Music
      Type, 1823   190
7.3   Publication Honoraria for Robert Schumann's
      Musical Works   192
1A.1 Estimated Annual Wages of English Building Tradesmen   209

TABLES

1.1   Composers Included in the Select Sample, by Year of Birth   11
2.1   Chronology of Significant Political, Philosophical, and
      Cultural Events over Two and One-Half Centuries   15
2.2   1700, 1820, and 1900 GDP per Capita and Growth Rates   30
4.1   Value of 23 Composers' Estates at or Near Time of Death   105
5.1   Europe's Largest Cities, Ranked by 1750 Population   128
1A.1 Units of Currency Exchanging for One English
      Pound Sterling   206
4A.1 Schumann Family Expenditures in 1841   211

FOREWORD

THAT a professional economist should write a book such as this requires some explanation.

The seeds began growing more than half a century ago. For someone raised in a small, culturally isolated, midwestern town, undergraduate life at the University of Michigan was magically transforming. I began learning about classical music in the music literature course taught by Professor Glenn McGeoch. In it, only in part because I lacked perfect pitch, I received the worst grade of my undergraduate career, but acquired something much more important—appreciation and love of an art that has been a continuing source of joy. In my freshman English course, one of the books we read was Aldous Huxley's *Point Counterpoint*. I was fascinated to see that the interaction of human lives could be likened to the interplay of voices in a Bach fugue (a point made also in an 1865 letter from Richard Wagner to Cosima Liszt von Bülow). I began buying Bach recordings, and from then on, I was hooked.

Reinforcing my love for music was the other love of my life, my wife. When I first met her on Christmas Eve in 1955, one of my first reactions was, "How beautifully she plays Mozart. She must be the person I have been looking for." That her ancestors two centuries earlier included Gottfried Silbermann, who built organs and pianos played by J. S. Bach, added interest. She discovered only relatively late in life that she could be a gifted piano teacher, but we shared innumerable happy musical experiences as her career evolved. It helped that among the many places we have lived, all were first-rank "music towns."

The seeds for this book were planted more firmly sometime during the late 1970s, when we acquired Wolfgang Hildesheimer's book *Mozart*. They took root around 1980, when we visited Mozart's birth house in Salzburg and were able to observe first-hand the musical manuscripts into whose margins Mozart had written numbers recording his mounting debts. Why did Mozart, arguably the most naturally talented composer who ever lived, die in debt? Was he really, as Hildesheimer argued, a pioneer in seeking his fortune as a freelance composer? And was his choice of market-oriented activity premature, so that economic failure was virtually inevitable? Answering these questions was a job for an economist, and perhaps for one like myself with a repressed urge to pursue economic history. From that time, I knew I had to write this book. But a stream of other challenges kept me from working seriously on the project until my retirement in 2000 from Harvard University's Kennedy School.

Despite years of neglect, the project's foundation was laid in the summer of 1982 or 1983, when I drew up a list of questions that interested me as an economist and asked my high-school-age daughter Christina to see whether relevant materials could be found in the music library of Swarthmore College. The treasure trove she assembled made it clear that the project would be feasible.

Following that crucial contribution, many additional debts have been incurred. Much of my research has been done in five music libraries, at Swarthmore, Harvard, Princeton, the University of Bayreuth, and the University of Pennsylvania. I am grateful to the staffs of all five, but especially to George Huber of Swarthmore, for their help in finding elusive documents. Leads to key works were also provided by William Cornish of the University of Cambridge, Ruth Towse of Erasmus University, Rotterdam, and Stefano Fenoaltea of the Università di Cassino. Valuable criticism was received from seminar participants at the Technische Universität Freiberg, the University of Bayreuth, Haus Wahnfried in Bayreuth, Harvard University, Princeton University, and Swarthmore College. The help of Joel Mokyr at several stages in the project has been invaluable. Useful comments were also received from William J. Baumol and Michael Aronson. Excellent copyediting by Genevieve Vaughn saved me from numerous errors and tightened my prose. From Dr. Stephen J. Savage of Mount Sinai Hospital, New York, and nurses Shannon Lawrence and Maxine Prescott, I received the gift of life at a time when it appeared that I would be unable to complete the project.

My debt is greatest to my wife for her inspiration, encouragement, criticism, and the use of her excellent musicology library. The book is dedicated to her.

Responsibility for errors is, of course, mine. For someone plunging into such a complex new field, the burden is heavy by more than the usual amount.

F. M. Scherer
November 2002

Quarter Notes and Bank Notes

Chapter 1

INTRODUCTION

Hat man nicht auch Gold beineben
Kann man nicht ganz glücklich sein.
Traurig schleppt sich fort das Leben,
Mancher Kummer stellt sich ein.
Doch wenn's in den Taschen fein klingelt und rollt,
Da hält man das Schicksal gefangen;
Und Macht, und Liebe, verschafft dir das Gold,
Und stillet das kühnste Verlangen.
Das Glück dient wie ein Knecht für Sold,
Es ist ein schönes, schönes Ding, das Gold!

If you don't have gold at hand
You can't be completely happy.
Life drags on sadly,
Many troubles intrude.
But when it jingles and rolls in your pocket,
The fates are at your command.
Gold brings you power and love
And satisfies the boldest desires.
Fortune serves you like a hired lackey.
Gold, it is a beautiful, beautiful thing!
— Beethoven, *Fidelio*

FEW would disagree with this admonition of Rocco the jailer to his new apprentice Fidelio. Beethoven considered the message sufficiently important that, after having removed Rocco's "Gold" aria from some performances of *Fidelio*, he restored it (with minor textual changes accepted here) in the 1814 version, where it remains for all eternity.[1] Even composers need money to be "completely happy"—or at least, some approximation thereto. The more difficult question is, how did composers, great and not so great, obtain their gold? And there scholars are not of one mind concerning the historical facts.

It is reasonably well accepted that at the outset of the eighteenth century, most musicians creative enough to be composers were employed either by the nobility or by the church. It seems clear too that by the middle of the nineteenth century, the situation had changed. The role of the church and especially the noble courts as employers had diminished appreciably, replaced by opportunities for composers to work as free-lance artists performing, teaching, and selling their creations through private market transactions. The change, it will be argued in this book, occurred largely because of economic and political developments that simultaneously strengthened the demand of middle-class citizens for music in all forms and weakened the feudal foundations of European noble courts and religious establishments.

Where consensus among scholars fades is on how and when com-posers made the transition from a court- and church-oriented system to a market-oriented system. Some, such as Wolfgang Hildesheimer, see Mozart as the first "free" composer in a sociological sense, who had to endure material poverty as a consequence of his freedom.[2] The sociolo-gist Norbert Elias argues that:[3]

> Mozart's decision to set himself up as a freelance artist came at a time when the social structure actually offered no such place for outstanding musicians. The emergence of a music market and the corresponding insti-tutions was only just beginning.

William J. Baumol and Hilda Baumol place Mozart within a broader trend, characterizing the second half of the eighteenth century as a time of transition "from the universal system of private patronage to the beginnings of a market mechanism under which the product of the com-poser and the performer became a commodity that could be bought and sold."[4] Howard Gardner similarly sees Mozart as "an important transi-tional figure in laying a foundation of independence and self-initiated creation."[5] Hansjörg Pohlmann, the leading student of intellectual prop-erty rights in music, views the trend toward freelance composition in a still broader time frame spanning the entire eighteenth century. In his schema Mozart occupies an intermediate role:[6]

> Composers' struggle for independent freelance status and their attempt to escape positions of dependence under employment relationships—an at-tempt that led to Mozart's tragic failure—found in Beethoven its first cli-max. Beethoven is thus the culmination of a long developmental process.

Consistent with Pohlmann's vision, a central argument of this book is that a transition from patronage-oriented to market-oriented freelance composition did occur, but that it was much more gradual and evolu-tionary than the focus on Mozart as a turning point implies. Antecedents can be found a century before the death of Mozart. And nearly a century after his death, remnants of the old system survived.

Some Examples

The complexity of the evolution is suggested by comparing thumbnail biographies of three important composers, all born in the year 1685 — Johann Sebastian Bach, Domenico Scarlatti, and George Frideric Handel — with three born a century and a quarter later — Frédéric Chopin, Robert Schumann, and Franz Liszt.

Bach provides the archetype of how composers earned their living in the early eighteenth century.[7] His entire adult life was spent as an employee — first as organist at churches in Arnstadt and Mühlhausen, then as organist and director of court music for the Duke of Weimar and prince of Köthen, and finally as cantor and director of music for the Thomasschule (School of St. Thomas) and four affiliated Leipzig churches. Like many employed composers of his time, he moonlighted in activities outside his main sphere of employment, dedicating compositions to hoped-for patrons, publishing (at his own expense) a few of his works, holding private lessons, inspecting new organs installed in other towns, and most importantly, between 1729 and 1741, directing an unofficial Leipzig orchestra, the Collegium Musicum, which charged admission for the concerts it regularly held in Zimmermann's coffee house during the winter and a coffee garden during the summer. Bach's Collegium Musicum association became important enough to lead Christoph Wolff (1991, p. 40) to conclude that "Toward the end of his life Bach came astonishingly close to the romantic ideal of the free-lance artist." But his compositions for and direction of the Collegium remained secondary to his salaried church and school duties.

What is known about Domenico Scarlatti's career shows fewer traces of freelance activity. He began as a composer of religious works and operas in the court of the King of Naples. After brief visits at other Italian courts, he spent four years in the free city of Venice. Virtually no historical record exists on that period. It would not be unreasonable to suppose that he engaged in freelance composition for one or more of the Venetian opera houses or for wealthy citizens, since there were no noble courts. His success in Venice must have been limited, however, since in 1709 he moved to Rome, where for a decade he was musician in the houses of local and visiting nobles and then presided over musical activities for a chapel associated with St. Peter's basilica. Around 1719 he migrated to Lisbon, becoming teacher and music master in the court of the King and Queen of Portugal, following them to Madrid in 1728 when marriage united the ruling families of Spain and Portugal. He remained a musician in the Madrid court throughout the remainder of his life.

George Frideric Handel learned the art of opera composing first in the free city of Hamburg, where the local opera was a private enterprise, and then in Rome, where he shared the hospitality of Cardinal Pietro Ottoboni with Domenico Scarlatti, Arcangelo Corelli, and other composers. Returning to Germany, he accepted a position as director of court music for the Elector of Hanover, but took a leave of absence to visit London and remained there, followed by his would-be Hanover patron, newly crowned as King George I of England. After residing for a while in the home of Richard, Earl of Burlington, Handel became musical director of a London opera company, The Royal Academy, which was a free-standing organization financed by wealthy Londoners who delegated operating responsibilities to an impresario. Handel worked first as salaried director of the opera company; then, when the original financial backers withdrew their support, as co-impresario; and finally as principal impresario for the public performance of his own works. In his impresario role, he lurched precariously between riches and ruin. His survival in lean years was facilitated by a generous annuity of £600 per year from the king's family. Thus, during much of his career, Handel was not only a freelance composer but also a risk-taking entrepreneur.[8] His early eighteenth century freelance activities, however, were supplemented by subsidies from the royal court.

We advance now in time to the years 1810 and 1811, when three representative nineteenth-century composers were born.

Frédéric Chopin was a freelance artist throughout his career. After being provided an excellent musical education by his upper middle-class Warsaw family, he presented a series of freelance concert performances in Berlin, Dresden, Prague, Vienna, Munich, and Stuttgart between 1828 and 1831. Continuing on to Paris, he achieved only limited financial success performing his compositions at public concerts. But his introduction by a Warsaw acquaintance into the salons of wealthy Parisians provided a network of contacts, through which he became the most sought-after and best-paid independent piano teacher in Paris. His earnings were augmented through honoraria from music publishers. When his health deteriorated, he could no longer continue his strenuous teaching schedule. A concert trip to England failed to solve his financial problems, and he died in poverty at age thirty-nine.

After completing his university studies, Robert Schumann settled in Leipzig, where in 1833 he founded a journal reporting on contemporary music developments and was supported at first through the income from an inheritance. After his marriage to Clara Wieck, his receipts from the journal, the inheritance, and publication fees proved to be insufficient to support a rapidly growing family. (See the Appendix to Chapter 4.) They were supplemented through Clara Schumann's freelance piano performance tours throughout Europe. An appointment to the newly founded Leipzig Conservatory faculty proved to be unsuccessful and short-lived. In 1850, at the age of forty, he assumed his first salaried position, as music director of a mostly amateur orchestra and choral society in Düsseldorf. Supervision of the sponsoring Musikverein (musical society) was exercised by representatives appointed by the city council. Schumann's relationship with orchestra musicians and the governing body was conflict-ridden. In 1852 his duties and salary were reduced, and in 1853 he was required to resign. Soon thereafter he lapsed into insanity and died in an asylum in 1856.

Following music studies in Vienna and Paris, Franz Liszt had four distinguishable careers that epitomized the experiences of composers living during both the eighteenth and nineteenth centuries. His first career was as a touring freelance piano performer. Initially his success was modest, but after he learned the art of spectacular performance by observing Niccolò Paganini, he became Europe's best-drawing concert pianist, performing both his own compositions and those of others (often transcribed) and amassing a substantial fortune. Then, in 1847, he ended his freelance touring and became director of music in the ducal court at Weimar, Germany—a position analogous to those held by the prototypal eighteenth-century composer. In 1858 he resigned his Weimar job and prepared for holy orders, becoming an abbé but not a priest, in Rome, which was his principal residence between 1861 and 1869. His desire to become music director at St. Peter's went unfulfilled. In 1869 he returned to a free residence provided by the Duke of Weimar without any official direction or performance obligations. From that time until his death in 1886, he traveled extensively, with principal bases in Weimar, Rome, and Budapest, teaching hundreds of students gratis and offering numerous public concerts, the proceeds of which were largely donated to charitable causes.

What we see from these six vignettes is a transition from court and church patronage to freelance activity, but the change was gradual, with elements of market-oriented efforts appearing early in the evolution and elements of the patronage and church systems remaining well into the nineteenth century. J. S. Bach and especially Handel exhibited early manifestations of market-oriented activity; Liszt reverted after success in the free market to noble and church support.

NUMBERS AND CREATIVE OUTPUT

Thus, the question, properly framed, is not whether composers earned their bread through patronage as compared to the polar alternative of

freelance activities, but the number of composers under one system vis-
à-vis the other, or even more precisely, the extent to which composers
divided their professional lives between the patronage and freelance
alternatives.

Numbers matter. Some authors have suggested that the patronage
system, at least as it existed in Germany, Austria, and Italy during the
eighteenth century, provided an environment uniquely conducive to
making music as a profession, and as a result, music composition experienced a kind of golden age.[9] The essence of their argument is that the
breakup of the Holy Roman Empire left central Europe divided into
hundreds of individual principalities and dukedoms, many of which, for
reasons to be elaborated in the next chapter and chapter 5, chose to
support musical ensembles and hence provide employment for musicians and would-be composers. Given widespread employment opportunities, more individuals became professional musicians than would
otherwise have been the case. And with more individuals employed as
musicians, more turned to composition as part of their responsibilities,
which in turn, it is argued, implies that more composers of superior
creative talent would emerge.

This book is written by an economist who recognizes that economic
analysis cannot predict the appearance of genius. True genius is an extremely rare phenomenon. Even if everything else could be held constant (the economist's standard *ceteris paribus* assumption), which can
hardly be assured, an increase in the number of individuals pursuing
musical composition as a profession implies at best in a very weak statistical sense that one or a few will be outstanding geniuses. A composer
as great as Mozart might emerge next year, or, as Joseph Haydn speculated on learning of Mozart's death a year before Beethoven moved
permanently to Vienna, "Posterity will not see such a talent again in
100 years!"[10]

Economic analysis can illuminate matters in another way. Economic
incentives affect the specific challenges to which individuals, creative or
not, allocate their time. A noble court might provide an ideal environment for the flourishing of creative talent. But the seignior might also
have strong preferences as to what kind of music he prefers and insist
that his hired composer hew to that line, suppressing compositions that
stray from the preferred norm. Alternatively, the free market might provide maximum opportunity for the composer to pursue his most creative instincts,[11] or it might reward disproportionately the composition
of unimaginative fluff appealing to some lowest common denominator.
A priori, it is not possible to say which of these plausible alternative
hypotheses comes closer to the truth. The question is an empirical one.
We cannot pretend to answer it definitively, but we will address the
evidence systematically and advance some new insights.

METHODOLOGY

To repeat, this book comes from an economist, not a musicologist. The methodological approach taken here is unorthodox by the standards of musicology and even to some extent by the standards of economics, as one might expect from a scholar who strays onto forbidden disciplinary turf.

One important difference is the systematic analysis of quantitative data. Although other qualitative and quantitative materials will be tapped as we proceed, the most unique new evidence comes from a sample of 646 composers born during the two centuries from 1650 to 1849 — that is, a period during which the transition from court and church employment to freelance activity is believed to have occurred.[12] The starting point for the sample was the "Composers" section of the *Schwann Opus* reference guide to recorded classical music (Fall 1996). An attempt was made to identify every composer with extant recorded music born during that time span. The criterion implied by this selection approach was survival in the ears and minds of posterity. Meeting this survival test was a matter of some concern to Leopold Mozart, who advised in a 1778 letter to his son:[13]

> Only your good sense and lifestyle will determine whether you will be a common musical artist forgotten by the entire world, or a famous Kapellmeister about whom posterity will read in books.

Or as Giuseppe Verdi wrote to a friend a century later, "History will tell us which epoch was good, and which bad."[14]

Altogether, 742 composers were identified in this way. Biographical information on each was sought in the *New Grove Dictionary of Music & Musicians* (Sadie, 1980). For 76 composers no entry was found in the *New Grove*. Compared to record listings in *Schwann Opus* averaging 25 centimeters (10 inches) in length for composers on whom information was found in the *New Grove* (with a *Schwann* range of from 1.8 to 1656 centimeters), only 4 of the 76 no-entry composers had record listings exceeding 3 centimeters. For 20 other composers listed in *Schwann*, the biographical information in the *New Grove* was too sparse to support coding of career patterns and locations. Excluding these 96 composers left a usable sample of 646. The sample is incomplete, omitting the explicitly excluded composers and also any others who failed to have recorded music memorialized by the *Schwann Opus*.[15] Among 91 composers of Italian operas born between 1650 and 1849 on whom information was tabulated by Elvidio Surian,[16] only 42 made it into the sample. Not surprisingly, the composers omitted from Surian's list wrote operas that are seldom, if ever, performed in modern times.

All of the 44 composers born in the 1650–1849 time span whose operas are reviewed in the *New Grove Book of Operas* (Sadie, 1996) were included in the sample. All but 17 of the sampled composers were born in Europe; the exceptions were born in North or South America. Fourteen of the 646 composers were female, motivating the use of "he" or "his" when a gender-dependent pronoun or adjective must be used without further information.

Among the data collected were birth and death years. From them, each composer's life span could be computed. The average age at death was 64.5, the median age 66. The oldest composer in the sample, Giacobbe Cervetto (1682–1783), died in London at the probable age of 101 (his exact birth date is uncertain). The youngest, Juan Arriaga (1806–1826), a student at the Paris Conservatoire, died a few days before reaching the age of 20. Nine composers lived for 90 years or more. There are two explanations for the remarkable longevity of our sample members, so contrary to accepted notions of high mortality in those days of bloodletting and other barbaric medical practices. First, a major reason for low life expectancies in the eighteenth and nineteenth centuries was high infant mortality. Those who lived long enough to become a composer of note had passed through some of the most perilous years and probably (as Mozart did with smallpox) developed resistance to many potentially lethal diseases. Second, there may be a selection bias in our sample. Composers who lived relatively long had more time to get their affairs in order and ensure that their musical manuscripts were preserved for posterity.

To estimate the relative creative output or "productivity" of sample members, the length in centimeters of the recorded music listings in the *Schwann Opus* catalogue was measured. This variable is analogous to the citations indexes widely used to measure the productivity of scholars and the value of invention patents.[17] The more music of enduring quality a composer wrote, the more items were likely to survive in recorded form, and hence the longer the *Schwann* listing. The better any given work was, the more likely it was to be recorded by multiple artists and groups, and so again, the longer the *Schwann* listing. To rub an old wound by way of illustration, there were 32 different full recordings of Mozart's *Die Zauberflöte* (The Magic Flute). Antonio Salieri's opera *La locandiera* (The Innkeeper) had two recordings; the only other recorded survivor among his 40 operas, *Azur, Re d'Ormus* (Azur, king of Ormus), which was performed 28 times in Vienna during the 1788 season, had one.[18] *Gloria transit.*

Figure 1.1 arrays the citations data for the 646 composers, letting each *Schwann* observation be located at the year of the composer's birth. Not surprisingly, a few composers tower over all the others. Wolf-

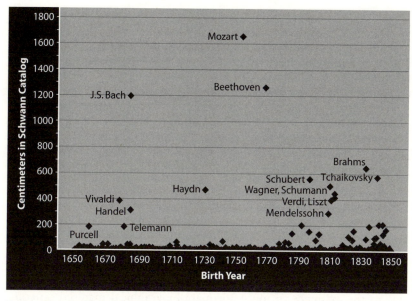

FIGURE 1.1 Recorded Music for the 646 Composers by Birth Year

gang Amadeus Mozart, Ludwig van Beethoven, and Johann Sebastian Bach are the leaders, trailed by the usual suspects. The distribution of observations is what statisticians call "skew," with many low-value observations (indeed, so many that it is impossible to distinguish individuals among those clustered along the horizontal axis) and a few with large outlying values. Statistical tests reveal the distribution to be less skew than the so-called Pareto distribution and more skew than the log normal distribution.[19] The top 65 composers, comprising 10 percent of the total number of composers, accounted for 86.4 percent of total *Schwann* catalogue lineage; the top 10 composers were responsible for 49.4 percent. This concentration of values is a bit lower than the concentration of economic valuations for German invention patents that were renewed to their full term, and somewhat higher than the distribution of stock market values resulting from equal investments in U.S. high-technology startup enterprises held from 9 to 13 years.[20] Thus, it lies within the observed distributional range of outcomes from highly creative activity.

A large sample such as the sample of 646 can illuminate broad trends and patterns, but it cannot yield much insight into how individual composers perceived their career opportunities and outcomes, or what strategies they pursued to advance their careers. To achieve depth of qualitative analysis along with quantitative breadth, a smaller sample of 50 composers was selected.[21] For each composer in this group, which will be called "the select sample" in subsequent references, at least one book-length biography was read and annotated, and for the more important composers, several biographies and correspondence collections were scrutinized. Altogether, 80 such biographical references along with numerous collateral works were consulted.

The composers included in the select sample are arrayed in order of birth dates in table 1.1. Also presented is the index that measures, in linear centimeters, the length of recorded music listings in the *Schwann* catalogue. The select sample included all composers ranked 1 through 26 in length of *Schwann* catalogue listings, along with 24 other composers, with the lowest *Schwann* ranking of 137, selected to provide representative coverage of time periods and geographic locations. There is a seeming coverage bias in terms of time periods. Among all composers in the large sample of 646, the select sample includes 7.1 percent of those born between 1650 and 1699, 6.1 percent of those born in 1700–1749, 6.5 percent of those born in 1750–1799, but 10.6 percent of the 1800–1849 birth cohort. This bias is only secondarily attributable to the existence of more adequate biographical material on composers born more recently. The main reason for the more extensive sampling of composers born during the nineteenth century is that 14 of the 20 in the nineteenth-century cohort were among the top 26 composers in terms of *Schwann* catalog listing length.

As perusal of table 1.1 reveals, some convention had to be adopted for the spelling of names. Two centuries ago spelling was under any circumstances a haphazard thing. Transliteration from the Slavic languages poses special difficulties. Many composers lived at diverse career phases in several different nations, where their names often came to be adapted to the local custom. Handel's given name in Germany, for example, was Georg Friedrich Händel. Most Englishmen were unable to cope with his umlaut, so he was frequently called Hendel. But when he acquired English citizenship in 1727, he registered himself with the spelling of table 1.1. The spellings adopted in table 1.1 and throughout this book are those found in the revised edition of *The Oxford Dictionary of Music* (Kennedy, 1994), except in a few cases where the *Oxford* is at odds with generally accepted practice.

A book about the economics of music composition can hardly be written without monetary measures. In Europe over the time span covered by this work, countless different currencies were in circulation. To make sense of the data, some common denominator is needed. We have chosen to use the English pound sterling, one of the most stable European currencies, as the benchmark. The appendix to this chapter provides tables of exchange rates among some of the more important cur-

TABLE 1.1
Composers Included in the Select Sample, by Year of Birth

Composer	Birth Year	Death Year	Schwann cm.
Johann Pachelbel	1653	1706	26.2
Arcangelo Corelli	1653	1713	33.9
Henry Purcell	1659	1695	178.1
Tomaso Albinoni	1671	1750	43.4
Antonio Vivaldi	1678	1741	378.2
Georg Philipp Telemann	1681	1767	179.8
Jean-Philippe Rameau	1683	1764	41.6
Johann Sebastian Bach	1685	1750	1190.2
Domenico Scarlatti	1685	1757	40.4
George Frideric Handel	1685	1759	306.5
Christoph W. Gluck	1714	1787	36.3
C.P.E. Bach	1714	1788	62.5
Leopold Mozart	1719	1787	17.3
Franz Joseph Haydn	1732	1809	460.5
Johann Christian Bach	1735	1783	44.0
Johann Michael Haydn	1737	1806	29.0
Johann Vanhal	1739	1813	10.5
Luigi Boccherini	1743	1805	72.8
Karl Stamitz	1745	1801	21.9
Antonio Salieri	1750	1825	11.6
Muzio Clementi	1752	1832	24.7
Wolfgang Amadeus Mozart	1756	1791	1655.8
Ludwig van Beethoven	1770	1827	1262.4
Johann Nepomuk Hummel	1778	1837	56.5
Niccolò Paganini	1782	1840	66.2
Carl Maria von Weber	1786	1826	135.4
Carl Czerny	1791	1857	8.4
Gioachino Rossini	1792	1868	197.7
Franz Schubert	1797	1828	552.5
Gaetano Donizetti	1797	1848	150.4
Vincenzo Bellini	1801	1835	84.2
Hector Berlioz	1803	1869	129.5
Johann Strauss Sr.	1804	1849	15.4
Felix Mendelssohn	1809	1847	290.6
Frédéric Chopin	1810	1849	497.4
Robert Schumann	1810	1856	414.9
Franz Liszt	1811	1886	398.2
Giuseppe Verdi	1813	1901	408.4
Richard Wagner	1813	1883	433.7
Clara Wieck Schumann	1819	1896	20.4
César Franck	1822	1890	104.7
Bedřich Smetana	1824	1884	88.2

TABLE 1.1 *Continued*

Composer	Birth Year	Death Year	Schwann cm.
Johann Strauss Jr.	1825	1899	153.8
Johannes Brahms	1833	1897	643.9
Camille Saint-Saëns	1835	1921	191.1
Modest Mussorgsky	1839	1881	104.0
Pyotr Ilyich Tchaikovsky	1840	1893	567.9
Antonin Dvořák	1841	1904	209.2
Edvard Grieg	1843	1907	197.0
Gabriel Fauré	1845	1924	159.0

rencies and explains how the conversions were made. Additional information is presented on annual earnings in a standardized job category (notably, for a building craftsman in southern England) and the purchasing power of those earnings.

PLAN OF THE BOOK

Chapter 2 begins by laying historical foundations for the analyses that follow. It traces the political, philosophical, and economic revolutions during the seventeenth through nineteenth centuries that transformed the markets in which composers sold their services. It shows how increasing prosperity raised the demand for musical performances, education, and instruments (with further changes during the 1920s as radio and electrical phonographs permitted passive enjoyment of music at home). It also reveals how musical performance audiences and venues changed in response to these developments. Chapter 3 explores further the diverse means of earning a living open to composers and uses the sample of 646 composers to discern how composers' occupational choices evolved over a period of two centuries. Chapter 4 collects insights from a host of qualitative materials on the family and educational backgrounds of composers, the role economic considerations played in their occupational choices, the risks of alternative choices, the strategies pursued to deal with those risks, and (for a limited sample of composers) the extent to which composers achieved economic success, measured in terms of net worth at the time of their death. Chapters 5 and 6 investigate the geography of composers' nativity and their choices of work locations. Among other things, chapter 5 tests the hypothesis that the fragmentation of the Holy Roman Empire into hundreds of more or less independent principalities and dukedoms created especially attractive employment opportunities for composers during the eighteenth century. Chapter 6 investigates how radical improvements in transportation media, occurring mostly during the first half of the nineteenth century, affected composers' geographic mobility. Chapter 7 analyzes the alternative means by which composers' work could be disseminated (often without permission), the emergence of copyright systems, the impact of copyright or its absence on composers' publication strategies, and how market opportunities shaped publishers' preferences for diverse composition forms. Chapter 8 concludes.

Chapter 2

THE POLITICAL, SOCIAL, AND

ECONOMIC MILIEU

THE GREAT FLOWERING of classical music took place between the years 1650 and 1900. Most of the important events occurred in Europe, which will be the principal geographic focus of our analysis. Those two and one-half centuries were times of astonishing political, intellectual, economic, and cultural change in Europe. To learn how the business of composing music evolved, we must begin with a broad understanding of the underlying political, intellectual, and economic currents. A chronological overview is provided by table 2.1.

WAR AND REVOLUTION

While the spirit of national identity within European lands was gaining strength, political boundaries and alliances changed through a breathtaking sequence of military encounters.[1]

The most devastating of the wars, the Thirty Years War, occurred just before the period on which we focus, leaving important legacies for, among other things, the development of music. The war's early roots lay in the unsuccessful revolt against Roman Catholic orthodoxy led by Prague's Jan Hus, burned at the stake in 1415, and the Protestant reformation initiated by Martin Luther in 1517. It was in the first instance a war over freedom of religion, augmented by great power disputes among the leading European nations. It began in 1618 when the Protestant estates of Bohemia, unhappy over the lack of tolerance shown them by the Holy Roman Empire, refused to acknowledge Habsburg-backed Ferdinand II as king of Bohemia and emperor-designate. Combat among armies raised within the Austrian empire and Germany escalated with the entrance of France, Habsburg Spain, England (active mostly through financial support), the increasingly powerful Scandinavian nations, and factions from the Spanish-dominated Low Countries. During the ensuing thirty years armies battled back and forth through much of Germany, Poland, Bohemia, and the Low Countries and parts of France, Italy, and Spain, living for the next engagement by plundering local populations. In what is now Germany, the focal point, deaths from

TABLE 2.1

Chronology of Significant Political, Philosophical, and Cultural Events
over Two and One-Half Centuries

1637	First Italian public opera house, Teatro San Cassiano, opened in Venice.
1642	Death of Galileo Galilei; birth of Isaac Newton.
1643	Death of Claudio Monteverdi in Venice.
1643–1658	Church organs and sheet music destroyed during civil war, followed by the protectorate of Cromwell in England.
1648	Thirty Years War ends with Treaty of Westphalia.
1660	Royal Society in London for Improving Natural Knowledge officially established.
1661	Louis XIV assumes full powers as king of France.
1666	Académie Royale des Sciences established in France.
1672	Académie Royale de Musique inaugurated in Paris under Jean-Baptiste Lully.
1683	Ottoman Empire's siege of Vienna broken.
1685	Birth of J. S. Bach, G. F. Handel, and Domenico Scarlatti.
1688	Collegium Musicum organized in Leipzig by Johann Kuhnau.
1688–1689	Glorious Revolution in England; William of Orange becomes king with powers limited by Parliament.
1689	Peter the Great assumes power as czar of Russia; begins opening to the west.
1690	John Locke's *Two Treatises of Government* published.
1694	Bank of England established.
1700	Death of Charles II separates Habsburg Austria from alliance with Spain, triggers war of Spanish succession.
1709	Statute of Anne is first general copyright law.
1709	Battle of Poltova consolidates Russia's power in north.
1713	Treaty of Utrecht makes Austria sovereign in Flanders, Milan, Naples, and Sardinia.
1719	Royal Academy of Music founded in London with Handel as music director.
1720	South Sea financial speculation bubble bursts.
1723	First opera theater of St. Petersburg inaugurated.
1725	Concert Spirituel founded in Paris by A. D. Philidor.
1733	John Kay invents the flying shuttle for looms.
1734	Voltaire's *Lettres philosophiques* and Alexander Pope's *Essay on Man* published.
1737	Death of Antonio Stradivari in Cremona.
1739	David Hume's *Treatise of Human Nature* published.
1740	Frederick II (the Great) becomes king in Prussia, Maria Theresia empress of Austria; Prussia seizes Silesia from Austria, triggering war of Austrian succession.
1748	Montesquieu's *De l'Esprit des lois* published.

TABLE 2.1 *Continued*

1755	Rousseau's *Discours sur l'origine de l'inégalité* published.
1756–1763	Seven Years War rages in central Europe.
1757	Diderot's *Encyclopédie* banned by French Parlement.
1760	Era of English canal-building begins.
1762	Premiere in Vienna of Gluck's *Orfeo ed Euridice*.
1762	Rousseau's *Du Contrat social* published.
1762	Catherine the Great becomes czarina of Russia.
1762	Hereditary feudal servitude abolished in Savoy.
1765	James Hargreaves invents the spinning jenny.
1772	Poland partitioned among Austria, Prussia, and Russia.
1776	First commercialization of Watt-Boulton steam engine.
1776	American declaration of independence from England.
1778	Elector Karl Theodor moves his orchestra, the best in Europe, from Mannheim to Munich.
1780	Joseph II becomes emperor of Austria.
1781	Immanuel Kant's *Critique of Pure Reason* published.
1781	Freedom of occupational choice proclaimed in Austria.
1783	Catherine the Great authorizes private printing presses in Russia.
1786	Premiere of Mozart's *Le nozze di Figaro* in Vienna.
1787	U.S. Constitution provides for copyright; enabling law passed in 1790.
1788–1791	War between Austria and Ottoman Empire.
1789	Storming of Bastille initiates French revolution.
1791	Haydn's first London concerts; death of Mozart.
1791	French copyright law adopted.
1792–1815	French revolutionary and then Napoleonic wars.
1796	French occupy territory east of the Rhine.
1805	First performance of Beethoven's Third Symphony (*Eroica*) in Vienna.
1805	French occupy Vienna briefly, returning in 1809. British defeat French fleet at Trafalgar.
1806	Napoleon defeats Prussia at the battle of Jena.
1810	Freedom-of-occupation law enacted in Prussia.
1812–1813	French forces retreat from Moscow and (reconstituted) are defeated in battle of Leipzig.
1815	Treaty of Vienna ends Napoleonic wars, brings back Austrian domination of northern Italy, and ends Austrian control of Belgium.
1816	Premiere of Rossini's *Il barbiere di Siviglia* in Rome.
1824	First performance of Beethoven's Ninth Symphony in Vienna.
1825	Stockton & Darlington railway opened in England.
1829	German music publishers enter no-copying accord; followed by political affirmation in German Bund.

TABLE 2.1 *Continued*

1831	Paganini's extended performance trip capped by triumphs in Paris.
1832	English middle classes enfranchised.
1834	*Zollverein* (customs union) reduces tariff barriers in Prussia and Saxony.
1839	Dresden-Leipzig rail link completed.
1840	Austrian copyright law extended to Italian possessions.
1842	Premiere of Verdi's *Nabucco* in Milan.
1842	Philharmonic Society of New York presents its first concert, including Beethoven's Fifth Symphony.
1845	Premiere of Wagner's *Tannhäuser* in Dresden.
1848	Popular revolutions in France, Germany, Austria, Italy. First war of Italian independence commenced, lost.
1854	New York Academy of Music creates opera venue.
1858	Premiere of Brahms's First Piano Concerto.
1859	Struggle for Italian unification escalated by Vittorio Emanuele and Giuseppe Garibaldi.
1861	Kingdom of Italy proclaimed, uniting most Italian states.
1861–1865	Civil war in the United States.
1861	Emancipation of Russian serfs.
1864	Schleswig-Holstein taken from Denmark by Prussia.
1870–1871	France defeated in Franco-Prussian war.
1871	Rome is named capital of united Italy.
1872	Johann Strauss Jr. conducts at Boston Peace Festival.
1883	Metropolitan Opera House opened in New York City.
1885	Berne convention initiates international copyright.
1891	Tchaikovsky presides at Carnegie Hall inaugural concert in New York City.

combat, starvation, and hunger-induced disease amounted to as much as one-third of the resident population.[2] Not atypical was the small town of Kleinbobritsch, located thirty kilometers southwest of Dresden and birthplace of the leading early eighteenth-century organ builders Andreas and Gottfried Silbermann. Four decades before the Thirty Years War began, Kleinbobritsch had 21 farm families and 6 other families in residence; when the war ended, there were only 10 families.[3] As a consequence of the population loss, land was cheap, so the grandfather of Andreas and Gottfried could make advantageous purchases that eventually facilitated the grandsons' entry into the organ-building profession. In what is now the Czech Republic, the war was even more devastating. Following the 1620 triumph of imperial forces at the Battle of White Mountain (three kilometers west of Prague's Hradčany castle), 27 barons, knights, and other local leaders were executed; the properties of 680 (mostly Protestant) Czechs were confiscated and turned over to supporters of Ferdinand; and thousands of others fled Bohemia rather than convert to Catholicism.[4]

The Thirty Years War ended with the Treaty of Westphalia, concluded at the towns of Münster and Osnabrück in 1648. Some of the warring parties, notably Sweden and France, gained territory through the settlement. Ownership of most lands, however, reverted to their prewar feudal lords. This left within what is now Germany some three hundred territorially sovereign principalities and dukedoms. Most were nominally under the jurisdiction of the Holy Roman Empire, but the emperor and his diet retained so little political power that the various entities' leaders were effectively free of imperial control, which had in any event withered even before the war as the emperor dispensed privileges in exchange for support in wars and conflicts with the papacy. In the century and a half that followed 1648, the courts of these feudal lords, we shall see, became magnets to musical talent. The religious division of Germany was largely frozen in the status quo ante bellum, since the Treaty mandated religious tolerance in Germany (but not in Habsburg Austria) and required local sovereigns to forfeit their lands if they changed religious affiliations. Switzerland and the Netherlands were guaranteed formal independence.

Among the many other wars that followed, only three can receive attention in this brief survey. The death of Spanish king Charles II without direct heirs in 1700 was followed by the accession of Philip V, grandson of France's King Louis XIV, marking the end of Habsburg family control in Spain, the start of a Bourbon dynasty, and acceleration of the decline of Spain's position as a world power. Terminating the War of Spanish Succession that followed, the Treaty of Utrecht in 1713 gave Austria sovereignty inter alia over Flanders, Milan, Sardinia, and Naples. During the next century and a half the territories and cities of Italy became military and political footballs, with control oscillating among Austria, France, Spain, the papacy, and status as independent cities or states. Italians' deep resentment over their subjection by foreigners was epitomized in the audience's tumultuous reaction to the liberation chorus, "Va Pensiero," during the 1842 premiere of Giuseppe Verdi's opera *Nabucco* (Nebuchadnezzar) at La Scala in Milan. Only when an Italian nationalist army seized Rome in 1870 after Rome's French protectors left to join their homeland's defense against Prussian invaders was full unification achieved under King Vittorio Emanuele.

When Maria Theresia became empress of Austria in 1740, King Frederick II of Prussia took advantage of what he perceived to be a momentary weakness by seizing control of Silesia, the most industrialized region of the Austrian empire. Episodic attempts by Austria to regain control escalated into a full-scale Seven Years War between 1756 and 1763, pitting against Prussia (with financial support from England) the allied forces of Austria, France, Russia, and Sweden. The war went badly for Prussia, leading to temporary occupation of Berlin, closure of the court opera established by Frederick, and disarray within his stellar court orchestra. Prussia's defeat was averted mainly by Russia's decision, during the brief reign of Czar Peter III, to change sides — an alliance that sowed seeds for the first partitioning of Poland among Russia, Prussia, and Austria in 1772. A truly independent Poland reemerged only with the Treaty of Versailles in 1919. The huge expenses incurred by Austria and some German states during the Seven Years War left many royal treasuries exhausted, leading to stringencies that underlay a reduction of support for musical activities.

Even more disastrous for the support of central European musical culture were the wars that followed the initial French revolution of 1789 and the French Assembly's declaration of war against Austria in April 1792. After initial setbacks, French troops advanced on the German front to Frankfurt before withdrawing, captured Nice and Savoy in 1792, and continued into Italy in 1793. Sporadic warfare also occurred in Spain. French forces again crossed the Rhein onto its east bank in Germany during 1796. After a period of relative quiet, the French won important battles at Ulm and Austerlitz in 1805, occupying Vienna briefly in 1805 and again in 1809.[5] They defeated Prussian forces decisively at Jena in 1806, killing in a precursor battle a gifted music composer, Prussian Prince and General Louis Ferdinand. In their march across Germany, they disrupted the courts of local principalities and dukedoms, levied heavy taxes on the nobles who remained, and began introducing, in the spirit of the revolution, new laws that abolished the subservience of peasants to their masters. Their fortunes were reversed only with their calamitous retreat from Moscow in 1812, followed by another loss to Russian and Prussian forces at the battle of Leipzig in 1813. After the resignation of Napoleon and his return, but before his defeat at Waterloo in June 1815, the war ended officially with the Treaty of Vienna. Austria regained its control over much of northern Italy, including Venice, which had been a free city until 1798; Poland was again partitioned; and Belgium was ceded to the Netherlands. More than one hundred previously independent German dukedoms and principalities were merged with neighbors.[6] Many of the legal reforms initiated by the French occupiers were rolled back, but the spirit of liberté and egalité introduced by France proved, as we shall see, more difficult to eradicate. Despite the French example, governmental repression of local citizens actually increased in some places, most notably, in Austria and its imperial possessions.[7]

Following the Treaty of Vienna, wars continued to plague Europe, but they were for the most part more narrowly concentrated geographically and less bloody. Prussia in particular regained the momentum it had achieved under Frederick the Great, seizing Schleswig-Holstein from Denmark in 1864, uniting through carrots and sticks the many fragmented states of Germany, and dispatching its armies to the gates of Paris in 1870. But the only additional event that can be added to this grim narrative was more in the nature of revolution than war. First in Paris during February 1848 and shortly thereafter in Austria, Germany, and Italy, spontaneous revolts by bourgeois and working-class citizens against established authority broke out.[8] In France, Austria, and parts of Germany, they were brutally repressed. One casualty was Richard Wagner, who had identified with the revolutionary elements and was forced in 1849 to flee a comfortable position as Kapellmeister in Dresden. For the next decade he remained a fugitive on the run from the Saxon police (as well as from debt collectors and cuckolded husbands). Another was Johann Strauss Jr., who was refused a position as director of the Viennese court's ball music for his sympathy with citizens seeking liberalization.[9] In Italy, the uprisings triggered renewed efforts to achieve liberation that succeeded two decades later.

THE ENLIGHTENMENT AND THE REFORM OF FEUDAL INSTITUTIONS

The century and a half that followed the Treaty of Westphalia was a time of intellectual ferment in tandem with struggles for military and political power. There arose during this time a new philosophical view that came to be known as the Enlightenment.[10]

The philosophical writings of the Enlightenment were rooted partly in the Protestant Reformation but most directly in advances in physical science and mathematics. Among the latter, the most important was the definitive recognition that the earth rotated about the sun, not the opposite. Originally based upon astronomical observations and hypotheses therefrom by Nicholaus Copernicus (1473–1543) of Crakow, the Copernican model triumphed with the publication of Isaac Newton's *Principia Mathematica* in 1686 and 1687. Newton's mathematical model of the solar system was built upon the painstaking experimental work of Galileo Galilei (1564–1642) and the laws of planetary motion derived by Johannes Kepler (1571–1630), whose work was in turn made possible by the unprecedentedly detailed astronomical observations of Tycho Brahe (1546–1601). From this and other advances in physics and biology, it became clear that the understanding of physical phenomena progressed best through the marriage of inductive theorizing with careful empirical research.[11] The value of this approach was anticipated presciently by England's Francis Bacon (1561–1626), whose writings inspired weekly meetings of an "invisible college" in London beginning in the 1640s and led in 1660 to the formal organization of the Royal Society of London for Improving Natural Knowledge. It was the Royal Society that published Newton's *Principia*, among other distinguished contributions. A similarly minded group, the Académie Royale des Sciences, was established in France under the patronage of Louis XIV in 1666.

The recognition that theory rooted in careful empirical observation could advance knowledge of the physical world so dramatically, and that scientific advances in turn led to new technologies that raised material standards of living, made a powerful impression upon philosophers who pondered the human condition and man's relationship to divine providence. The first in a brilliant line of contributions came from England's John Locke, who tried to apply the methodology of the physical sciences to questions such as how the human mind reasoned (in his *Essay Concerning Human Understanding*, 1690) and how social relations between men and their rulers were structured (in initially anonymous *Two Treatises of Government* (1690) and *Letters of Toleration* (1690)). One theme sounded by Locke and reiterated by most of the Enlightenment philosophers was rejection of theological authority as a basis for settling the great questions of human existence. Rather, answers were to be obtained through empirical observation (to be sure, as Immanuel Kant stressed a century later, a treacherous guide to human behavior) and careful independent reasoning.[12] Enlightenment writers were unwilling among other things to let popes suppress the evidence compiled by scientists such as Galileo to maintain the theologically convenient fiction that earth and hence the human beings Jesus Christ came to save were the fixed center of God's universe. An aggressively doubting stance toward traditional theological doctrine was, sociologist Robert Merton has shown, a characteristic preponderant among the early members of England's Royal Society and France's Académie Royale des Sciences.[13] Not surprisingly, advocacy of religious toleration was virtually unanimous among the Enlightenment writers.

Equally important for the analysis that follows here was the view of many Enlightenment philosophers, as expressed in America's 1776 Declaration of Independence, that all men are created equal.[14] Among the important contributors to this view were Charles Louis de Montesquieu (1689–1755) and Jean-Jacques Rousseau (1712–1778). In his *De l'Esprit des lois* (on the Spirit of the Laws) (1748), Montesquieu traced historically the development of law in ancient and modern societies and found that the most successful systems of law were adapted to meet the needs of the people governed. In his 1749 essay, *Discours sur les arts et sciences*, Rousseau surveyed evidence from societies Europeans considered primitive and found, contrary to popular conceptions, that the "noble savages" enjoyed an admirable "natural liberty," despite their meager command over worldly goods and services. This led him to conclude in a later work:[15]

> Look into the motives that have induced men, once united by their common needs in a general society, to unite themselves still more intimately through civil societies: you will find no other motive than that of securing the property, life, and liberty of each member by the protection of all.

More generally, most philosophers of the Enlightenment shared a view that "natural law" required the civil laws and systems of government to be structured so as to benefit the great mass of a nation's inhabitants, and not merely a privileged elite.

At the time of these writings, the political structures prevailing in Europe could scarcely have departed more from the ideals postulated by the Enlightenment philosophers. During the eighteenth century, most of Europe's inhabitants—probably 80 percent, averaged across the various territories—worked in agriculture or belonged to farm families.[16] Most agricultural lands of Europe at the time were held by a small minority of landowners with property rights often dating back to the middle ages. The lords' or seigniors' land was worked by peasants toiling under feudal master-servant relationships that varied widely from region to region, but that for tens of millions of peasants differed little from chattel slavery.[17] Under the best conditions outside England and the Netherlands, notably in what is now France and the western parts of Germany, peasants had hereditary tenure in the land they worked and in their residences, but had to turn over an appreciable part of their produce to the master and devote a specified number of days of personal service per year to the master's estate operations. Under the less favorable conditions typical of agriculture east of the Elbe river and extending into Russia, the peasants either lacked tenure or could easily be dispossessed of their lands and were unable to pass residual rights on to their children, who, however, were often bound under a legal doctrine known as *mainmorte* to remain on the master's estate and continue their servitude from generation to generation. Indeed, in European Russia, the 90 percent of the population who labored as serfs were commonly bought and sold by their masters or transferred to repay gambling debts.

For readers familiar mainly with current living standards in Western Europe and the Americas, the conditions under which the typical European peasant subsisted at the outset of the eighteenth century are virtually inconceivable.[18] There were to be sure some wealthy peasants, found more often in the west than the east, but most peasants lived in abject poverty and misery, sharing small huts with their often sizable families and the few animals they happened to possess. Their nutrition consisted primarily of grains, commonly in the form of porridge or soup, supplemented by legumes or (especially in the East) cabbage. Bread was expensive; fines were imposed unless it was baked from flour ground at exploitive monopoly tariffs in the landlord's mill (like beer brewed in the seignior's brewery). Meat and (outside southwest Europe) wine were rarities reserved for important feast days. The potato, a crucial dietary supplement in later periods, began gaining acceptance only in the second half of the eighteenth century. Among peasants' few blessings was the absence of physicians, who in those unenlightened times were as apt to kill their patients as to heal them. But disease and early mortality were rampant. Indeed, to articulate a theme that will emerge later, compared to the peasant status under which most inhabitants of European nations toiled, the economic opportunities open to musicians, however meager on average, were quite attractive.

It can hardly be surprising, therefore, that among the philosophers of the Enlightenment who stressed the dignity of all individuals, the systems of feudal tenure prevailing in Europe were a prime target for reform.[19] Because the relatively few landlords had powerful influence over existing legal institutions (courts of first jurisdiction were typically staffed by landlord-appointed judges) and could block reform efforts, constitutional changes were considered necessary to make government and the judicial system more responsive to the needs of the common people and to provide checks against abuses by the powerful.

For Enlightenment philosophers, England served as a model. The king's power was limited by the accord reached in the Glorious Revolution of 1688, through which James II was driven from the throne and replaced by William of Orange, with the express understanding that tolerance would be exercised toward dissenting religions and that Parliament, and not the king, would have decisive power in such matters as taxation. The power of Parliament was in turn constrained, despite the ultimate appellate role of the House of Lords, by a relatively independent judicial system. In England too, a substantial share of agricultural production came from yeomen who owned the fields they cultivated. To be sure, many yeomen lost their traditional access to common pasture lands during the enclosure movements of the sixteenth, seventeenth, and eighteenth centuries.[20] But they were at least not burdened by onerous feudal servitude obligations, and in most instances, they received appreciable compensation when larger landowners fenced in common lands against the incursion of others' grazing cattle. During the eighteenth century, the enclosure movement was accompanied by intensified interest in a more scientific approach to farming, facilitating a considerable increase in agricultural productivity and hence better nutrition for most English citizens. Greater agricultural productivity and rapid population growth together encouraged migration of agricultural families' children to the cities and made it possible to feed the enlarged urban work force required for an emerging Industrial Revolution.[21]

The more intelligent European sovereigns were keenly aware of these developments. Some recoiled in horror against proposed changes in the ancien régime, but others embraced the Enlightenment enthusiastically. Most notable among the latter were Frederick II (The Great) of Prussia and Joseph II, kaiser of the Austro-Hungarian empire. Voltaire (1694–1778), by common consent the best-known popularizer of Enlightenment views, was guest at the court of Frederick the Great in 1743 and again in 1750–1753, and throughout most of his adult life Frederick maintained a lively correspondence with Voltaire on philosophical and political questions.[22] Pursuing an Enlightenment agenda, Frederick (among other things, a passionate composer of flute music) abolished torture and the punishment of women who had aborted, fostered freedom of religious practice, encouraged the educational work of Jesuits in his captured Silesian territories, and sought to eliminate the Prussian serfs' feudal obligations (but succeeded in doing so only on state-owned lands). Frederick's beliefs were partly in keeping with the views of Enlightenment philosophers, but he also had more pragmatic goals. He saw a liberated and prosperous peasantry as the best source of tax revenue and well-nourished conscripts for his armies, and in his view, the military power he sought for Prussia flowed from the size and prosperity of the mostly agricultural population. In this he was at odds with Prussian land barons, who sought to preserve their advantageous feudal institutions, and not until Prussia was almost prostrate economically during the Napoleonic wars were the Prussian serfs emancipated and freedom of occupational choice authorized.

Joseph II of Austria was perhaps even more progressive, discussing Enlightenment philosophy with Frederick the Great at meetings in 1769 and 1770 and with Catherine the Great of Russia in 1781.[23] While co-sovereign with his mother Maria Theresia, he initiated a program of peasant legal rights and tenure reforms, conferred after Maria Theresia's death in 1780 freedom on peasants to learn a trade and leave the estate, and confiscated for the benefit of the poor the property of many monasteries.[24] He too experienced sharp conflict over land tenure reform with his noble landowners, who viewed his policies as a threat to their feudal dues, and after his death in 1790, many of his initiatives were nullified. It is well known, if only from the motion picture *Amadeus*, that Joseph II pushed through, over the opposition of an anti-

Mozart cabal, the production of an opera, ultimately *Le nozze di Figaro* (The Marriage of Figaro), from the controversial play of the same name (in French) by Pierre-Augustin Beaumarchais. The play was controversial not because it turned on the sexual licentiousness of noblemen, which shocked no one in that enlightened time, but because it depicted a humble barber as shrewder and more intelligent than Count Almaviva. This was seen as a serious affront to the noble establishment. It is said that Joseph supported Mozart's efforts because he perceived the need for reforming the system of feudal privileges (including the count's right of first nuptial access to Susanna) and wanted to send a message of warning to the landed gentry who would be the opera's principal listeners.[25] The message was ignored, leaving unresolved in Austria as well as France many of the feudal grievances that precipitated the French Revolution and carried Joseph's sister Marie Antoinette to the guillotine in 1793.

Reforms did come, but only gradually, over the course of a century on the European continent.[26] Some occurred because progressive individual landowners recognized from the British demonstration that the feudal system was hopelessly inefficient, and that it was more profitable to rent land to well-motivated peasants than to compel their activity. Some were the result of actions by enlightened despots such as Frederick the Great, Joseph II, Duke Leopold I of Lorraine, and Karl Friedrich of Baden. The first formal proclamation abolishing *mainmorte* was issued in Savoy (now the northwest corner of Italy) during 1762. Louis XVI of France followed with a proclamation in 1779 affecting only crown lands. In 1771 the king of Savoy established a commission to recommend compensation to lords whose peasants were emancipated, but its efforts were desultory, and when revolutionary French forces invaded Savoy in 1792, the remaining peasant holdings were emancipated without compensation. Duress resulting from the revolution within France, French military occupation outside it, and the threat or actuality of peasant uprisings were important inducements to change. In Hessen, the Hanover region, and Westphalia, the old systems were restored when Napoleon retreated, but along the Rhine's west bank and in northwestern Germany, the lands had already been sold, usually to their tillers, and it was impossible to undo what had been done. The reforms initiated in Austria by Joseph II that affected landowners' pocketbooks most directly were reversed by his successors Leopold II and Franz II. Only under the threats posed by the 1848 revolution did Austria complete the emancipation of its peasants. Among the 38 initial European territorial emancipation decrees tabulated by Jerome Blum, 42 percent followed the outbreak of the 1848 revolution.[27] The Danubian principalities of Romania were the last on Blum's list to begin emancipation—in 1864, a year after Abraham Lincoln issued his Emancipation Proclamation for the United States.

The provisions made to compensate landlords for the rights they surrendered to their peasants varied widely. Emancipation achieved under force of revolution or occupation sometimes carried no compensation. In Austria, the government issued bonds to pay landowners two-thirds of the estimated value of their losses; the peasants who benefitted were expected to repay half of the government's outlays with interest over the course of forty years.[28] In Prussia, peasants with hereditary tenure to till certain plots could become unencumbered freeholders by surrendering to their landlords one-third of the land they worked; those without tenure had to give up half their land.

The consequences of feudal tenure reform for landlords varied equally widely. Some landlords, especially in Austria, received large sums of money that could be invested in improving their farming operations or in commencing industrial endeavors or could be squandered on consumption. Some who could no longer extract involuntary service from their peasants, like many who embraced land reform by assembling larger, more efficient holdings, began to take a more active interest in farming, conferring less discretion upon hired managers and introducing reforms that raised agricultural productivity. An exodus of peasants from the land to the cities led to higher wages for the farm workers who remained, increasing the incentive for landlords to rationalize their farming operations. Still others found themselves with greatly reduced wealth and were forced to cut back consumption—among other things, for the support of musical activity as a part of their court life.[29] On this, more will be said both here and in later chapters.

The Enlightenment philosophers were also strong advocates of open intellectual discourse and opposed its antithesis, government censorship. As an enlightened despot, Frederick the Great was less sympathetic. For instance, he wrote to Voltaire in 1766:[30]

> In society tolerance should guarantee to everyone the liberty to believe what he likes; but this tolerance should not be extended so far as to authorize the effrontery and license of young scatter-brains who audaciously insult what the people revere.

Censorship included among its targets the production of operas. Joseph II greatly reduced censorship during his reform regime, transferring censorship duties in Vienna to Mozart's champion (and Haydn's librettist), the liberal Baron Gottfried van Swieten. Emperor Franz II reinstated systematic censorship, shifting the responsibility for its implementation to the police in 1801. Between 1803 and 1805, a "recensoring commission" banned 2,500 books.[31] Virtually all operas produced in

northern Italy from the end of the Napoleonic wars up to Italian unification were prescreened. Verdi's *Rigoletto* was banned totally by the
censors of Austrian-occupied Venice. Its 1851 premiere took place only
after considerable high-level persuasion, demotion of the libertine principal from king to duke, and a change of title to avoid the theologically
sensitive word *maledizione* (curse). The original version of Verdi's *Un
ballo in Maschera* (A Masked Ball) memorialized the assassination of
Sweden's King Gustavus III in 1792, but to escape prohibition by Neo-
politan and then Roman censors, the opera had to be rewritten in 1858
to depict assassination of a less sensitive Governor of Boston.

DEMOGRAPHIC AND ECONOMIC CHANGES

Paralleling the intellectual, political, and military changes surveyed here
were significant demographic and economic developments.

The population of Western Europe, excluding Russia, Bulgaria, Romania, Turkey, Greece, and the Balkans, increased from nearly 80 million in 1650 to 101 million in 1750 and then to 182 million in 1850.[32]
The average annual population growth rate for the first of these cen-
tury-long intervals was 0.25 percent; for the second interval, it accelerated to 0.58 percent. Figure 2.1 graphs population trends for seven important nations or national groups. The four Scandinavian nations
together were excluded because their trend line coincided almost exactly
with the trend line for Belgium, the Netherlands, and Luxembourg.
Among the groups sampled, the United Kingdom (excluding northern
and southern Ireland) had the most rapid population growth, averaging
0.64 percent per year over the two centuries.[33] European Russia was
second most rapid at 0.63 percent.

To support a growing population requires increased food output. As
we have seen, in the typical continental European nation during the
eighteenth century, roughly 80 percent of the population was engaged in
agriculture.[34] One farm family fed 1.25 families, including itself, on average. With Holland and England leading the way, spectacular increases
in agricultural productivity were achieved. For some nations, food imports also permitted increasing cross-national specialization. By the
1890s, the fraction of the economically active population engaged in
agriculture, forestry, and fishing dropped to 10.7 percent in the United
Kingdom.[35] In France during the 1890s, an average farm family fed 2.22
families. The Austro-Hungarian empire's progress was more modest.
With 65 percent of the work force still engaged in agriculture and forestry, one farm family fed 1.54 families.

During the period on which we will focus, another of the great revo-

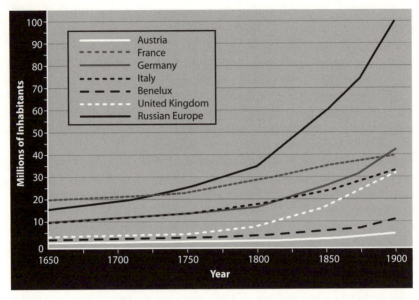

FIGURE 2.1 Trends in Population: Seven European National Groups

lutions in human history — the first Industrial Revolution — occurred. It was not unrelated to the developments in agriculture, since a reduction in the fraction of the work force required to feed the population facilitates industrialization.[36] But in addition, science and technology were harnessed on an unprecedentedly broad front to create new goods and services and to increase workers' productive efficiency.[37] How revolutionary the industrial and agricultural revolutions were is suggested by David Landes' rough estimates of changes in economic output per capita in western Europe over long periods. Between the years A.D. 1000 and 1700, he reports, output per capita trebled, implying an average 0.16 percent rate of growth per annum.[38] Between 1700 and 1750, the apparent growth rate rose to 0.4 percent and then accelerated into the range of 1 percent per year by the second half of the nineteenth century. Estimates by Nicholas Crafts based on more recent and more complete data for the United Kingdom imply productivity growth — that is, growth in output per person employed — of 0.3 percent per year between 1780 and 1801, 0.5 percent from 1801 to 1831, and 1.2 percent per year between 1831 and 1873.[39] Since that time, even higher productivity growth rates have become commonplace in the industrialized world.

Because the concepts needed to measure real gross national product were invented only during the 1930s, long-term statistics on the growth of output per capita for individual European nations must be painstakingly reconstructed, and data series comparable across nations are

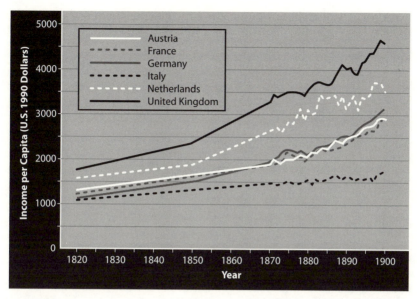

FIGURE 2.2 Trends in Income per Capita: Six European Nations, 1820–1900

exceedingly rare. The most wide-ranging series have been compiled by Angus Maddison, beginning in an early version with 1820 and containing long gaps (notably, 1821–1849 and 1851–1869) before annual estimates are offered. Figure 2.2 charts the original Maddison data series on real gross domestic product (GDP) per national resident (roughly, income per capita) for six important European nations, with linear interpolations for missing data years.[40] Output is measured in U.S. dollars at 1990 purchasing-power levels, with exchange rate conversions at purchasing-power parity. With a head start on the Industrial Revolution, England is shown to have had the highest GDP per capita in 1820, continuing its lead as the twentieth century dawned. The original Maddison data series used for figure 2.2 put the Netherlands, with Amsterdam as a principal world trading and banking center surrounded by productive agricultural lands, in second place. His later reconstruction elevated the Netherlands to first place for 1820, but not at later benchmarks. Germany started from a trailing position (at least, among the relatively prosperous nations sampled) but moved ahead through superior industrial growth to third place in 1900. In 1820 average incomes per capita in Austria exceeded those of Germany, mainly from the concentration of government officials and commerce in Vienna, but what is now modern Austria industrialized more slowly than Germany during the rest of the nineteenth century.[41]

From early fragmentary estimates by Maddison and his later reconstruction extending back in some cases to the year 1000, real per capita GDP averages in 1700, 1820, and 1900 and annual growth rates for those intervals can be extracted to cover a wider sample of 13 nations.[42] The data, which, especially for nations whose borders changed significantly, entailed considerable guesswork, are presented in table 2.2. They are arrayed in descending order of estimated 1820 GDP per capita. Of the 13 nations, 8 achieved growth rates of 1.0 percent per year or more in the 1820–1900 interval. Although most of the surveyed nations (with the notable exception of the U.S. colonies) began with fairly similar GDP per capita, reflecting similar initial technological conditions and the plodding growth that was typical before the Industrial Revolution, the nations' varying success in implementing the fruits of modern technology led to greater cross-national inequality of income levels by the dawn of the twentieth century.

Economic historians have widely divergent views on how output increases were divided among the citizens of industrializing nations. The most complete data on this point exist for the United Kingdom, vanguard of the agricultural and industrial revolutions, but even for it, there is disagreement. Rapid population growth and improvements in agricultural productivity induced large numbers of workers to seek jobs in the towns and cities. Although mechanization of industrial production increased output per worker greatly, increases in the supply of in-

TABLE 2.2
1700, 1820, and 1900 GDP per Capita and Growth Rates (Maddison Estimates, in Dollars of 1990 U.S. Purchasing Power)

Nation	1700 GDP per Capita	1820 GDP per Capita	1700–1820 Growth Rate	1900 GDP per Capita	1820–1900 Growth Rate
United Kingdom	1286	1756	0.26%	4593	1.20%
Netherlands	1809	1561	−0.12	3533	1.02
Austria	1056	1295	0.17	2460	1.01
Belgium	1120	1291	0.12	3652	1.30
United States	540	1287	0.72	4096	1.45
Denmark	1000	1225	0.17	2902	1.08
France	976	1218	0.18	2849	1.06
Sweden	977	1198	0.17	2561	0.95
Germany	940	1112	0.14	3134	1.30
Italy	1075	1092	0.01	1746	0.59
Spain	900	1063	0.14	2040	0.81
Czechoslovakia	n.a.	849	n.a.	1729	0.89
Russia	666	751	0.10	1218	0.60

Source: Maddison (1995), pp. 194–200; and (2001), p. 264.

dustrial labor offset what would otherwise be tendencies for the real wages of common workers, and especially those who lacked special skills, to rise. In one of the most ambitious studies, Jeffrey Williamson found that the real wages of common laborers in England increased hardly at all up to about 1820, after which they rose rapidly and workers began sharing in the fruits of the Industrial Revolution.[43] Despite this reversal, he found, income distribution became increasingly unequal up to about 1860, with relatively well-paid and especially highly skilled employees gaining more rapidly than unskilled workers. For all adult male blue-collar workers, real full-time earnings were found to have nearly doubled between 1797 and 1851. For white-collar workers — individuals more likely to attend orchestral music concerts and operas and to perform music at home — earnings more than quadrupled, with especially strong gains after 1820.[44] Solicitors and barristers were found to have fared particularly well, moving from an estimated average real income (assuming 1850 consumer goods price levels) of £119 in 1797 to £1,838 in 1851.

Williamson's estimates have been challenged, most notably, by Charles Feinstein (1988, 1998). Feinstein charges Williamson among other things with applying incomplete and badly timed cost-of-living indexes and tapping unrepresentative samples, especially for the best-paid occupational specialties. After adjusting for these and other perceived problems, Feinstein concludes that the average working-class family's standard of living improved by less than 15 percent in Great Britain between the 1780s and the 1850s and that, since inequality of workers' incomes increased little, middle-class employees fared hardly better. After the 1850s, all scholars agree, the fruits of the Industrial Revolution began to benefit working-class individuals. To the extent that Feinstein's criticism is valid, a puzzle remains. The best-accepted estimates, for example, those of Nicholas Crafts, show average real income per capita at the economy-wide level to have been rising briskly during the first half of the nineteenth century. If employees did not reap the gains from industrialization, who did? A plausible answer is that important early gainers from the Industrial Revolution in Great Britain were the entrepreneurs who built thriving new businesses and the bankers who financed them. For that core component of the middle classes, the data tapped by Williamson and Feinstein provide little insight.

An alternative way of seeing how increasing prosperity affected, among other things, the potential demand for music is to examine changes in wealth instead of changes in income. Individual wealth in centuries past is typically estimated through the analysis of probate records assessing estate values at the time of death. This is an approach to which we must resort when we ask in chapter 4 how well composers fared economically. There were clearly changes in the distribution of British wealth at

the time of the Industrial Revolution. Their analysis is complicated by
the fact that by far the greatest concentration of wealth in the United
Kingdom during the eighteenth century came from the ownership of
land. Landholdings became less important over time, however, both because industrial production grew more rapidly and because landlords'
rents were held back by output-increasing technological changes and
the phasing out of the Corn Laws, which protected English farmers
from import competition, between 1828 and 1846. From the most careful research on asset holdings, Peter Lindert found that the wealthiest
10 percent of English and Welsh households held 58.3 percent of all
wealth, excluding the value of landholdings, in 1670; 57.7 percent in
1740; 60.9 percent in 1810; and 77.1 percent in 1858.[45] Thus, wealth
holdings, excluding land, became increasingly unequally distributed as
the Industrial Revolution progressed. When land values are added in,
most of the trend toward increasing inequality fades because of the relative decline in the holdings of the wealthiest landowners relative to
wealth holders generally. However one construes the evolution of inequality in wealth holdings, it is clear that the upper and middle classes
fared well as the Industrial Revolution progressed. This is shown by the
following average holdings of wealth (excluding land) for selected groups
at various points in time.[46] All holdings are estimated in Pounds Sterling
at purchasing power levels prevailing in 1875:

	1670	1740	1810	1858	1875
Titled gentry	£552	£563	£2032	£3036	£9855
Merchants	296	573	608	5917	11804
Professionals	n.a.	n.a.	607	1073	1201
Shopkeepers	149	195	304	641	606
Industrial tradesmen	101	110	345	687	523
Yeomen	199	178	256	314	465

The number of professionals and merchants (the latter category including industrialists and financiers) — the core of an increasingly affluent
upper middle class — rose from 81,000 in 1670 to 360,000 in 1875,
remaining at approximately 5 percent of all households for which wealth
estimates could be hazarded. Meanwhile, the number of titled gentry fell
from 1.45 percent of all surveyed households in 1670 to 0.35 percent in
1875.[47]

INCOME, WEALTH, AND THE DEMAND FOR MUSIC

The industrial and agricultural revolutions made it possible for Europeans to enjoy — possibly only after a substantial lag — material stan-

dards of living much higher than they had experienced during the first half of the eighteenth century. First in England and then on the European continent, the average citizen eventually became better fed, better clothed, better housed, and better able to enjoy an occasional luxury. A crude index of progress is the consumption of sugar, regarded in Mozart's time as a luxury.[48] Average sugar consumption per capita in Great Britain (excluding Ireland) has been estimated for the mid-1790s at 16.03 pounds per year. By the mid 1850s, average consumption had doubled, with nearly two-thirds of the increase occurring in final decade. By 1900–1904, it had risen further to approximately 79 pounds.[49]

A basic hypothesis of this book is that as Europeans and later Americans became increasingly affluent, their demand for music in diverse forms increased and spread to an ever-widening fraction of the population. Hearing music performed professionally and having the means to perform it oneself were luxury goods, defined by economists as goods whose consumption rises more than proportionately with advances in real income.

The consumption of music, of course, is not the same as the consumption of sugar. Music is not a single granular product; it is a composite of many integrated products, some based upon others. Music is normally "consumed" by hearing it performed, either by amateurs or professionals, and through the pleasure one derives from performing it oneself. To perform it requires training, instruments, and musical scores. Economists say that the demand for inputs used in producing another desired product is a *derived* demand; thus, the demand for musical instruments and training is derived from the demand for musical performance, and the demand for music publication services is derived from the demand for sheet music, which in turn is derived from the demand for music performance. The demand for music, moreover, calls for something other than a static, never-changing, narrowly conscribed product. Consumers seek variety in the music they hear, and they may tire of hearing the same old thing over and over again. Thus, there is a demand for innovation in the composition of music — innovation in the sense that new and variegated products are forthcoming on a more or less regular basis. During the last four decades of the twentieth century there emerged a substantial literature in economics showing both theoretically and empirically that changes in demand *induce* innovative changes in products to satisfy the altered demands.[50] Changes in the music provided to consumers in turn generate derived demands for musical instruments that are improved to confer greater versatility, better intonation control, superior timbre, and other characteristics. These complex interrelationships must be kept in mind in the chapters that follow.

It would be pleasant if we could use standard economic tools to carry out statistical tests of how concert attendance or the purchase of sheet music changed with increasing per capita incomes and wealth during the eighteenth and nineteenth centuries. It is hoped that appropriate data may become available from research in London.[51] Meanwhile, however, we must settle for a crude and indirect test, relating the demand for a particular musical instrument — the piano — to changes in real incomes in the United States over an extended period.

From Cyril Ehrlich's estimates[52] of U.S. piano production in the years 1850, 1870, and 1890 and U.S. Census Bureau statistics[53] for intermittent years thereafter up to 1939, a data series on U.S. piano production, reproduced in figure 2.3, was compiled. Circles mark the years for which production estimates were available; the connecting lines are interpolated. We see an acceleration of piano output up to 1909 and a sharp decline after 1925 — in the middle of an economic boom. Economic theory asserts that the quantity demanded depends upon (1) the price of the product (the higher the price, the smaller the quantity demanded); (2) consumers' income (usually a positive influence); (3) the size of the relevant population, or the number of families; (4) the prices or quantities of substitute goods (the lower substitute prices or the higher substitute quantities are, the lower the demand for the product in question); and (5) for durable goods like pianos, the stock of the product already in consumers' hands (the larger the stock, the smaller current sales tend eventually to be, all else equal).

The statistical technique used to analyze piano production data here and other quantitative indicators in subsequent chapters is known as multiple regression analysis. In essence, one seeks to find an equation or set of equations that best explains variations in some variable, known as the dependent variable — in the present case, the variations over time in U.S. piano production. (In other regression analyses conducted later in this book, the dependent variable's variation often occurs among subjects at a fixed interval in time; these are called cross-section analyses, whereas the piano problem requires time-series analysis.) The explanation is embodied in a set of independent, or explanatory, variables whose variations can plausibly be hypothesized to affect the dependent variable's value. Through multiple regression analysis one estimates a set of coefficients, one for each independent variable. The coefficients reveal the impact of an independent variable on the dependent variable's variation (holding other explanatory variables momentarily constant). Because many readers may be unfamiliar with this method of analyzing data and some may be put off by the use of mathematical equations, we consign the regression equations and their accompanying notation to end notes, using the text to identify the variables analyzed and interpret the results.

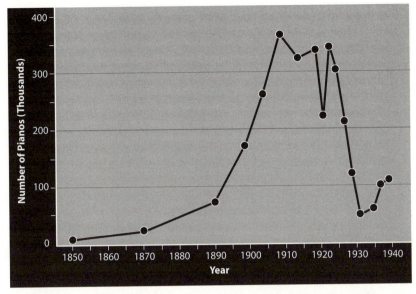

FIGURE 2.3 Production of New Pianos in the United States, 1850–1939

For those who wish to pursue the end notes, some additional comments are in order. The strength and precision of the explanatory variables' impact on the dependent variable are assessed using so-called *t*-ratios, which will be uniformly enclosed in brackets []. *T*-ratios in excess of 1.7 are presumed to reveal statistically significant relationships, in the sense that they are likely to survive with 95 percent or higher confidence the chance elements that invade virtually all quantitative measurements. How well the equation "fits" the data is revealed by a coefficient known as R^2, which can vary from zero (indicating no relationship between the dependent and explanatory variables) to 1.0 (indicating that the regression equation explains all of the variation in the dependent variable). Before squaring, R is the correlation coefficient with which statistical associations are often described.

Data on GDP per capita at 1990 purchasing-power levels, reflecting consumers' average incomes, are drawn from the Maddison series used for figure 2.2. The stock of pianos in homes and other locales was estimated by interpolating linearly from the observed production values and assuming that newly produced pianos were added to a stock that began at 160,000 in 1850 and depreciated at an annual rate of 3 percent of any given year's stock level. The principal likely substitutes to the use of pianos at home were phonographs and radios. Estimates of the number of U.S. families with phonographs and radios (each in thousands) were derived from Census reports.[54] Variables denoting the number of families in the United States and accumulated piano stock values were too highly correlated to yield separately meaningful insights. Therefore, a variable measuring the stock of pianos as a percentage of the number of families was substituted in some analyses. Cyril Ehrlich observes that the introduction of mass-production methods into piano making between 1851 and 1883, first in the United States and then elsewhere, led to sharp declines in piano prices, along with improvements in quality.[55] Unfortunately, a usable piano price series was available (from Sears Roebuck catalogues) only beginning in 1897. Thus, prices can be included in estimating the demand relationships only from 1899 through 1937, so regressions for that restricted sample were also computed. Even then, the price data are crude. The number of pianos offered in particular Sears catalogues varied from one to half a dozen, with the number diminishing considerably after 1925, apparently in response to generally reduced consumer demand. Qualities varied widely, and so the reported prices were adjusted not only for changes in economy-wide price levels (using a Bureau of Labor Statistics wholesale price series)[56] but also for quality differences, classified into top, medium, and low quality classes.[57] All piano prices were for uprights, without self-playing features.

Specific variable definitions and the regression results are reported in an extended end note.[58] In all variants, income per capita proved to be an important explanatory variable, permitting one to infer income elasticities of demand. In the regressions using observations for 17 years within an 1850-to-1939 interval, the estimated income elasticities ranged from 3.16 to 4.32, indicating that as income per capita increased by 1.0 percent, the purchase of pianos rose by 3.16 to 4.32 percent. Products with income elasticities greater than 1.0 are called "luxury goods" in economic analysis; thus, pianos clearly fell into the luxury category. For the less complete time series on which prices were available, the estimated income elasticities were lower, in the range of 2.40 to 2.75. The estimated price elasticities in those regressions failed to pass conventional statistical significance tests, but lay in the plausible range of -0.62 to -0.78, suggesting that with lower prices, quantities sold rose, but less than proportionately.

A particularly noteworthy result is found in the statistically powerful negative coefficients associated with the number of radios in American homes, or, in the truncated time series, with the number of phonographs. It would appear that the invention and sale of phonographs in their original acoustic form had little impact on the purchase of pianos. The appearance of home radios beginning in the early 1920s, accompanied by the introduction in 1924 of electrical phonographs, with fidelity far superior to that of purely mechanical phonographs, had a powerful negative impact on piano purchases.[59] No longer did home entertainment have to consist of family members performing music on the parlor piano. The family could hear the Columbia (CBS) Orchestra (from 1926), the Metropolitan Opera (from 1931), the NBC Symphony Orchestra, led by Arturo Toscanini (from 1937), and much else on the radio or listen to 78-rpm records of their favorite music. One is hard put to find an alternative explanation for the abrupt decline in piano purchases beginning during the mid-1920s. A new way of consuming music (and much else) had emerged, changing radically the character of American family life.

THE INSTITUTIONALIZATION OF MUSIC PERFORMANCE

Music performance requires a venue. For music performed outside the home, venues have varied over time with changes in political, religious, and economic conditions. We survey briefly here the historical evolution of some principal supporting institutions, notably, churches, noble courts, opera houses, town governments, and privately organized concert locales.[60]

Church Music

Music played a significant role in formal religious services from at least the time of King David three millennia ago. David played several musical instruments, wrote many of the traditional Hebrew psalms, and is said apocryphally to have organized formal musical activities in the Temple. The tradition of music was carried forward in Christian churches. Before the Protestant reformation, the varieties of music performed depended to a considerable degree upon the whims of ruling popes. Church music advanced by fits and starts from the sixth-century plainsong associated with Pope Gregory I to the magnificent a capella antiphony and polyphony of Giovanni da Palestrina (1525–1596), called by Giuseppe Verdi "the true Prince of sacred music and the Eternal Father of Italian music."[61]

By allowing differences in taste to flourish, the reformation proved to be an important turning point. Martin Luther (1483–1546) believed that music should have a central role in religious devotion and wrote many great Protestant chorales. His counterpart Huldrych Zwingli (1484–1531) banned musical performance from church services and had organs removed from Swiss churches. The Formula of Concord, endorsed in 1577 by most of the German-speaking Protestant principalities and dukedoms, decentralized decision making on musical questions to local governments, allowing one hundred flowers to bloom. In Protestant England too there were differences of opinion. In 1563, during the reign of Elizabeth I, a resolution to remove organs from Anglican churches was defeated in the lower House of Convocation by a single vote.[62] Organs were in fact banned from the churches and, when not removed to safer locales, demolished during the protectorate under Puritan Oliver Cromwell from 1649 to 1658, but returned with the Restoration of Charles II and his successors to facilitate inter alia the religious anthem writing of Henry Purcell.

Struggling to cope with the challenges of the reformation, the Roman Catholic Church debated among other issues at the Council of Trent the question of its position toward church music. There were pressures to withdraw from complex polyphony to monophonic music whose words "may be clearly understood by all."[63] This approach was weakly endorsed by the Council in 1562 and more firmly by a Liturgical Commission in 1563, but it was opposed by Holy Roman Emperor Ferdinand I, and as a result, subsequent popes chose not to arouse further controversy by demanding uniformity of local practices. Again, variegated flowers were permitted to bloom, leading to conservative church music rules in jurisdictions such as Spain while in Germany and Austria, local prelates encouraged luxuriously orchestrated Masses by the Haydns, Mozart, Schubert, Beethoven, and (for dedication to Roman Catholic King Friedrich Augustus II of Poland and Saxony) Johann Sebastian Bach. Deploying church music as a weapon against Protestantism was advocated especially actively by the Jesuits, who made musical training a significant component of education in the schools they maintained.[64]

As a result of these developments, most churches, Protestant and Catholic, retained an organist, and the more affluent parishes supported professional orchestras to accompany their choirs. Although the ability of churches to maintain elaborate orchestras was weakened by the confiscation of revenue-yielding religious-order properties (for example, by an Enlightenment-minded Joseph II in the Austrian dominions and in France following the 1789 Revolution), the performance of music continued to be an important element in Roman Catholic and Protestant worship.

Orchestras of the Nobility

During the Middle Ages, church and state fused in the musical groups maintained by emperors and kings. It was not uncommon for a sovereign to employ musicians for his or her royal chapel, and then to draft them into duty accompanying dinners and providing dance music for festive occasions.[65] Gradually, specialization emerged, so that individuals were designated to perform as either chapel musicians or court musicians, but not necessarily both. During the seventeenth century the support of court orchestras spread throughout Europe. Thus, among the most prominent composers born between 1650 and 1699, Arcangelo Corelli was employed in the court of ex-Queen Christina of Sweden in Rome as well as in the households of two cardinals, the equivalent of royalty in Rome; Henry Purcell doubled as royal chapel organist and (erratically paid) composer of secular music for the English kings; Marin Marais was viola da gamba player in the court of France's Louis XIV, for whom François Couperin served as court (and chapel) organist. Georg Philipp Telemann was employed in the tiny ducal courts of Sorau and Eisenach; Johann Sebastian Bach in the courts of Weimar and Köthen; George Frideric Handel (briefly) by the Elector of Hanover; Domenico Scarlatti by the royal family of Portugal (and earlier, by a Corelli benefactor); and Johann Quantz played the flute in the court orchestras of Frederick the Great of Prussia and the king of Poland and Saxony. By 1705, the court orchestra in Vienna under Emperor Leopold I included 107 members.[66]

Indeed, what happened in central European noble courts during the half century that followed the end of the Thirty Years War and the early decades of the eighteenth century was akin to a cultural arms race.[67] Maintaining a court orchestra (or even better, a court opera) added to the sponsoring noble's prestige. Most nobles drew their wealth from the peasants working their landed estates. Initially, the availability of unworked land depressed land rents, but as population levels were restored by the start of the eighteenth century, the proliferation of mouths that needed feeding placed increasing pressure on food supplies, driving up food prices and the rents landowners levied upon those who tilled their lands.[68] Nobles' return to affluence, together with the prestige derived from supporting one's own musical establishment, combined to induce a vast number of courts, large and small, to hire or train musicians and build up an orchestra (in German, *Kapelle*) or at least a band (*Harmonie*). Although no exact census exists, it is scarcely an exaggeration to say that by the middle of the eighteenth century, no self-respecting noble court could be seen without its in-house musical performance ensemble.[69]

In the second half of the eighteenth century, however, the cultural arms race abated, and many of the courtly orchestras were disbanded. Just as our theoretical understanding of how deadly arms races wind down is imperfect,[70] we do not have exact information on the dynamics of the cultural deescalation. There are at least five plausible explanations, most consistent with the theory of arms races and all supported by at least some evidence. First, once most noble courts had orchestras, little distinction was to be had from maintaining one's own ensemble — even though withdrawing could be difficult, since prestige might be lost by not having one. Second, interest in music, like many other attributes, varies widely over generations within a family, and when the more enthusiastic patrons died, they were often followed by heirs who chose not to carry on the tradition. Third, as the competition for a less than completely elastic supply of first-rate musicians intensified, the cost of maintaining a prestigious ensemble mounted, and this "fatigue and expense"[71] discouraged continued expenditure. In some instances budgetary cutbacks were compelled by financial distress attributable more or less directly to excessive outlays for (and in some cases borrowing to support) conspicuous consumption.[72] Fourth, assertive leadership can help break out of a high-expenditure equilibrium. Empress Maria Theresia and her son Emperor Joseph II of Austria were notorious skinflints. They economized visibly on expenditures for their own court musical establishments and encouraged others within their ambit, and especially religious prelates, to follow their lead. And an important lead it was, given the large number of noble courts in the Austrian empire and adjacent Germany. Finally — although one set of events occurred too late to explain the principal wave of court orchestra abandonments — the Seven Years War and then the Napoleonic wars, along with feudal reforms instigated by French occupying forces, reduced the wealth of many noble courts, inducing them to implement economy measures. Already by 1796, before Napoleon's troops overran Austria, Baron von Schönfeld, a Viennese nobleman and publisher, lamented:[73]

> It was formerly most usual for our princely houses to maintain their own *Hauskapellen.* . . . Now . . . to the detriment of art, this praiseworthy practice has been lost, and one Kapelle after another is extinguished, so that aside from that of Price Schwarzenberg, hardly a one still exists.

The baron's observation provides useful perspective, but his "hardly a one" assertion was too pessimistic, since in both the Austro-Hungarian empire and other European lands, a substantial number of noble courts continued to maintain orchestras well into the nineteenth century. Thus, among the 85 Austro-Hungarian-Czech Kapellen identified by Julia Moore, at least 9 — including those associated with two separate Colloredo family members, Count Joseph Erdödy, the Esterházy family, two branches of the Haugwitz family, Prince Liechtenstein, Prince Franz Joseph Lobkowitz, and Prince Schwarzenberg — were still in existence during 1796.[74] In Germany, noble courts maintained *Hauskapellen* during at least part of the nineteenth century in Dresden, Hanover, Stuttgart, Weimar, Kassel, Breslau, Darmstadt, Wiesbaden, Meiningen, Hechingen, and Donaueschingen, among others.

The Organization of Opera

Among the varieties of secular musical performance supported by the nobility, chamber music and music for larger ensembles enjoyed precedence in time, but a latecomer, opera, was both more spectacular and more costly. Musical tableaus and dramas that foreshadowed what we now call opera were first sponsored by the Medici family, rulers of Florence, during the closing decades of the sixteenth century.[75] Opera took a significant step forward with the initial performance of Claudio Monteverdi's *Orfeo* at the Gonzaga court in Mantua during 1607. From there it spread throughout Italy, facilitated in part by Monteverdi's departure from service to the Gonzagas and his move to the free city of Venice in 1612.[76] Venice premiered its first opera theater, San Cassiano, in 1637. By 1640, Venice had three opera houses; by the end of the century, the number of opera houses has been variously reported between six and sixteen.[77] The first opera performance in Rome occurred at the Barbarini family palace in 1631. The first Roman theater dedicated to opera was completed in 1671, but it was closed under an order from Pope Innocent XI in 1674, after which opera performance returned temporarily to the homes of wealthy Romans.[78] The Naples royal court mounted its first opera performance in 1650. By the last two decades of the seventeenth century, virtually every Italian city of any size had, or was constructing, a theater dedicated to opera, and regular opera seasons were the norm.[79] From Italy the support of formal opera establishments spread northward, to Vienna (linked to the Gonzaga family by marriage) in the 1620s, Dresden in 1667, Hamburg in 1678, and Paris (with the first performance of an opera by Jean-Baptiste Lully at the new Académie Royale de Musique) in 1673. Henry Purcell wrote operalike scores for London theaters during the 1690s. In 1719 a formal London opera company, the Royal Academy of Music, was established, with George Frideric Handel as music director.

The first operas were produced under noble auspices. Organizing opera in a house financed and controlled by the local sovereign continued to be the custom in Naples, Turin, Paris, Vienna (until the Napoleonic wars), St. Petersburg, and German capital cities such as Berlin (where Frederick the Great built an opera house in 1742), Dresden, Darmstadt, Stuttgart / Ludwigsburg, Munich, and Mannheim / Schwetzingen. Under this organizational mode, the local king or duke built the opera house with money from the state treasury, appointed an official or com-

mittee to manage the program, intervened frequently in artistic decisions to impose his own artistic tastes, and provided generous subsidies
to keep the costly enterprise afloat. In some cases admission was restricted to members of the court and guests invited by the sovereign; in
others, the places left after the official pecking order had been satisfied
were offered at little or no charge to military officers and properly at-
tired citizens in good standing.

The trouble with this organizational approach was that it generated
incentives systematically biased on the side of incurring extravagant
cost. During the eighteenth and nineteenth centuries, opera in Europe
and especially in Italy was the moral equivalent of football, television,
and social clubs all rolled together in modern Western society—it was
the main source of entertainment for individuals with money and leisure. When the opera was produced by a noble house, the noble's reputation and prestige hinged on the quality of the performances mounted.
As Raynor observes:[80]

> Expense was no object, for no nobleman would stint himself and his
> guests when he had an opportunity to impress his peers and possibly his
> betters.

Even in the nineteenth century, the heavily subsidized Paris operas were
known for spectacular stagings, resulting from "gold tossed in with two
hands—subvention and fashion."[81] In many locales an alternative organizational approach was sought that balanced quality and cost more
judiciously. Also, court bureaucracies sometimes lacked the competence
or flexibility to implement the expected multiplicity of operas successfully, and so, as Patrick Barbier states:[82]

> The Italians realised from the beginning of the seventeenth century that
> in order to satisfy their passion it was better to expect nothing of the au-
> thorities; they must organize the building and running of the theatres
> themselves.

The solution to these problems, beginning with Venice's San Cassiano
in 1637 and emulated through much of Italy, London, some German
cities such as Hamburg, and eventually Vienna, was to organize opera
production as an essentially private venture. The funds for building an
opera house were provided by groups of wealthy, often but not always
noble, families. For their contributions they obtained a permanent title
to the best boxes, just as U.S. sports stadiums are financed by selling
preferred boxes to well-heeled corporations. The financiers typically selected from their numbers a governing committee, which contracted
with an impresario to whom was delegated responsibility for planning
the opera season (usually with the advice and consent of the commit-

tee), recruiting singers, selecting composers and librettists, contracting with scenery producers, and attending to the countless details that must be resolved to mount good performances. Financial responsibility was divided between the governing families and the impresario in ways that were not always crystal-clear, creating a lively business for the profession dignified by Portia in Shakespeare's *Merchant of Venice.* Special levies on the original financiers helped cover perennial losses, but some impresarios were driven into bankruptcy and/or were forced to flee, under cover of darkness, creditors who were accompanied by the local police. Impresario suicides were not unknown. In short, from the seventeenth century on, opera in Europe was often organized as a quasi-private enterprise—a point that will become important when we consider the career paths of opera composers.

Instrumental Concert Venues

Private organizations dedicated to the professional performance of instrumental music emerged more slowly than privately organized operas. Their genesis appears to have been linked to two phenomena—a vacuum left by the absence, or default, of the noble establishment in satisfying local demands, and the growth of prosperity, which created non-noble audiences eager to hear instrumental music performed.[83]

London, the largest and one of the wealthiest European cities, provided leadership in this respect. After the Restoration, King Charles II and his successor King James II employed court musicians, but paid them so badly that they were forced (and allowed) to pursue freelance opportunities outside the court. Consequently, during the 1680s and 1690s Henry Purcell, John Blow (1649–1708), and their contemporaries secured rooms, often associated with inns and taverns, where they performed music for paying listeners.[84] With the passage of time a more systematic organizational approach evolved. In 1697 Thomas Hickford opened a "Great Dancing Room" in which concerts were regularly offered. In 1739 Hickford moved to larger (1420 square feet) and more fashionable quarters off Soho Square, where nine-year-old Wolfgang Amadeus Mozart performed with his sister Nannerl in 1765. Nearby was Carlisle House, where Johann Christian Bach and Karl Friedrich Abel initiated a popular concert series in the same year.[85] During the second half of the century several more concert halls were opened, including the Hanover Square Rooms (2530 square feet, accommodating 500), in which Franz Joseph Haydn's first London concerts were held in 1791. After the second round of Haydn concerts in 1794, interest in concert attendance ebbed, possibly because no contemporary composer could replace Haydn, but almost surely also because of the economic burdens of the Napoleonic wars. In 1813, however, the Royal Philharmonic Society was organized to present a regular and continuing concert series, performing among other works many of Beethoven's most important orchestral compositions.

Germany inherited a tradition of concerts, often presented on Sundays and holidays in town squares, by *Stadtpfeiffer* (town pipers) who were paid by the towns to participate in ceremonial festivities and military marches.[86] Paralleling that tradition was the emergence in the sixteenth century of amateur music performance groups. These evolved during the seventeenth century into more formal organizations, one of the most important being the Leipzig Collegium Musicum, initiated in 1688 by Johann Kuhnau (1660–1722). Leipzig was distinctive in at least three respects. For one, as a "free city" it had no resident nobility, and hence no court concert life, but it harbored an affluent middle class. When a visiting Franz Liszt complained about the absence of countesses and princes, Robert Schumann is said to have retorted, "We too [have] our own aristocracy here, namely, 150 bookstores, 50 printing establishments, and 30 newspapers."[87] Second, it was home to the Thomasschule, considered the best musical training school for young Germans during the seventeenth and eighteenth centuries. Third, it harbored a great university, many of whose students had musical talent. Kuhnau brought together university students, pupils of the Thomasschule, and talented Leipzig residents into the Collegium Musicum, whose mostly amateur musicians offered regular paid-admission concerts to Leipzig residents. Later the Collegium, whose activity was mirrored in other German cities, often by organizations with the same name,[88] was led by Georg Philipp Telemann,[89] and between 1729 and 1741, by Johann Sebastian Bach. Its concerts in the Bach era were held at Zimmermann's coffee house. Little evidence has survived on the Collegium's program, although it is virtually certain that many of Bach's secular works from that period were written for it. Through several further organizational adaptations, the Collegium Musicum evolved into a regular concert series located from 1781 on in Leipzig's Gewandhaus, whose orchestra incorporated professional musicians during the next two decades and remained one of the world's great musical organizations over the next two centuries.

In Vienna the holding of private concerts emerged in less independent ways because Vienna enjoyed such a rich array of nobility-backed concert opportunities. During the eighteenth century, halls financed by the monarchy or the many resident nobles were made available, sometimes gratis or at nominal charges, for freelance musical performances by composers such as Mozart and (in his later years) Franz Joseph Haydn. The Tonkünstler-Societät (Society of Musicians), founded in 1772 to organize periodic concerts for the benefit of Viennese musicians, appears to have been the first self-governing concert organization, using, however, halls provided by the monarchy. Mozart's start as a Viennese resident composer was also facilitated by the availability for public summer concerts of the Augarten, a park with pavilion ceded to public use by Emperor Joseph II. Only during the nineteenth century did additional instrumental concert venues emerge that were independent of the Imperial establishment.

In Paris, a larger and wealthier capital city, concert life was at first concentrated in facilities maintained by the monarchy and then, especially after the revolution, in private salons. A partial exception was the Concert Spirituel, which occupied royal premises but operated largely independently of the monarchy, presenting between 1725 and 1790 instrumental and secular vocal music concerts for the public. Up to the time of the Revolution, staging public concerts required a royal privilege. After the Revolution independent venues began to emerge, many short-lived. The Paris Conservatoire, organized officially in 1795, opened a concert hall in 1811 that became a prime locus for public concerts by both its students and outsiders. The Société des Concerts du Conservatoire, founded in 1828, helped build public concert life through frequent concerts by an orchestra comprising Conservatory students and alumni. Also important was the Salle Pleyel, opened in 1830 by the Pleyel music publishing firm, which among other things provided a forum for Frédéric Chopin's Parisian public debut in 1832.[90] By 1866, Paris was the setting for nearly 200 significant concerts annually.[91]

Amsterdam, probably Europe's richest city in terms of income per capita during the eighteenth century, opened its first opera house in 1680 and its first public concert hall, sponsored by the Felix Meritis Society, in 1777.

Russia joined the ranks of private-concert-giving nations relatively late. In 1718, Czar Peter the Great issued a *ukase* encouraging private individuals to hold in their homes mixed-gender *assamblei* analogous to Parisian salons.[92] The practice took root, and musical entertainment became a regular component of the gatherings, among others, those initiated around mid-century by Count A. G. Razumovskii.[93] The first Russian musical society offering weekly concerts for its 300 dues-paying members was established in St. Petersburg in 1772. Its successors included the Philharmonic Society, founded in 1802.

The Spread to Broader Audiences

As the decades advanced and the real income of the average citizen increased, innovative venues for music performance began to emerge, catering to audiences that had not been served by traditional performance approaches.

During the first two centuries of opera performance in Italy, it was customary for the leading theaters to present only operas that were new or at least reworked so that they appeared to be new. In the typical season, three to five new operas would be performed. Following the democratizing events of 1848, however, there was a movement toward repertory opera — that is, the performance of operas that had proved successful in the past. This saved the cost of new librettos and musical scores, and scenery built for previous performances could often be stored and recycled. These cost economies in turn permitted lower subscription or admission fees to be charged, drawing in a broader range of spectators. By the 1870s, the repertory strategy had become the norm in Italy.[94]

In England the democratization of opera took an earlier and quite different turn. The decisive event was the premiere in 1728 of John Gay's *Beggar's Opera*, an irreverent musical extravaganza featuring popular tunes sung in English, contrary to the Italian tradition of conventional London operas. Gay's offering is said to have been the greatest theatrical success of the century in England,[95] precipitating a decade-long craze for ballad operas and draining away potential spectators from London's two Italian opera houses and aggravating their chronic financial difficulties. *The Beggar's Opera* and its derivatives provided a precedent for the highly successful Gilbert and Sullivan operettas during the last three decades of the nineteenth century.

Making an early transition to industrialization and enjoying (with Holland) Europe's highest national per capita incomes in the latter part of the eighteenth century, England also pioneered other means of making music available to a wider spectrum of the public. Three are noteworthy. In 1735 Vauxhall Gardens, southwest across the Thames from today's Victoria Station, began presenting open-air orchestral concerts during the summer — under cover of a roof when it rained.[96] Low admission fees permitted wide participation. Other garden locales soon imitated the Vauxhall initiative, making it possible for London's citizens to hear many of the best-known singers and instrumentalists perform.[97] The increasing popularity of George Frideric Handel's English-language oratorios provided another vehicle for concerts drawing large numbers of listeners. In 1750, the first of various annually repeated performances of Handel's *Messiah* was presented at, and for the benefit of, London's Foundling Hospital. These concerts drew audiences in excess of 1,000 persons.[98] In 1784, a year before the centennial of Handel's birth, the first four gigantic Handel Commemoration concerts were held at Westminster Abbey. The orchestra and chorus totaled 525. The series was repeated during the next three years and again in 1790 and 1791. The audience count at a 1791 performance was 1,067, including Franz Joseph Haydn, who was inspired from his experience to write his *Creation* and *Seasons* oratorios.[99] Later, between 1840 and 1880, the popular demand for music performance was met by the establishment of hundreds of music halls, which offered working-class patrons instrumental and vocal music lubricated by the sale of alcoholic beverages.[100]

In Vienna the democratization of music anticipated the English music halls in a somewhat different form. The waltz, which evolved in preceding decades from Austrian ländler folk dances, was enthusiastically received during the 1814–1815 Congress of Vienna. As Austria resumed its economic growth in the years that followed, ballrooms proliferated in Vienna to the point where, it is said, they could accommodate 50,000 participants simultaneously.[101] Music was provided by orchestras headed at first by Joseph Lanner (1801–1843) and, after he left the Lanner group, by Johann Strauss Sr. The demand was so great that Strauss expanded his forces and began serving multiple ballrooms at the same time. By 1830 he had 300 musicians under contract, who were typically deployed in groups of 25. The attraction of the Strauss and Lanner orchestras was so great that it is said to have impaired attendance at Vienna concerts by Frédéric Chopin in 1830 and 1831.[102] Johann Strauss Jr. later formed his own ensemble to carry on the family tradition independently and, after its success was assured, turned to the composition of operettas paralleling the offerings of Gilbert and Sullivan. To the Viennese operettas of Strauss one can trace a complex lineage from John Gay through the Singspiele — including Mozart's *Magic Flute* — produced to popular acclaim in Vienna's Freihaus-Theater auf der Wieden by Emanuel Schikaneder (1751–1812), and to the French-language operettas of Jacques Offenbach (1819–1880).

Johann Strauss Jr. played a starring role in what may have been the pinnacle of large-scale popular music performance during the nineteenth century. In 1872 he was paid $100,000 plus traveling expenses to conduct his own compositions and those of Mendelssohn and Wagner, performed by an orchestra of 2,000 and a chorus of 20,000, before audiences of 100,000 persons in a huge wooden shed erected for the Boston (Massachusetts) Peace Festival of 1872.[103]

AUDIENCES AT PUBLIC PERFORMANCES

We suggest in this book that as average incomes per capita rose in the various European nations (and later in the United States), the demand for music in diverse forms increased and spread to an ever-widening fraction of the population. This notion and the supporting assertion made by some authors that in Vienna at the onset of the nineteenth century "there was a piano in every house" have been questioned. Perhaps the most pointed challenge was mounted by Julia Moore, who shows inter alia that the "piano in every house" inference was drawn carelessly from a contemporary guidebook that actually said "A piano is found in the home of every educated family" — a major difference, since relatively few families could be called educated in the year 1800.[104] Moore goes on to dispute the contention that, for Vienna at the time of Beethoven, "leadership in musical patronage was wrested from an impoverished aristocracy . . . by an increasingly large and powerful middle class."[105] Moore's critique is joined by sociologist Tia DeNora, who argues that "the actual participation and power of the middle class and second society in musical affairs at the end of the 18th century was still relatively insignificant."[106] DeNora advances the more subtle argument that in Vienna, the aristocracy was more distinct from the upper middle classes, and that it opposed the spread of concerts to the middle class more successfully than in London, where a thriving concert life existed.[107] As a leading biographer of George Frideric Handel (who lived in London mainly during the first half of the eighteenth century) observed:[108]

> There was . . . a growing public for musical performances. Mercantile England was bringing into being large numbers of people who were strange to the uses of their own wealth and leisure and who were eager to know how to live.

But even in London, Simon McVeigh asserts in the preface to his magisterial study of eighteenth-century concert life in London, "it would certainly be a mistake to attribute the rise of the modern symphony concert to a welling-up of middle-class energies."[109]

The differences here are really more matters of timing and location than existence. This is recognized by McVeigh, who observes that the middle classes did demand music performance during the eighteenth century, but had their own preferred concert venues different from those of the nobility. For instance, the wealthier middle-class members had a concert life centered on the City (that is, the banking district).[110] And for others, the public garden concerts were a draw. At Vauxhall Gardens in 1786, for example, according to a contemporary account quoted by McVeigh:[111]

> There were last night above 6000 persons present, among them some of the first people in the kingdom, but as is always the case at Vauxhall, it was a *melange*; the cit and the courtier jostled each other with the usual familiarity; the half guinea was no repellant to the middling order; John

Bull loves to shoulder his superiors in rank . . . and where he pays as much for admission, he never considers them to be more than his equals.

As we have seen, the Industrial Revolution came later to some nations than to others, and from the data in figure 2.2 and table 2.2, it should be clear that changes in income per capita and wealth were in any event gradual rather than revolutionary. And some nations such as England were less socially stratified and class-conscious than others such as Austria. The Viennese nobility may have continued to favor their salons and the Imperial concert halls, but the middle classes attended concerts first in the Augarten and the Freihaus-Theater auf der Wieden and then, by the 1830s, in the ballrooms served by the Lanner and Strauss orchestras.

The gradual spread of piano ownership to the middle classes, and hence the gradual increase of demand for sheet music, can be seen quantitatively from our estimates (used earlier to derive demand elasticities) of the number of pianos owned relative to the number of families residing in the United States. In 1850, the ownership rate was approximately 5 percent; in 1900, it was 12 percent. It reached a peak in 1923 at 23 percent (by which time the United States had become the world's richest industrial nation) before declining under the onslaught of competition from radios and phonographs.

On attendance at and support for important public musical performances, we have fragmentary evidence that fills out the picture more completely. During his time in Vienna, Mozart brought many of his works to public notice through subscription concerts — concert series for which admission tickets were sold in advance by subscription. In March 1784 he sent to his father a list of the 176 subscribers to his first series of three concerts, for which the subscription price was 6 Viennese florins (at prevailing exchange rates, roughly 15 English shillings).[112] The more detailed biographical information that Mozart scholar Otto Erich Deutsch derived from the list permits the following breakdown by social class:

Prince, count, baron, lord or other titled nobility	111
Diplomats without noble title	3
Generals	2
Names with "von" or "de" prefix	55
Other, without evident distinction	5
Total	176

Clearly, Mozart attracted an audience heavily weighted toward the nobility. Interpreting the "von" and "de" designations is more problematic. As an acute observer of Viennese life, Johann Pezzl, noted in 1786, the prefix "Frau von" was used at the time for "wives of merchants, wives of lesser government clerks, of artists, well-to-do professional men and house officers of great families."[113] This is consistent with the occupational descriptions provided by Deutsch. Thus, roughly a third of the participants in Mozart's concerts came from what might be called a bourgeois background — wealthy middle class, to be sure.

For London we have nearly contemporary information on the box holders for subscription concerts held by Johann Christian Bach and Karl Friedrich Abel in the King's Theatre, probably in the spring of 1775.[114] The participants can be broken down as follows:

Prince, Duke, Count, Lord, Marquis, etc.	60
"Honorable"	1
"Mr." or "Mrs."	24
Total	85

At 29 percent, the fraction of commoners appears slightly lower than among Mozart's subscribers. However, the Bach-Abel list is for box subscribers only. Individual admissions were also sold for the pit (what Americans would now call the orchestra) and the galleries — the latter at 5 shillings threepence, half the single-concert box price. Those places usually went to the "lower orders," so it seems likely that the Bach-Abel concerts attracted a larger proportion of commoners than Mozart's Vienna concerts, for which, we know from an estimate of total receipts, few if any single-admission tickets were sold.

An earlier sample of London's music-loving public can be gleaned from a May 1719 list of original subscribers to the Royal Academy of Music, for whose opera presentations George Frideric Handel became music director.[115] Here, however, the stakes were not a handful of shillings, but a minimum guarantee of £200, augmented over the years by calls for mandatory supplements to cover the opera's recurrent losses. My classification of the list is as follows:

Earl, duke, count, viscount, and lord	32
Esquire and sir	11
Other untitled	22
Total	63

Roughly half appear to have been "gentlemen," without titles of nobility (granted more sparingly in England than in Austria) but with sufficient wealth from practicing a profession or from property holdings to guarantee, in backing a costly, risky venture, an investment equivalent to the annual income of six building-trades craftsmen.[116]

Thus, in both London and Vienna during the eighteenth century, the nobility played a leading role in supporting public musical performances, but there is evidence of substantial upper-middle-class participation too. In free cities without a resident nobility, such as Hamburg, Frankfurt, and Leipzig, where a vigorous public concert life nevertheless emerged, we must assume that middle-class participation was much greater. In Italy, too, some cities harbored a preponderance of middle-class operagoers. For instance, Franco Piperno writes concerning attendance at the public opera founded by a rich Padua noble during the seventeenth century:[117]

> In Padua the audience (from the back rows to the front) included "the citizenry," "students" at the university and "aristocratic foreigners," "rectors and nobles of the Veneto," and "gentlewomen" and "gentlemen." We know little about the precise social composition of the audience at court theaters, but what is striking about this testimony from a university city in a republican state—aside from the hierarchical seating arrangements, which much resembled the custom of the courts—is the presence of people of modest social rank . . . who presumably would not have been admitted to court spectacles in the capital city of a monarchical state.

By the nineteenth century, as we have seen already from the emergence of new venues for music performance, the situation was changing significantly. Of his concerts during 1846 in Prague, a city with many nobles who frequently absented themselves to Vienna, Hector Berlioz recalled:[118]

> My concert was attended not only by the lower classes but even by the peasants, to whom certain places were rendered accessible by the low prices; and I was able to judge the interest this audience took in my musical efforts by their singularly naive exclamations at the more unexpected effects, a proof that their memory was sufficiently well stocked to allow of their forming comparisons between the known and the unknown, the old and the new, the good and the bad.

In Birmingham—an industrial center where the English nobility rarely chose to congregate—a performance of Felix Mendelssohn's Elijah in 1846 was attended by an audience of 2,000.[119] Even at La Scala in Milan, the seat of Austria's government occupying Lombardy during the 1820s, the less costly seats were taken by the "black cape" servants of the nobility, soldiers, "well-bred men and women" who did not dress elegantly, and the "lesser people" such as artisans and petty service providers.[120] What one did not find in the La Scala galleries, Rosselli continues, was representation of the lower classes as a whole—for instance, laborers and peasants. But that too changed with the advent of repertory opera during the 1850s. The combination of lower prices and gradually increasing prosperity made opera—still much more important in Italy than symphonic music—so widely accessible that when Giuseppe Verdi left Turin by train for Paris in 1894, ordinary citizens and workers staged a demonstration to bid him farewell.[121] Thus, by the end of the nineteenth century, at least in many parts of the world, good music had become available for widespread popular consumption.

Chapter 3

MUSIC COMPOSITION AS A PROFESSION

WE SHIFT our focus now from broad socioeconomic trends to the particular choices composers made, or were impelled to make, among alternative ways of keeping body and soul together. Chapter 1 identified hypotheses advanced by earlier writers that provide broad themes for the analysis here. In particular, it is said that the late eighteenth century in general, and the experience of Wolfgang Amadeus Mozart in particular, marked a transition from the support of composing activity through patronage and church employment to private market alternatives, which in turn meant that composers became freelance artists accepting the risks of creating for the market. We shall find here that changes did occur, but they were more gradual and evolutionary.

THE EMPLOYMENT ALTERNATIVES

Composers earned their bread in many ways. They included working for the church, serving in noble courts, securing support in other ways from wealthy (mostly noble) patrons, and engaging in freelance activities, which in turn took a diversity of forms. It should not be surprising that many composers availed themselves of more than one such opportunity, sometimes simultaneously and sometimes at differing career stages. As Simon McVeigh observes in his excellent book on concert life in eighteenth-century London, "No musician working in London for any length of time made his entire living from concert work, and the career of most musicians was an ever-varying cocktail of different enterprises."[1] In pursuing multiple activities, composers had to allocate their limited time and energy among competing alternatives.

Church Employment

From at least the time of the Renaissance, European musicians found countless opportunities to be employed in the churches as organists, choir directors, and (in the most affluent churches) Kapellmeister presiding over music ranging from a capella singing to full orchestral performances. Virtually all Roman Catholic parishes of any size and most of the Protestant churches, except those following the most conservative

Calvinist and Puritan precepts, needed at least an organist, who in the seventeenth and eighteenth centuries was expected to perform some of his own compositions as well as using public-domain materials.

In the smaller parishes the persons who filled these jobs were poorly paid, but they were at least assured, as a nun who taught the author in elementary school used to say, of "three squares and an oblong." In the more important churches and cathedrals, the Kapellmeister's position was highly attractive and eagerly sought. Had he been blessed with better health, Mozart's career need not have ended in a morass of debt. Mozart had applied successfully for a position that would have made him the successor to Leopold Hoffmann (1738–1793), Kapellmeister of St. Stephan's cathedral in Vienna.[2] Hoffmann's salary was 2,000 florins per year (£205, or five times the annual income of a fully employed building craftsman in southern England) plus generous emoluments, which, with his various other sources of income, would have allowed Mozart to live comfortably. But Mozart died before he reached his thirty-sixth birthday while Hoffmann, whose health was not considered good at the time, lived on unexpectedly until 1793. Half a century later, the thirteen-year-old Camille Saint-Saëns chose to concentrate on organ performance at the Paris Conservatory instead of piano because it offered better employment prospects at a French church.[3]

The level of musical performance that churches could sustain was adversely affected by the confiscation of income-earning church lands in Austria under reforms initiated by Emperor Joseph II and in France following the revolution of 1789. But as the Mozart and Saint-Saëns examples testify, employment opportunities remained.

Support from the Nobility

A second major source of support for composers during the seventeenth and eighteenth centuries was found in the noble courts, many of which, we have seen in chapter 2, competed to outdo one another in the excellence of their orchestras and operas. Actually, support came in two main forms: from employment in the court and from subsidies more or less detached from work obligations.

Employment opportunities in court orchestras or Kapellen ranged from instrumental performance positions to directorship of a court's musical establishment, with salaries steeply graduated according to the responsibilities attached. Usually those who were proficient enough to be remembered as significant composers rose to the top of the ranks and enjoyed substantial salaries—for example, Johann Sebastian Bach at Köthen, Johann Stamitz in the famous Mannheim / Schwetzingen musical organization, Joseph Haydn at the Esterházy palaces, and Haydn's brother Michael under the Prince / Archbishop of Salzburg. Occasionally a musician rose even further by modern-day values, becoming political adviser to a sovereign, as castrato Farinelli (Carlo Broschi, 1705–1782) did in the court of Spain's Kings Philip V and then Ferdinand VI.[4]

Some nobles and other wealthy individuals were also patrons of the arts, and as such provided outright subsidies or continuing pensions to particularly worthy composers. Sometimes these required a quid pro quo, such as delivering a commissioned work, but in other cases none was required.

During the seventeenth and eighteenth centuries and well into the nineteenth century, composers commonly dedicated a work to a wealthy hoped-for patron and sent it to him, unsolicited, accompanied by profuse flattery. The etiquette of the times called for the would-be patron to provide in return an appropriate honorarium, but this was not obligatory, and many ignored the gesture. The Elector of Brandenburg failed to acknowledge J. S. Bach's gift of the six Brandenburg concerti and let them lie, unplayed and unknown, in a musty cupboard. Bach is believed to have been sorely disappointed when he traveled in 1747 to Potsdam, improvised on a theme given him there by Frederick the Great, and then dedicated to Frederick his magnificent *Musikalisches Opfer* (Musical Offering), but received neither an honorarium nor travel expenses from the king.[5] On the other hand, he was handsomely rewarded with a golden goblet containing 100 Louis d'or (= £114) for dedicating to Count Hermann von Keyserlingk the so-called Goldberg Variations.[6] While in London Joseph Haydn performed twenty-six musicales for the Prince of Wales, but received nothing in return. When the British Parliament later settled the prince's substantial debts, Haydn sent a bill for 100 guineas, which the Parliament paid.[7] Beethoven sent to King George IV of England a dedicated copy of his *Wellington's Victory* battle symphony, but heard nothing in return. He did not let the matter rest, however, and through his musician friends in London, a payment of £600 was finally negotiated ten years later.[8] He was less successful in dedicating his Ninth Symphony (*Choral*) to King Friedrich Wilhelm of Prussia. The king sent him in return what was purported to be a diamond ring, but proved on careful examination to contain a cheap stone worth 300 paper florins (£12).[9]

Subsidies with little or no return performance obligation were not unusual. During much of his London career, George Frideric Handel received from the royal family an annual pension of £600, only £200 of which was tied to musical instruction Handel provided members of the family.[10] Beginning in 1787, Mozart received from the court of Emperor Joseph II a stipend without duties of 800 florins per year (£46, or 1.2

times an English building craftsman's annual earnings). During the early years of his stay in Vienna, Beethoven received from Prince Karl von Lichnowsky an annual pension of 600 florins (£50), which ended in 1806 after a dispute over a requested performance at the prince's summer estate. In 1809, when Beethoven was about to accept a position in Kassel, Germany, three patrons persuaded him to remain in Vienna by guaranteeing him an annual pension of 4,000 florins. Its purchasing power eroded dramatically owing to inflation and currency reforms in the wake of the Napoleonic wars, but the renegotiated pension continued to provide significant support to Beethoven through the rest of his life.[11] Perhaps the most generous royal subsidy known went to Richard Wagner from King Ludwig II of Bavaria. During the last two decades of Wagner's life Ludwig conferred upon him personal cash gifts estimated at 500,000 marks (£25,000) along with substantial loans, later repaid, to finance the construction of and heavy losses incurred by Wagner's Festspielhaus in Bayreuth.[12] Even so, the criticism aroused in Munich over Ludwig's generosity forced Wagner to ask his publishers for supplemental loans.[13]

Members of the nobility were not the only ones who provided financial support to struggling composers. Tchaikovsky, for example, received between 1877 and 1890 an annual pension of 6,000 rubles (approximately £700) from Nadezhda von Meck, a widow whose deceased husband had accumulated a fortune through railroad building. The annuity is said to have contributed a third of Tchaikovsky's yearly income.[14] Perhaps the most unusual subsidy was from one composer to another. In 1838 Niccolò Paganini, recognizing that he was dying but not that unwise investments would bring him financial difficulties, gave the struggling thirty-seven-year-old Hector Berlioz 20,000 French francs (£782, or 13 times an English building craftsman's annual earnings).[15]

FREELANCE AND OTHER PRIVATE SECTOR ACTIVITY

The increasing prosperity of a music-loving public opened up many opportunities for composers to earn a living through activities supported by neither the church nor noble patrons. Gradually, privately organized orchestras came to replace the orchestras and chamber concerts supported by the nobility. These provided employment for composers as performers and directors. In accepting such positions, however, composers continued to be employees. A more important departure was the pursuit of freelance opportunities in which the composers were in effect independent agents with the discretion to choose at arm's length which tasks they would undertake and which they would decline.[16] These free-lance activities assumed numerous forms.

Composition and Publication Fees

For one, there was a demand for the composition of specific works in exchange for a fee or honorarium. Already at the start of the seventeenth century, we have seen in chapter 2, the creation of new operas was organized in this way throughout much of Italy and in England. Opera impresarios negotiated with composers case by case for composition to a particular libretto, sometimes suggested by the composer but usually by the impresario. Fees and other terms of the agreement were individually negotiated. Analogous commissions were given out by private individuals and orchestra associations. Mozart's commission in 1791 from an anonymous nobleman (much later discovered to be Graf von Walsegg) for the composition of a Requiem is a famous early example. The Philharmonic Society of London negotiated with Beethoven (in the end unsuccessfully, because of coordination and health difficulties) for first performance rights on Beethoven's still-to-be-composed late symphonies.

Fees could also be earned by selling compositions to a music publisher. A few composers born in the seventeenth century, such as George Frideric Handel in London, Georg Philipp Telemann in Hamburg, and François Couperin in Paris, earned appreciable sums through the publication of their music. The market for serious works was thin, however, and the fees offered by publishers were modest. Publication became an important source of income only a century or so later in the time of Beethoven. It was so important that we devote to it a special chapter, chapter 7, and leave it without further discussion at this point.

Performance Income

Composers often earned at least a part of their living by serving as featured guest performers, either with an orchestra that needed special talent, as in concertos, or in performances that emphasized the composer as a solo or accompanied artist.

An early representative of the guest artist school was Jean-Marie Leclair (1697–1764), who travelled widely in northern Europe, appearing as guest violinist with various orchestras, before he received a standing appointment as musician in the court of King Louis XV. Although guest artists were occasionally used in earlier concerts, the idea of paying a star instrumentalist a large fee to enhance concert attendance may have originated with London impresario Johann Salomon (1745–1815) in 1793 (two years after Salomon's first concert series featuring Joseph Haydn as resident composer and conductor). Salomon retained composer Giovanni Viotti (1755–1824), considered Europe's leading violinist, to appear as soloist in his orchestral concert series for the unprecedented season fee of £578.[17] (Higher fees had been commanded by opera singers, but not by instrumentalists.) By the second half of the nineteenth century the guest artist tradition was well-established, with soloists such as Joseph Joachim (1831–1907) and Johannes Brahms playing violin or piano solo parts with numerous European orchestras.

Much more prominent were the artists who embarked upon a grand tour to feature themselves as performers, often in conjunction with accompanists and/or vocalists. A well-known early example was the 1763–1765 tour of Wolfgang Amadeus Mozart and his family to arrange child prodigy performances in Munich, Stuttgart, Mannheim, Paris, Brussels, and The Hague, among other locations. At the age of ten, Johann Nepomuk Hummel undertook a similar trip with his father, returning home only five years later. Netting nearly 11,000 Reichsthaler (£2,200) after deduction of expenses, the tour was much more successful financially than that of the Mozarts.[18] The difference, it would appear, lay in more patient and careful planning of concert locations by father Hummel. Hummel's later adult tours, while on leave from Kapellmeister duties at Weimar, are said to have brought him "a modest fortune."[19] After a limited youthful tour with his father, cellist Luigi Boccherini embarked in 1767 upon a freelance concert tour with violinist Vincenzo Manfredini (1737–1799) that carried him eventually to Paris and then to a permanent position in Madrid. John Field (1782–1837) travelled widely through western Europe demonstrating pianos manufactured by his mentor, Muzio Clementi, before settling in Russia during 1803. The grand tour tradition reached a pinnacle with the spectacularly successful and lucrative European tours of Niccolò Paganini and Franz Liszt. The successes of the two were related, since Liszt is said to have learned his audience-pleasing showmanship from attending a Paris concert by Paganini in 1831.[20] So spellbound were listeners by the solo performances of Liszt that Clara Schumann, who supported her sizable family through extensive concertizing, arranged her early tours to avoid appearing in venues where Liszt had played, or was scheduled to play, during the same time period.[21]

Some well-known composers were adept at solo performances and enjoyed giving them; others lacked the crowd-pleasing gift or were unwilling to make the sacrifices necessary to succeed. Beethoven had substantial early success as a piano soloist in Vienna, but had to end his performance career in 1808 as his deafness progressed. Carl Czerny, an excellent pianist and composer of unusually challenging piano études, is said to have done little concertizing because his playing lacked spectacular effects.[22] Frédéric Chopin's public performances were infrequent and confined with few exceptions to small halls, in part because his sublime playing was quiet, projecting poorly in a large room. To Franz Liszt he explained, "I am not fit for concerts. Crowds intimidate me. I feel poisoned by their breath, paralyzed by curious glances, and confused by the sight of strange faces."[23] Johannes Brahms was an outstanding pianist, but limited his public performances in his early career, partly because, as he explained in an 1855 letter, "my aversion to playing for people has got quite out of hand. At times I am seriously frightened."[24] To earn a living, however, he overcame his apprehensions and commanded considerable sums as a solo performer. After he achieved financial security, he cut back his concertizing sharply because, as he explained to his father in 1862, "I could now go on giving fine concerts, but it's not what I want to do; for it would take up so much of my time that I wouldn't get to much else" [such as composing].[25] During the 1860s and 1870s, Richard Wagner went on concert tours to alleviate his chronic financial needs, earning 18,000 florins (£1,800) from 1875 performances, but feared the concerts would so delay his work on *The Ring* and other operas that he would die before completing it.[26]

Entrepreneurship

Most freelance composer-musicians of the eighteenth and nineteenth centuries were content to offer their works to patrons, publishers, and impresarios and to perform in concerts organized by others. Some, however, accepted more or less extensive entrepreneurial functions for the performance of their compositions.

Georg Philipp Telemann directed regular concerts of Leipzig's Collegium Musicum in the early 1700s, as did Johann Sebastian Bach between 1729 and 1741. Admission was charged, but little is known about the division of proceeds among Telemann and Bach as organizers, the (mostly amateur) performers, and Zimmermann's Coffee House, where the concerts were held. From the 1720s to the time of his death in 1767 Telemann performed similar entrepreneurial functions, organizing concerts as a sideline to his duties as church and school music director in Hamburg.

As we have seen in chapter 2, London during the eighteenth century was the scene of many privately organized concert series.[27] Among the most famous of them was the Bach-Abel series beginning in 1765. Organization and risk-bearing for the series were undertaken by Johann Christian Bach, the son of Johann Sebastian Bach, and Carl Friedrich Abel (1735–1782). At first the concerts were highly successful. But then the rent was trebled at their concert hall; a move to a different location failed to attract remunerative audiences; and the purchase by Bach of a large house at Hanover Square was even more unprofitable. Receipts fell from £3,959 in 1774 to £1,505 in 1775 and further in later years. As losses accumulated, Abel dropped out of the partnership, leaving Bach heavily in debt.[28]

A conventional way of bringing one's compositions and often also one's performance skills to the public's notice in eighteenth-century Vienna and other parts of continental Europe was the subscription concert, also known as an *Académie*. Mozart pursued the method with considerable success during his early years as a resident of Vienna. As we saw in chapter 2, his first series of three self-initiated concerts in 1784 attracted 176 advance subscriptions at a package price of 6 florins. The standard procedure was for the composer to announce in advance the contemplated program, seek subscriptions, and if all went well, rent the hall (or preferably, have it provided gratis by a nobleman), hire the necessary orchestral players, and proceed. If subscriptions were inadequate, the series could be cancelled. This means of hedging proved important for a concert series announced by Mozart in 1789, by which time Austria was at war with the Ottoman Empire, many Viennese residents were absent from the city, and taxes had been raised. Only a single person — Mozart's faithful backer, Baron Gottfried van Swieten — subscribed, and the series was cancelled.[29]

Beethoven sold subscriptions for some of his self-organized concerts in Vienna, usually offered as single events, and for others he depended mainly on box-office receipts. Julia Moore reports that use of the subscription approach declined sharply during Beethoven's early Vienna years — a phenomenon paralleled nearly simultaneously by a drop in London concert series.[30] The timing coincidence suggests that war worries and increased taxes due to the Napoleonic wars were important contributing factors. From a meticulous study of Beethoven's finances, Moore concludes that "even though half of his concerts were failures financially, a few profitable concerts sustained Beethoven's optimism for many years."[31] She infers more generally (p. 286) that "public concerts were risky ventures during this period, and the composers who dared to organize their concerts were either optimists or gamblers in spirit."

One-off concerts were undertaken by composers without a formal subscription mechanism, although it was customary to sell tickets in advance. The experience of Hector Berlioz illustrates the range of conditions. When Berlioz traveled through central Europe during the 1840s and thereafter, his concerts were usually arranged by local impresarios or nobles, who paid all the expenses and typically offered Berlioz half of the receipts.[32] In Paris, however, the principal concert venues — the Opéra and (later) the Salle du Conservatoire — were frequently denied him, at least partly in reaction to his sharply worded articles as a music critic. He therefore had to arrange and finance most of his own Parisian concerts, including a series of several concerts annually between 1834 and 1842 at which both his own music and that of others was presented in the Salle du Conservatoire (from which he was systematically excluded after 1843).[33] Serving as impresario for the performance of his own music posed special problems because, unlike Mozart and the youthful Beethoven but like Beethoven of the *Missa solemnis* and Ninth Symphony, his works typically required massive orchestral and choral forces, most of whom had to be paid. In 1844, for example, he secured a temporary building used for an industrial exhibition, recruited a thousand instrumentalists (including 36 double basses) and singers, and advertised the advance sale of tickets for a "gigantic concert" that would feature selections from his own works (including *Symphonie fantastique* and a *Hymne à la France*).[34] On the morning of the concert, after one partial and one full rehearsal, advance ticket sales amounting to 12,000 francs were sufficient to defray only half of the expenses already sunk. But as the day advanced, eight thousand Parisians streamed in to hear the concert,[35] raising total ticket sales to 32,000 francs, out of which, after all performance expenses, taxes, and police fees were paid, 800 francs remained for Berlioz as organizer and composer.[36] Large losses incurred when he hired the Opéra Comique for the premiere of his *Faust* in 1846 were recouped only through a profitable concert tour in Russia. This and similar experiences led Berlioz to write about a nightmare he had during the 1850s:[37]

> I dreamt that I was composing a symphony. . . . I had gone to my table to begin writing it down when I suddenly reflected: "If I write this part I shall let myself be carried on to write the rest. The natural tendency of my mind to expand the material is sure to make it very long. . . . When the symphony is finished I shall be weak enough to allow my copyist to copy it out, and thus immediately incur a debt of 1,000 or 1,200 francs. Once the parts are copied I shall be harassed by the temptation to have the work performed; I shall give a concert in which, as is sure to be the case in these days, the receipts will barely cover half the expenses; I shall lose what I have not got; I shall want the necessaries of life for my poor invalid [wife], and shall have no money either for myself or for my son's keep on board ship!" . . . I threw down my pen, saying, "Bah! I shall have forgotten the symphony tomorrow." But the following night the obstinate symphony again presented itself . . .

Berlioz's experience was extreme, but it illustrates a more general point: that organizing and financing one's own concerts could be a nightmarishly risky business.

Opera during the seventeenth and eighteenth centuries, we observed in chapter 2, was typically organized in much of Italy and in London when groups of wealthy individuals joined to build an opera house and subsidize regular performance seasons, entrusting to a private impresario responsibility for bringing together the various forces required and assuming many contractual risks.[38] The impresario's function was a specialized one, demanding skills more like those required in the realm of business than for musical performance. Composers contracted with the impresario to write the score, participate in rehearsals, and often to conduct, typically from the harpsichord, the first three performances. But there were occasional exceptions in which composers served also as impresarios.[39]

The most important early case was that of George Frideric Handel.[40] After several years as a freelance composer of operas and diverse other works in London, Handel was named salaried musical director of the newly organized Royal Academy of Music in 1719, which became for a while London's principal opera company. The Academy was financed initially by subscriptions of at least £200 each from 63 wealthy individuals (by other accounts, 73), who were called upon repeatedly in subsequent years for additional levies to cover operating losses. At first Handel's responsibilities were largely creative, writing operas, recruiting talent, and overseeing the opera program. By 1729, however, the Academy's subscribers had tired of being dunned for additional funds, and their participation ended. Financial responsibility was thereupon taken over by Handel in partnership with Swiss émigre John Jacob Heidegger (1666–1749). Their productions lurched perilously between profit and loss. Crucial to the group's survival were subsidies from the royal family, which in the 1732–1733 season comprised 20 percent of total receipts.[41] The situation was made even more difficult by the formation in 1733 of a second competing opera company, the Opera of the Nobility, which among other things lured away from Heidegger and Handel several of their most talented singers and imported from Italy the most renowned of all castrati, Farinelli. In 1734 Heidegger ended the partnership. Handel then continued to stage operas on his own initiative, with occasional help from Heidegger, relocating to Covent Garden and developing a new and more successful format, English-language oratorios. The oratorios rescued him from what otherwise would have been financial ruin and in the end, after numerous reverses, made him a wealthy man. In serving as entrepreneur and impresario for his own operas and oratorios, Handel among other things sold tickets from the residence he had purchased at 21 Brook Street (now a Handel museum). In 1739, Handel began selling individual entrance tickets, permitting attendance by middle-class citizens who could not afford the traditional season's subscription.

Even without the difficulties of presenting Italian-language opera to uncomprehending Londoners, Handel's contemporary Antonio Vivaldi was less fortunate in taking on impresario functions. Vivaldi claimed to have written 94 operas, many of them lost to posterity, as a sideline to his teaching and *maestro di cappella* duties at the Ospedale della Pietà orphanage.[42] He also served occasionally as impresario at some of the lesser Venetian opera houses, producing both his own and other composers' operas. In 1736, however, he overstepped his luck, accepting a commission to produce a three-year series of operas, some written by others and revised by him and another original to him, to be performed in the papal city of Ferrara, 114 kilometers from Venice. All of them failed, in part because he was forbidden to enter Ferrara by the local cardinal on grounds of alleged immorality — that is, for not fulfilling his priestly duties by saying Mass regularly, and because he was accompanied on tours by a female opera singer-companion. Thus, he was forced to entrust local production functions to a substitute, who managed them badly. And after the obstinate cardinal's transfer from Ferrara, Vivaldi's own Ferrara opera failed artistically. He became mired in litigation over alleged contractual debts amounting to 6,000 Italian ducats (very roughly, £1,200), 60 times his annual salary at the Ospedale.[43] In 1738 he lost his Ospedale position and was reduced to selling freelance works to the Ospedale and wealthy patrons. In 1740 (some accounts say 1741) he travelled to Vienna, hoping to revive his fortunes by writing operas for a Viennese theater. In this too he was unsuccessful. He died there in 1741 and was given a pauper's burial.

Richard Wagner served as impresario and manager of his own opera productions after he settled in Bayreuth. He, too, incurred substantial losses. The first Bayreuth festival of 1876 recorded a net loss of 150,000 marks (£7,250). Unlike Vivaldi, however, Wagner was saved by the generous patronage of Bavaria's King Ludwig II.

Teaching

Many composers earned a living through teaching. As economic growth enriched the middle class, we have seen, individuals who wanted to perform music at home demanded instruction in the art and skills of playing instruments. Also, as noble establishments reduced or eliminated their court orchestras, opportunities shrank for learning instrumental playing by doing, increasing the need for alternative ways of training professional musicians.

Some musicians such as Franz Schubert and Bedřich Smetana turned to teaching as a last resort, because they found it difficult to earn a living through music in other ways.[44] Julia Moore concludes from a study of Viennese estate records that during the Napoleonic wars, as noble courts were retrenching, there was a marked increase in the number of musicians who described themselves as *Klaviermeister*, which she interprets to mean that they derived most of their income through teaching.[45]

For a few musicians, providing private lessons was a successful means of accumulating wealth. When he returned to London in 1784 after a long piano performance tour on the continent, Muzio Clementi took up teaching and claimed to have given lessons 16 hours per day. By the turn of the century, he had amassed a fortune of some £15,000 — capital to finance his entry into music publishing and later piano manufacturing, which increased his wealth even more.[46] As one of Vienna's leading independent piano teachers, Carl Czerny gave private lessons for some 12 hours per day, leaving at his death a fortune of 100,000 silver florins (£10,000).[47] In 1818, Beethoven asked Czerny to play the solo in the premiere performance of the Fifth Piano Concerto (Emperor), but Czerny was too busy teaching to prepare adequately.[48] Twelve years later, however, when his finances were solid, Czerny reported to Felix Mendelssohn that he was spending less time teaching and more composing, since the latter yielded a better financial return.[49] Thanks to his entrée into the most fashionable Paris salons, Frédéric Chopin became the favorite piano teacher of wealthy Parisians and, until his health failed, earned sufficient income to live stylishly.[50]

A good reputation among the wealthy citizens of a major city permitted piano teachers to command substantial fees for an hour's instruction. Clementi normally charged one guinea per hour. Coming to London from Austria in 1791, Joseph Haydn was astonished to find that, like Clementi, he could command a guinea (£1.05) per hour — more than a week's earnings for an English building craftsman.[51] Chopin's standard fee was 20 francs per lesson, which in the 1830s was equivalent to three-fourths of a guinea. For more run-of-the-mill piano teachers in Vienna at the beginning of the nineteenth century, Moore reports, the standard fee appears to have been one florin, or one-tenth what Haydn charged in London.[52] From his more affluent Viennese students, on the other hand, Mozart obtained one-half gold ducat per hour, or about £0.25.[53]

Composer-teachers engaged in price discrimination, charging lower rates to less affluent students. Particularly promising but impoverished students were often given free lessons. Mozart not only charged the nine-year-old Johann Nepomuk Hummel no tuition, but also took the youth into his household (in 1787) and let him reside there without compensation for nearly two years.[54] Antonio Salieri asked fees only of his noble and rich middle-class students; others, such as W. A. Mozart's son Franz, Beethoven, Carl Czerny, Franz Schubert, Ignaz Moscheles (1794–1870), and Franz Liszt, received free instruction.[55] Czerny also instructed Franz Liszt without pay; Liszt in turn charged his students in Weimar nothing. In Leipzig Clara Schumann had a less philanthropic approach. She would not accept Leipzig students at all because she apparently believed she would lose respect engaging in commercial transactions with her fellow citizens, but she consented to take on visitors from abroad at a fee of two thaler (£0.3) per hour.[56]

Teaching students of mediocre talent was an onerous task, and composers begrudged the time teaching took from more creative work. As Mozart wrote to his father from Paris in 1778:[57]

> Out of good will I gladly give lessons, especially when I see that someone has talent, enjoyment, and the desire to learn. But to have to go to someone's house at a particular hour, or to wait at home for someone, that I cannot do, even if it brings in money. That's impossible for me. I leave it to other people who can't do anything but play the piano. . . . The talent that a kindly God gave me in such abundance I can use composing.

Soon after his arrival in Vienna during 1781, Mozart informed his father that he had taken on four students but wanted no more:[58]

> I can have as many as I like, but I'd rather not have so many — I want to be better paid than the others, and in that respect I'd rather have fewer. . . . I'd rather have three pupils who pay me well than six who pay me poorly.

After his financial fortunes worsened, however, he told a benefactor in 1790 that he had two students currently and wished to raise the number to eight.[59]

Beethoven had numerous students (including Czerny) during his early Vienna years. As his health deteriorated, however, he limited his teaching mainly to his patron Archduke Rudolph, and even then, he observed in a letter, if he didn't show up for the Archduke's lesson, it was a crime against majesty, but if he did show up, all he got was a stamp to be displayed when he collected his 1,500 florin yearly pension.[60] Chopin complained about students who left for their summer holidays and failed to pay their past-due fees — a problem with which the husband of a twenty-first-century piano teacher can readily empathize.[61] When his strength ebbed as a result of tuberculosis, Chopin's teaching manner with middle-class students became testy and ironic — but not for his high-society students, with whom he was always charming and considerate.[62] Edvard Grieg is said to have looked back with bitterness on his early years in Norway, "when almost all his energy went into instructing young ladies who wished to play the piano, instead of being available for more creative work."[63]

In addition to giving private lessons, composers could earn their bread teaching in schools. A few composers, such as Tomaso Albinoni, Jean-Philippe Rameau, and Bedřich Smetana opened their own formally organized schools. Most, however, worked in schools organized by the church, the nobility, or local governments.

The existence of formal music schools can be traced back to church choir schools established at York, England, in A.D. 627, Salzburg in 774, and Lüneburg, Germany, in 995.[64] By the sixteenth century in England, as many as 40 choir schools could be counted, the best of which was the Chapel Royal in London.[65] Some European universities offered courses in music, and musical training was an accepted part of grammar schools' curricula on the European continent. Especially important to the development of music in the seventeenth through nineteenth centuries were schools in a few key continental cities — notably, Leipzig, Venice, and Naples. The Thomasschule of Leipzig was founded in 1212 to train boys to sing in the local churches. It was not the only such school in Germany, but stood out for its distinguished cantors during the seventeenth and eighteenth centuries — notably, Johann Sebastian Bach and Johann Kuhnau (1660–1722). In Venice, a significant contribution was made by four orphanages (ospedali), which initially housed orphaned or abandoned girls, but which later accepted girls from middle-class families drawn by the excellent education the ospedali provided in both music and the liberal arts. During the seventeenth and early eighteenth centuries the ospedali had as faculty members many of the most distinguished Venetian composers, including Antonio Vivaldi, Giovanni Legrenzi (1626–1690), Nicola Porpora (1686–1768), Johann Hasse (1699–1783), Baldassare Galuppi (1706–1785) and Niccolò Jommelli (1714–1774). Their orchestras gave weekly concerts for the citizens of Venice and performed at civic and religious events. The modern term "conservatory" stems from the four conservatori of Naples, founded during the seventeenth century. Initially they, like the ospedali of Venice, were founded as orphanages and as schools for the poor.[66] During the seventeenth century they began to emphasize musical education, training composers inter alia for the Neapolitan opera and drawing from all over Italy young castrati, who were given a superb musical education to start them on careers as opera singers. Students from poor families were admitted free after rigorous screening; others paid fees. By the outset of the eighteenth century they were considered Italy's leading institutions of musical education. Political and economic instability then precipitated closures and mergers, so that by the first decade of the nineteenth century only a single conservatory, the Real Collegio di Musica, survived.

Meanwhile other conservatories were being opened. In 1795, the Conservatoire National de Musique et de Déclamation was established in Paris, inheriting and adding to functions from the earlier École Royale de Chant. Additional conservatory foundings occurred at Bologna in 1806, Milan in 1807, Prague in 1811, Vienna in 1817, London (the Royal Academy of Music) in 1822, and many others in successive years, including Leipzig in 1843, Berlin in 1850, St. Petersburg in 1862, both Venice and Rome in 1877, and Amsterdam in 1884.[67] Music education had become a systematic public undertaking spread throughout the world, drawing important composers onto faculties and turning out new generations of musicians, some of whom would become composers.

A Systematic Enumeration

Musicians also earned their living through work largely unrelated to composition or performance. We now advance, however, to investigate the choice of career paths from a more quantitative perspective. We analyze data on the sample of 646 composers born during the two centuries from 1650 through 1849.[68] How the sample was compiled is described more fully in chapter 1.

In interpreting the data that follow, it is important to recognize that there was a slight upward trend over time in the number of composers drawn into the sample, which was 141 for those born between 1650 and 1699, 148 for 1700–1749 birth dates, 168 for 1750–1799 birth dates, and 189 for the 1800–1849 cohort.

For each sampled composer, a battery of information was coded on birth and death dates and locations, years worked in diverse nations, and occupational experiences. This chapter draws mainly on the occupational information, with categories including church and noble court employment, freelance activity of various types, employment as a performer or director of a private sector orchestra, and various other categories that will be explained as we progress. Each coded activity was given a score of 3 (principal activity), 2 (secondary activity), or 1 (tertiary activity), taking into account both intensity and duration. Subjective judgments had to be made, but the process was reiterated until there was no longer reason to believe that serious systematic biases had intruded.[69] Needless to say, many composers pursued multiple means of earning a living, sometimes switching principal occupations in mid-career and often carrying several jobs simultaneously.

Composers' Occupational Experiences

We begin our analysis of how composers earned their living by examining the support they received from the nobility, ranging from counts to emperors and czars. The historical data were coded in three main ways: to show employment as director (for instance, Kapellmeister) of court musical activities and/or performances; as a performer in a court musical organization; and as recipient of noble subsidies for supplying occasional compositions or (as with the annuities received by George Frideric Handel from the English kings or Mozart from the Austrian emperor) for adorning the royal domain. Figure 3.1 shows how support of these types varied over fifty-year birth-date intervals, taking as the measure the percent of all composers born in a particular cohort so engaged. In each case, only activities that were primary or secondary to the composer's means of support are tallied. Tertiary codes were for the most part sparingly utilized and probably underestimate the amount of sporadic or occasional activity by composers. Brahms's three multimonth visits enjoying the hospitality of the duke of Detmold, for instance, were considered insufficient to merit a tertiary code. It must be noted again that a composer can be coded in more than one category. It was not at all unusual, for example, for an individual to begin as a court performer and remain in that primary role for several years before being promoted to Kapellmeister. But some continued in performance positions throughout their careers.

From figure 3.1 we see that composers born between 1650 and 1749 experienced substantial employment as court performers and directors. Employment dropped markedly for composers born during the second half of the eighteenth century, consistent with the evidence that the "arms race" among central European nobles for prestige through the maintenance of court orchestras began ebbing during that interval. Following the tumultuous events of the Napoleonic wars and the reform of feudal institutions, employment in noble courts declined precipitously for composers born in the first half of the nineteenth century.

All the composers employed in noble courts were engaged at least part-time in composing, so the right-hand bars in figure 3.1, representing employment for composition per se, include only those composers who received stipends merely to compose, without any concurrent performance or directoral obligations. These elite subventions were much fewer in number and dropped steadily over time to 7.4 percent, covering 14 composers, by the last fifty-year interval.

A few composers were employed in courts mainly to teach music to the noble offspring. An example is Franz Schubert's employment at the summer residence of Count Johann Esterházy in Zeliz, Hungary. It is coded as "secondary" despite its relatively short time duration because it was the only real employment Schubert enjoyed after leaving his father's school. Eleven composers were coded as having primary or secondary court employment of this type, which is not counted in figure

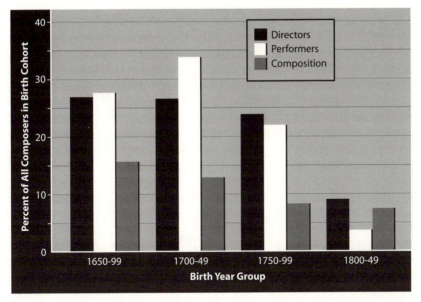

FIGURE 3.1 Percentage of Composer Cohorts with Support from Nobility

3.1. There were 4 cases for composers born in the first fifty-year interval, 2 in the second, 4 in the third, and 1 in the fourth.

Figure 3.2 summarizes the history of composers' employment with the various churches. The data are divided into only two categories, for directoral positions and for performance responsibilities (such as church organists). Church employment opportunities were embraced most extensively by composers born during the second half of the seventeenth century. After that, decline set in, especially for church choir or music director jobs. One possible reason for the decrease in directoral opportunities was the loss of revenue needed to maintain extensive musical organizations as properties were taken from the churches, especially in the Austria of Joseph II and revolutionary France, during the late eighteenth and early nineteenth centuries.

A few composers such as Antonio Vivaldi, Francesco Bonporti (1672–1749), (Abbé) Georg Joseph Vogler (1749–1814), Archduke (and Cardinal) Rudolph of Austria (1788–1831), and Franz Liszt received support as ordained priests or other officers of the church without necessarily having to discharge musical duties. If their compensation was unrelated to musical duties, their church support was not recorded in figure 3.2. There were 9 such cases for the 1650–1699 birth cohort, 6 for the second fifty-year birth interval, 1 (Rudolph) for the third, and 1 (Liszt) for the fourth.

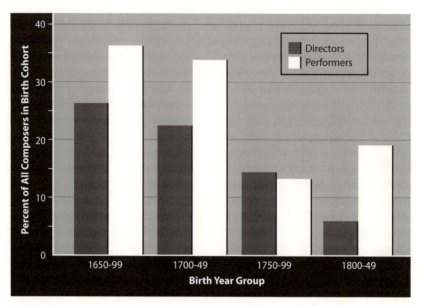

FIGURE 3.2 Percentage of Composer Cohorts Employed by the Church

Freelance Activity

As we have seen, composers engaged in various forms of freelance activity. Two of the most important categories were freelance performance and freelance composing. The coding for freelance composing was deliberately conservative. Activity was not counted as freelance when an artist composed for the sake of creation per se or when an individual employed to perform, direct, and/or compose music dedicated an occasional work to someone other than his employer, published an occasional work, or sporadically performed his works outside his employer's ambit. Rather, a composer was inferred to have been freelance only when he regularly composed to earn fees from publishers or impresarios, or when he composed works for performance at concerts organized or planned by the composer in the expectation of remuneration whose magnitude would depend upon the size and willingness to pay of the audience attracted. Altogether, 287 of the 646 sample composers, or 44.4 percent, were found under these criteria to have engaged in freelance composing. Among them, 186 pursued freelance composing as a principal activity, 95 as a secondary activity, and 6 (sparingly coded) as a tertiary activity.

Figure 3.3 arrays by fifty-year birth-date cohorts the data on cohort fractions engaged in freelance composing and freelance performance as

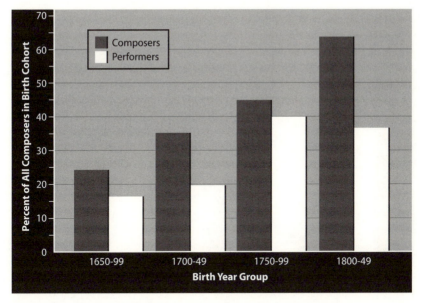

FIGURE 3.3 Composers Engaging in Significant Freelance Activity

primary or secondary activities. Composers were deemed to have been freelance performers when they went on tour to earn money through solo performances or when they regularly earned a living by appearing as guest soloists in a typically large home city such as London, Paris, Milan, or Vienna.

For both freelance composing and freelance performance, there is a marked upward trend over time. The trend is more consistent for composing than for performance, and for composers born during the first half of the nineteenth century, the relative growth of freelance performance activity is found to cease. There is double-counting across the two groupings. The fraction of birth-date-cohort composers who pursued *both* freelance composing and freelance performance to a significant degree rose from 5.0 percent for the 1650–1699 period to 8.8 percent for 1700–1749, 17.3 percent for 1750–1799, and 18.6 percent for 1800–1849.

As we observed both in chapter 2 and earlier parts of this chapter, an important source of freelance composing opportunities during the first century covered by our sample of composers was composing operas, especially in Italy and England but also to some extent in Paris and other parts of Europe. It is useful therefore to draw a distinction between composers who pursued opera composition to a significant degree and those who did not, and especially to see the extent to which

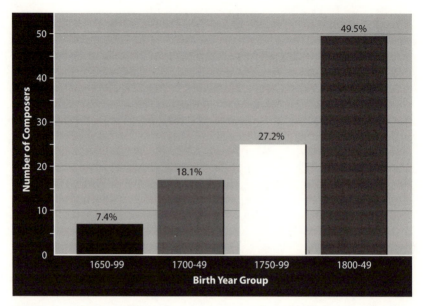

FIGURE 3.4 Number of Composers with Fewer Than Two Operas Pursuing Significant Freelance Activity

freelance composition thrived outside the world of opera. To do so, composers who wrote at most one opera, not counting cantatas and oratorios, were segregated from those who wrote two or more operas. Completion of only one opera was viewed as evidence that the composer found, as Beethoven did after his painful experience with two early versions of *Fidelio*, that his comparative advantage lay in other directions. Of composers born during the 1650–1699 interval, 47 wrote two or more operas; 54 of those born in the 1700–1749 interval did so, along with 76 from the 1750–1799 interval and 88 from the 1800–1849 cohort.

Figure 3.4 traces the growth of freelance composing for the sample members who wrote no operas or at most one. The vertical axis now measures the number of composers in each fifty-year birth-date cohort. The numerals above the frequency bars provide additional information, showing the percent of composers with fewer than two operas in a relevant birth-date cohort who engaged in primary or secondary freelance composing activity. Both the numbers of nonoperatic freelance composers and the cohort percentages rise sharply over time. Nearly half of the composers born during the first half of the nineteenth century who wrote fewer than two operas engaged in significant amounts of freelance activity. At the other extreme, among the opera-shy composers

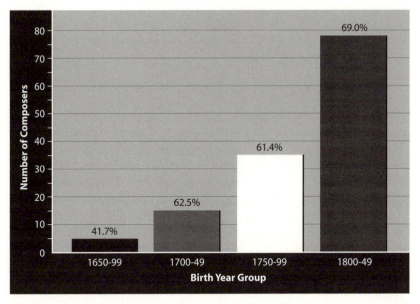

FIGURE 3.5 Number of Composers with Minimal Church or Court Employment Pursuing Significant Freelance Activity

born in the earliest fifty-year period, only two, Pietro Locatelli (1695–1764) and Jacques-Christophe Naudot (1690–1762), were found to have pursued freelance composition as a primary activity. After being employed by both church and court institutions in Italy, virtuoso violinist Locatelli emigrated at the age of thirty-four to Amsterdam, a hub of enterprise and international trade, where he earned a living by teaching, directing a private orchestra, and publishing his compositions. He was one of the relatively few composers in the sample to gain a state privilege (the forerunner of copyright, as we shall see in chapter 7) for the exclusive publication of his chamber compositions. Naudot taught flute-playing, performed in Parisian salons, earned money by dedicating his works to wealthy patrons, and aggressively published his flute compositions. His biography contains no evidence of church or court employment.

Freelance composing might be viewed as either a complement to or substitute for church or court employment. Figure 3.5 focuses on the composers who were coded as having no primary or secondary employment with either the church or noble courts. From figures 3.1 and 3.2, we might expect to find relatively few primary or secondary freelance composers with this history in the earliest birth cohort but a rising number in later periods. Our expectation is confirmed; 5 such individuals were born during the second half of the seventeenth century, 15 in the second fifty-year interval, 35 in the third, and 78 in the fourth. Among them, figure 3.5 shows, both the number who pursued freelance composing and the percent of those without church or court employment engaged in freelance composing rose over time, the former much more rapidly than the latter. The five primary or secondary freelance composers born during the first interval and without significant church or court employment were Tomaso Albinoni, a Venetian who inherited independent wealth from his merchant father and who supplemented his income by teaching and writing operas; John Gay (1685–1732), who adapted music composed mainly by others in musical performances for the London market, including the sensationally successful *Beggar's Opera*, first staged in 1728; Joseph de Boismortier (1689–1755), who composed both operas and instrumental music in Paris and was particularly successful in publishing instrumental works; Francesco Barsanti (1690–1722), who emigrated as a youth from Italy to play the flute and publish numerous compositions in London and Edinburgh; and Jacques-Christophe Naudot, whose activities in Paris are described above.

Was there something different about the composers who braved the vicissitudes of the freelance market? And in particular, were freelance composers more productive, in terms of having more recordings listed in the *Schwann Opus* catalogue, than composers who remained content with church or court employment? To explore this question, a regression analysis was performed. Variables used to explain variations in *Schwann* listing lengths included composers' birth years and four career path categories introduced in this chapter.[70] Those who embarked upon freelance composing were found to be significantly more productive than those who did not, all else equal. Composers who served as noble court music directors and/or received subsidies from noble patrons were also more productive. Evidently, the composers accorded the greatest following by posterity gravitated toward prestigious court appointments as well as, or as a substitute to, engaging in freelance composition. Composers born later in our two-century time span tended also to be more productive.[71] Opera composers achieved *Schwann* listings insignificantly longer than peers whose forte was instrumental music.

The form of freelance activity with the strongest element of entrepreneurship is acting as impresario, supervising and organizing the performance of one's own or others' musical works and acting as residual risk-bearer, reaping the profits if the performance succeeds economically and incurring the losses if it does not. In this category, 26 composers were coded as having been impresarios as a primary activity, 18 in a secondary role, and 19 in a tertiary role. Across birth cohorts, the number of primary and secondary impresarios was relatively stable at 7 for 1650–1699, another 7 for 1700–1749, and 8 for 1750–1799. The count then surged to 22 for composers born between 1800 and 1849. Prominent among the primary-activity impresarios during the earliest time period were Antonio Vivaldi, Georg Philipp Telemann, and George Frideric Handel. The others with primary impresario designations were Johann Kusser (1660–1727), who staged his own opera when he was denied access to the Hamburg opera and then directed a traveling opera house company performing throughout Germany; Reinhard Keiser (1674–1739), who was a leading figure in Hamburg opera production and composition; and Jean Baptiste Loeillet (1680–1730), who emigrated from Belgium to London, where he offered a weekly instrumental concert series from his Covent Garden residence. Included among the impresarios in the 1800–1849 cohort were Joseph Lanner (1801–1843) and his popular Vienna orchestra imitators Johann Strauss Sr., Johann Strauss Jr., and Eduard Strauss (1835–1880), as well as Richard Wagner and Jacques Offenbach (1819–1880).

Other Means of Support

Composers earned their keep in a vast variety of ways other than freelance composing and performance and service with the nobility or the churches. Figure 3.6 provides a broad overview, showing seven clusters of occupations and the fraction of composers in the relevant fifty-year birth cohort receiving primary or secondary income support within the cluster. The most impressive growth is observed in three categories, conservatory teaching, private orchestra direction, and as we have seen, serving as impresario.

The conservatory vocations, whose growth coincides with the creation of numerous formal conservatories during the late eighteenth and early nineteenth centuries, were coded sparingly. Thus, the teaching of Johann Kuhnau and Johann Sebastian Bach in the choir school of Leipzig's St. Thomas Church was excluded, in part because their duties extended in principle to other subjects; but Antonio Vivaldi's duties at the Ospedale della Pietà in Venice were included. Nor was Bedřich Smetana viewed as a conservatory teacher for operating his own private music schools in Prague and Gothenburg, Sweden; rather, his role was coded as that of a primary freelance teacher. Among the seven primary conservatory teaching occupations recorded for the first fifty-year period, five were at Naples, from which the concept of the modern conservatory evolved, and one (Vivaldi) at Venice.

No appreciable growth is observed in the private teaching category, perhaps in part because in later periods formally organized conserva-

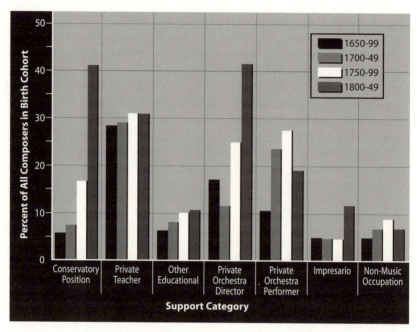

FIGURE 3.6 Percent of Composers in Birth Cohort with Other Means of Support

tories attracted many of the most able composers with an inclination to teach.

Similarly, we observe a substantial increase in service as music directors for private-sector orchestras (that is, those not associated with a noble court or church), whose formation paralleled the expansion of a prosperous middle class desiring to hear public performances of orchestral music. Service as performers in such private-sector orchestras increased during the eighteenth century but then declined, probably because individuals able enough to earn their spurs as memorable composers moved rapidly into directorship positions rather than having to remain in the hired-performer ranks.

The "other educational" category includes composers who taught music in educational institutions not primarily oriented toward music education, such as John Knowles Paine (1839–1906) at Harvard or Sir Charles Hubert Parry (1848–1918) at Oxford; part-time composers who taught other subjects at the university level (Alexander Borodin (1833–1887), chemistry, and César Cui (1835–1918), engineering); composers such as Jean-Philippe Rameau, Leopold Mozart, and Carl Czerny, who wrote musical theory or technique books; composers such as Robert Schumann, Hector Berlioz, and Charles-Marie Widor (1844–

1937), who regularly wrote columns of music criticism; writers on philosophy such as Jean-Jacques Rousseau (1712–1778), and fiction, such as E.T.A Hoffmann (1776–1822); and Giuseppe Verdi's librettist Arrigo Boito (1842–1918).

Not surprisingly, the nonmusic occupation category spans a wide array of other occupations pursued by composers. They range from leading a nation (Frederick the Great of Prussia); serving as a military leader (Prince Louis Ferdinand of Prussia, killed in 1806 during the Battle of Saalfeld, and Alexander Borodin); other high-level governmental service (such as Farinelli, Benjamin Franklin, and Benedetto Marcello); diplomacy (Agostino Steffani and Johann Mattheson); midrank civil service (Emmanuel Chabrier, E.T.A. Hoffmann, Johan Hartmann, Modest Mussorsky, and Alexander Dargomyzhsky); legal practice (Johann Kuhnau); royal astronomer (William Herschel); general newspaper publisher and physicist (Benjamin Franklin); stonemason (Carl Friedrich Zeller); wine merchant (Giovanni Viotti); and managing a glass factory (Franz Berwald).

Some composers pursued business occupations more closely related to their musical abilities, notably, music publishing and the manufacturing of musical instruments. Among the composers with music publication as a primary activity were Ignaz Pleyel (1757–1831), Muzio Clementi, Johann Baptist Cramer (1771–1858), Franz Anton Hoffmeister (1754–1812), Anton Diabelli (1781–1858), Joseph Elsner (1769–1854), and Leopold Kozeluch (1747–1818). The music publishing business will be analyzed at greater length in chapter 7. The most important producers of musical instruments were Ignaz Pleyel and Muzio Clementi, both of whom manufactured pianos, and Theobald Boehm (1794–1881), who invented important improvements in flute design and founded a flute-manufacturing enterprise.

Of the 646 composers in the sample, 24 enjoyed during at least a significant part of their careers sufficient wealth that they did not have to earn their living through musical activities (although some did in any event). Among those who were independently wealthy through inheritance were Tomaso Albinoni, Benedetto Marcello, Frederick the Great of Prussia and his nephew Louis Ferdinand, Archduke Rudolph of Austria, Felix Mendelssohn and his sister Fanny Hensel, John Marsh, and Marcial del Adalid y Gurréa. Marrying into independent wealth were, for example, John Stanley, Peter Heise, and Marianne Martinez. Some found themselves at the other extreme, without independent means and, through ill health, bad luck, or personal choice, forced by lack of income to depend upon others for their existence. Among these bohemians were Franz Schubert, Norbert Burgmüller, Samuel Wesley, Antal György Csermak, and Wilhelm Friedemann Bach.

Finally, a few composers benefitted during at least parts of their careers from generous prizes allowing them to pursue music composition without having to seek remunerative employment. Of the 646-composer sample, 11 received the prestigious French (or in one case, Belgian) Prix de Rome. Edvard Grieg won a similar prize and later a continuing stipendium from the Norwegian government.

CONCLUSION

To sum up, the way composers of enduring merit earned their living changed significantly over time. Consistent with the conventional wisdom, the principal sources of income in the late seventeenth and early eighteenth centuries were positions as employees with the churches and noble courts. Contrary to the assertion of some scholars, however, the pursuit of musical composition as a freelance profession did not emerge suddenly, notably with Mozart, during the second half of the eighteenth century. A considerable number of composers born between 1650 and 1699 engaged in substantial freelance work, mostly by competing for opera composition commissions, although even within this early cohort there were composers who kept body and soul together through freelance activities in nonopera fields. During the eighteenth and nineteenth centuries, the pursuit of freelance composition increased fairly steadily as growing general prosperity raised the demand for music performance at home and in public concerts and as the feudal system atrophied. Thus, the transition to freelance composing was a gradual evolutionary process, not a punctuation of otherwise static equilibria. Composers also earned a living in countless other ways, in many cases viewing composition as a part-time avocation apart from their principal occupations. Important complementary changes included the expansion of opportunities to earn a salary teaching in conservatories and directing the private orchestras created to meet the demand for music performance in public fora.

Chapter 4

COMPOSERS' BACKGROUNDS, ASPIRATIONS,

AND ECONOMIC REWARDS

HAVING SECURED a broad quantitative perspective on how composers earned a living, we advance now to micromotive questions. From what social and family backgrounds did individuals embrace the profession of music composition? How did they hone their musical talents? What were their aspirations and motivations? How well did they succeed in achieving their economic goals? What choices, strategies, and intervening variables affected the degree to which they succeeded economically?

FAMILY BACKGROUNDS

Career choices are influenced by the family circumstances in which individuals grow to maturity. An obvious variable is the role music occupied in the families of those who became composers. For the sample of 646 composers analyzed at many points in this book, individuals were coded as to whether a parent or other relative serving in loco parentis (such as a residentially proximate uncle or aunt) earned a living at least in part as a professional musician. Excluded were many other cases in which a parent or near relative was an enthusiastic amateur performer. For 137 of the 646 composers, insufficient information was available to determine whether the specified family criterion was satisfied. Since the presence or absence of professional musicians in the family is one of the most commonly recorded details in the biographies of composers whose early lives were otherwise obscure, this typically implies the absence of parental antecedents. For 263 of the sample members, or 40.7 percent of the total, one or more members of the parental family did function as professional musicians. This estimate, which probably errs mildly on the undercount side, implies that the serious pursuit of music was an important formative variable in a near majority of composers' career choices. It is not inconsistent with Elvidio Surian's estimate for 81 Italian opera composers on which reliable information was available, with birth dates extending on both sides of our 200-year sampling frame, that 46.9 percent of the composers came from musical families.[1]

During most of the two centuries framing our sample composers'

birth dates, economic activity in Europe was preponderantly agricultural. Approximately 80 percent of the population lived in rural areas
during the seventeenth and eighteenth centuries, many, especially before
1814 and in the more easterly parts of Europe, in servile peasant status.
Systematic information on possible peasant origins was not collected for
the sample of 646 composers. However, for the more select sample of
50 on which book-length biographies were examined, it is clear that
most composers did not stem directly from peasant stock. Only two of
the 50 came close. The father of Christoph Willibald Gluck was a for-
ester, but his principal duties were those of a forest manager for noble
landowners, so he is classified below as an estate official.[2] About the
family background of Johann Baptist Vanhal little is known, but peasant family origins are implied by the fact that Vanhal used his earnings
from music performance in Vienna to purchase his freedom from the
indentured servitude he inherited from his father in Bohemia.[3] For the
other 49 members of the select sample, no evidence of peasant origins
was found.

For those 49, the fathers' principal occupations were recorded as
follows:

Professional musician	20
Merchant or banker	9
Mechanical and artisan trades	5
Civil servant or estate official	5
Teacher or educational administrator	3
Physician or surgeon (e.g., barber)	2
Landowner	2
Clerk	1
Clergy	1
Showman-speculator[4]	1

These are largely what might reasonably be called middle-class occupations. Thus, most composers in the period studied here found their
roots in the middle classes—some, to be sure, from the least affluent
strata, such as Gaetano Donizetti, a weaver's son; some from the opposite extreme, such as the banker father of Felix Mendelssohn or the
wealthy Venetian paper merchant who sired Tomaso Albinoni.[5] Although some additional traces of peasant origins were found for composers in the broader 646-person sample, it is safe to generalize that for
young people with origins in the typically bleak life of Europe's peasants, the odds against becoming a composer were very high. Only the
most extraordinary talent and determination could overcome them.

Educational Background

Characterizing the educational backgrounds of the sampled composers is even more difficult. By any criterion, higher education — notably, at the university level — was a rarity during the time period within which our sample composers were born. Less than one percent of the European population attended university during most of that period, and even fewer obtained terminal degrees. But attending or not attending university was hardly a clear delineator between being well-educated or not. For many university students, lectures were seldom attended and a life of socializing and dissipation was common.[6] On the other hand, Johann Sebastian Bach did not attend university, and mainly because he lacked that credential, he was the third-ranked candidate for the cantor's position at Leipzig's Thomasschule when it was filled in 1723, securing the job only because it was refused by university-educated individuals (including Georg Philipp Telemann).[7] But Bach was an outstanding secondary school student, ranking first among the pupils in the second-to-last year of his secondary studies and obtaining a classical *Abitur* in a German Gymnasium — the equivalent of graduating from a top-notch American high school.[8] Although he sought to focus his energies on music and secured a substitute to avoid taking on nonmusic subjects, he was well-equipped to teach the Latin grammar and theological courses that were a normal part of the Thomasschule cantor's teaching responsibilities.[9]

Recognizing these limitations, the biographies of the 646 composers in our sample were searched for evidence of higher education. For 133 of the 646, there were no clear indications, which probably means that university-level studies were not pursued. For another 282, the evidence pointed strongly to a lack of higher-level studies. But for 114 of the 646, or 17.6 percent, some form of higher education was pursued. A more detailed breakdown is as follows:

University studies alone	83
University plus seminary or conservatory	6
Seminary alone	25

Evidently, those who became composers productive enough to enter our sample were on average much better educated than the average European of the relevant era.

Musical Training

A related analysis sought to determine how sample members obtained the training that laid a basis for their performance and composing activities. For 114 composers, the evidence available in the *New Grove* was insufficient to attempt any classifications. The information lacunae narrowed for each successive cohort. Owing to insufficient information, it was necessary to exclude from the analysis 32.6 percent of the composers born between 1650 and 1699, 23.6 percent for the 1700–1749 cohort, 12.5 percent for the 1750–1799 cohort, and only 6.3 percent for those born between 1800 and 1849.

Educational backgrounds were coded into eight main categories, including mentoring within the family, private tutoring (such as by non–family members outside a formal institutional context), education in a conservatory or private music school, education connected with participation in a church choir or choir school, musical training in conventional primary or secondary schools, musical training at the university or seminary level, on-the-job training, and self-teaching. No one can become a capable musician without arduous self-teaching, and most undergo on-the-job training. These categories were coded selectively. A sample member was considered self-taught only where there was evidence of explicit efforts by a youth to teach himself theory and/or performance outside a relationship with experienced tutors. The youthful Handel's surreptitious practice on a clavichord in his attic when his surgeon father forbade it is an extreme example. On-the-job training was coded mainly for individuals who before reaching the age of seventeen were regular or apprentice members of a performance group.

Not surprisingly, many composers learned their trade in multiple ways — typically, by beginning to play one or more musical instruments, then by trying their hand composing simple pieces, and only later by studying music theory systematically. Altogether, 971 codes were assigned to the 532 individuals for whom there was sufficient evidence to attempt a coding. Even then, the evidence is incomplete. Family mentorship is almost surely undercounted, and private-lesson experience may be. It is inconceivable, for example, that 34 composers could have gained admission to conservatories without any recorded evidence of prior training. Family members or private tutors must have sowed the seeds.

Figure 4.1 traces the principal modes of career preparation by 50-year birth-date cohorts. Family mentorship was evident in at least 40 to 48 percent of all cases, with known understatement and no clear trend over time. Private tutoring occurred in an even larger fraction of cases, with a slight upward trend. Although no systematic attempt was made to evaluate the credentials of teachers named in the *New Grove* biographies, an impressively high incidence of well-known names played a formative role in the early training of sample members. As in present-day musical training, there was a reciprocal dynamic: youngsters exhib-

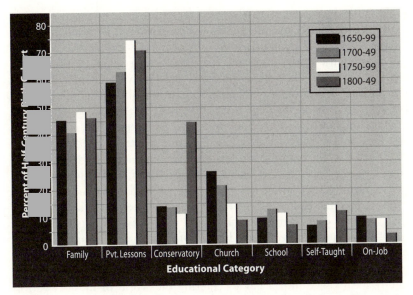

FIGURE 4.1 Percent of Half-Century Cohorts with Selected Career Preparation Modes

iting talent are attracted to and attract talented teachers, who in turn pave the way for later professional success.[10] From a modest level associated mainly with the famous Naples conservatories and the Thomasschule in Leipzig, there was a striking increase in conservatory training for the 1800–1849 birth date cohort. Conversely, training in church choirs and associated choir schools declined steadily as the profession of music became increasingly secularized. Self-teaching may have risen over time with the greater availability of published theory and performance treatises. On-the-job training declined as feudal institutions atrophied and court orchestras not averse to child labor were disbanded. Among the 7 to 12 percent of composers who received noteworthy musical education in nonspecialized primary and secondary schools, two-thirds lived in Bohemia, Moravia, and Germany, where musical education was a staple, especially in Jesuit and other denominational schools. University or seminary training in music (not explicitly graphed in figure 4.1) was recorded in from 0.7 to 5.3 percent of all cases.

Family training was coded as the sole career preparation in 34 cases (including Wolfgang Mozart, C.P.E. Bach, and Clara Schumann); private tutoring in 88 cases. The combination of those two modes was more frequent, encompassing a total of 149 cases, including 94 in which family training plus private tutoring were the only two forms of preparation in evidence. It is a wise teacher who recognizes that her own talented child's musical career is best advanced by a mentor insulated from internal family tensions.

There is little evidence on the compensation received by the private music teachers of successful composers. As we saw in chapter 3, it was not unusual for lessons to be offered free to the gifted children of families with modest means — for instance, when Mozart had Johann Nepomuk Hummel live in his household for nearly two years as a tutee. Antonio Salieri provided free lessons to a youthful Beethoven, who charged little or nothing for lessons given initially "several times a week" to ten-year-old Carl Czerny,[11] whose tutoring of Franz Liszt was free. Czerny turned away less promising candidates, including sample member Stephen Heller (1813–1888), unable to pay his usual high fees. Liszt in turn extracted no tuition from countless students.[12] Children from poor families also received tuition-free scholarships and residence privileges at the Naples conservatories during the seventeenth and eighteenth centuries. Thus, for young people with unusual promise, limited family means were not a bar to entering the world of musical performance and composing.

Differences in the sources from which composers received their early musical training appear to have had little systematic influence on the composers' subsequent productivity, measured by the length of listings for their recorded works in the Fall 1996 *Schwann Opus* catalogue. A regression analysis using the diverse codings as independent variables had little explanatory power.[13] Family training, private tutoring, and conservatory education exhibited the strongest (albeit weak) positive influences.

PECUNIARY ASPIRATIONS

We advance now onto more treacherous ground, asking what role prospective financial rewards played in composers' choice of music as a profession and the intensity with which they pursued it. There are two main problems. For one, all human beings, and not just composers, vary widely in their pecuniary aspirations. Some are content to live like the proverbial church mouse, some are drawn to a life of affluence. Second, people often dissemble about their true motives. Thus, the evidence must be read cautiously, and we must be satisfied with little more than an impressionistic mosaic characterizing general tendencies and the range of variation. Composers also varied in the levels of consumption to which they aspired. The appendix to this chapter provides detailed evidence on the consumption expenditures of a composer-performer family, Robert and Clara Schumann, for the year 1841. Among other things, it supplements the appendix to chapter 1 on the cost of maintaining a middle-class standard of living.

For all the composers whose detailed biographies were read, performing music and composing new music were activities pursued with enjoyment and even passion. Many composers such as Berlioz, Handel, Robert Schumann, and Smetana embraced music as a profession despite opposition from their parents. Where they varied was mainly in the intensity with which they devoted themselves to creating music for pay. The difference is characterized nicely in a remark attributed to Johann Christian Bach, comparing his motivation with that of his brother Carl Philipp Emanuel: "He lives to compose, I compose to live."[14] Even when the financial rewards were meager, performing and composing music undoubtedly provided for most if not all composers greater satisfaction than they could derive from feasible alternative employment opportunities.

There is also no composer among the 50 whose detailed biographies were examined for whom it can be said that money did not matter at all. Beethoven was surely being self-referential when he declaimed, through Rocco the jailer, that "If you don't have gold at hand you can't be completely happy."[15] He negotiated fiercely over the fees publishers paid for his compositions, and he litigated for recompense when inflation eroded the value of the pension three noble families promised to induce him to remain in Vienna rather than accepting a generous salaried offer to relocate in Kassel.[16] Yet money matters were a bother to him:[17]

> I do not understand any other money than Viennese ducats; how many thaler and gulden that makes is no affair of mine, for I am a bad business man and reckoner . . . There ought to be an artistic depot where the artist need only hand in his art work in order to receive what he asks for. As things are, one must be half a business man, and how can one understand — good heavens! That's what I really call troublesome.

It would be equally wrong to conclude that financial reward was a sole or principal objective for Beethoven or indeed for many composers. Like most if not all successful composers, the instinct to create was for Beethoven a fundamental motivational force. As Beethoven responded to his student Carl Czerny, who had alluded to the master's worldwide fame:[18]

> Ah, nonsense! . . . I have never thought about writing to achieve fame and honor. What is in my heart must come out.

Long after he had retired from composing operas for pay, Gioachino Rossini continued to write incidental music, observing that "I compose because I can't help myself" and that he couldn't get out of the habit of

composing.[19] Or as Hector Berlioz explained his tendency to write
works that brought little remuneration:[20]

> I often find it pleasanter to smash through a gate than to jump it. . . .
> But this is the natural result of my passion for music—a passion which is
> always at white heat, and never satisfied for more than a moment or two.
> With this passion love of money has never, under any circumstances, any-
> thing to do; on the contrary, I had never any difficulty in making any kind
> of sacrifice in pursuit of the beautiful, or in keeping clear of the miserable
> commonplaces which are the delight of the crowd. Offer me a fortune to
> compose some of the most popular works of the day, and I should refuse it
> angrily. It is my nature.

Extremes

The emphasis placed by composers on financial rewards varied over a
broad spectrum. The extremes are approximated by comparing father-
in-law with son-in-law: Franz Liszt and Richard Wagner.

Wagner's attitude is epitomized by his reaction in 1864, the year
when his luck turned and he began receiving generous subsidies from
King Ludwig II of Bavaria, to the assurances of a friend that the future
held great things for him:[21]

> How can you speak to me of the future, if my manuscripts are locked away
> in some cabinet! Who will produce the works of art that I, only I, with the
> help of friendly spirits, can create. . . . I'm differently constituted—I have
> sensitive nerves—I must have beauty, splendor, and light! The world owes
> me what I need! I can't live in a miserable organist position like your Mas-
> ter Bach! Is it an unreasonable demand, therefore, when I ask for that bit
> of luxury which I may crave? I, who prepare for the world a thousand
> pleasures!

Wagner's quest for ideal working conditions and an affluent lifestyle led
him almost constantly to live beyond his means, squeezing as much
support as he could from wealthy benefactors, publishers, and finally
King Ludwig, and fleeing debtors when the desired funds were lacking.
To one publisher, he complained in 1859 that his lack of both property—specifically, a quiet place in the country that could be purchased
for some £1,600—and financial means robbed him of his "sense and
appetite for work."[22] To another publisher's rejection of pleas for further monetary advances and implication that hungry artists were more
productive, he replied angrily in 1862:[23]

> You are in error, my best Herr Schott! You err seriously on how to deal
> with a person like me. Through hunger one can induce much, but not

works of a higher type. Or do you believe that when my nights are filled with worries, during the day I'll bring cheerfulness and good ideas to my work?

Five years later, he complained to the same publisher that with more generous financial support, he would have completed his opera *Die Meistersinger* three years earlier.[24]

Near the other extreme was Franz Liszt, the father of Wagner's second wife Cosima. In his early days, to be sure, Liszt, following the example of Niccolò Paganini, amassed a small fortune tirelessly crisscrossing Europe to perform his magic on the piano. But at the age of thirty-six, he announced a change of life and never again concertized for his own benefit, first accepting a salaried position in the ducal court at Weimar, later being ordained an abbé in Rome, and finally combining those roles with that of fundraiser for charitable causes.[25] He turned down among other things offers for a season performing in the United States that (at roughly £20,000) would have more than doubled his assets. From the end of his for-profit concert career, according to one of his biographers:[26]

We . . . see him, at the height of his renown, abandon that career, in order to devote himself to his music and what he considered to be the best interests of his art. The unselfishness and the true humanity of his life for the rest of his days are without parallel. He gave his services free, raising great sums of money for others, and teaching hundreds of pupils without asking payment for his pains.[27] He lived contentedly upon some three or four hundred pounds a year, having no luxuries, drinking the cheapest and coarsest of wines; and even where his one weakness was concerned, in the matter of cigars, he would give away the good ones that had been presented to him and smoke, for preference, the cheapest sorts he could buy.

The difference between the cases of Liszt and Wagner is less than complete, however, for Wagner was incessantly overextended financially, while Liszt enjoyed the security of an account with the Rothschild Bank of Paris that, wisely invested, allowed him to accumulate by the time of his death a balance exceeding £8,000.[28]

An even sharper contrast is found in the life of Franz Schubert. After leaving a nine-hours-per-day teaching job he disliked at his father's school, Schubert enjoyed only brief periods of poorly paid employment, with Count Johann Esterházy in Hungary. A biographer observes:[29]

[H]e had no exaggerated opinion of his general importance to the universe, and probably asked for little more from life than enough to eat and drink, a decent bed, a sympathetic friend or two, an occasional sight of the country (his letters show how sensitive he was to beautiful scenery), and money

enough to pay for the vast amount of paper he needed for the absorbing
business of writing music.

Unlike Beethoven, Schubert did not try (or considered himself unable)
to extract high fees from publishers. Ten years after he completed his
first for-pay work, he sought publication of his works "for a moderate
price" by Leipzig publishers because, he explained, "I very much want
to become as well known as possible in Germany."[30] In this he was
unsuccessful, at least during his brief lifetime.

Two further examples illuminate intermediate cases. With a large
family to support, Johann Sebastian Bach was zealous in efforts to enhance his income. He petitioned the king of Saxony to intervene and
mandate payment of a part of his Leipzig salary he considered his just
due, but which had been denied him in a reorganization of functions.[31]
He petitioned the city council of Leipzig to receive the fee he would
have earned had a Leipzig merchant married at home, rather than outside Leipzig.[32] Seeking (unsuccessfully) in 1730 an alternative to his
Leipzig position, he complained that "when a healthy wind blows," he
lost as much as 100 thaler (£16) in fees for presiding over the performance of funeral music.[33] Nevertheless, he had originally accepted the
Leipzig position and an apparent decline in purchasing power (despite
the provision of free housing) when his earlier patron, the prince of
Köthen, married a woman with no interest in music, leading Bach to
believe that his services had become less appreciated aesthetically, even
if not financially.[34] (At Köthen, he had been the second most highly paid
employee in the prince's court.[35]) An additional nonpecuniary motive
for the sacrifice of income at Leipzig may have been the better opportunities there for providing his children with a university education.

Shortly after he took up residence in Vienna during 1781, Wolfgang
Amadeus Mozart assured his father by letter that he had changed his
previously easygoing view on life and that "excepting my health, I
know nothing more necessary than money."[36] His critical assessment of
various employment possibilities reflected among other things the advice of his father that "one must always be conscious of one's reputation and keep oneself a bit expensive."[37] Although he composed many
pieces without regard to marketability, he worked hard and assiduously
sought commissions, performance opportunities, dedication patrons,
and other ways of composing for income—drawing the line mainly
against teaching mediocre students who diverted time from composition.[38] Unlike Wagner, he was too proud to beg for financial support
throughout most of his career, and when would-be patrons disappointed
him, he took leave in silent anger. During the last three years of his life,
however, when his income fell far below the cost of living to which he
and his family had become accustomed, he was reduced to write a series

of heartrending letters seeking ever-increasing loans from a Masonic brother.[39]

Insights from Economic Theory

Standard economic theory makes two simple predictions about how the supply of an individual's market-oriented work effort varies with income: as the rate of pay for a given task rises, more effort is forthcoming; but as income rises with higher pay, *eventually* effort is reduced.[40] "Eventually" is italicized here because activities that in modest quantities are pursued with pleasure can become burdensome as increasing fractions of one's waking hours are devoted to them.[41] The evidence on composers for the first of these hypotheses is far too unsystematic to permit meaningful tests. For the second, however, some useful insights emerge.

For lower income levels, it is also hazardous to extract generalizations. Mozart composed furiously (including his operas *Così fan tutte* (They All Do It), *La Clemenza di Tito* (The Clemency of Titus), and *The Magic Flute* during the last two years of his life, when his income fell; but it is not clear that he worked harder than in his halcyon Vienna years.[42] One reason why Christoph Willibald Gluck responded enthusiastically to a lucrative opera composition offer from Paris in 1774 is that he saw his own and his wife's fortunes dwindle as a result of losses at Vienna's Burgtheater, in which he was an equity-holder.[43] Clara Schumann observes in her diaries (with Robert), on a visit to Leipzig by the aging Norwegian composer Ole Bull, "How striking it is when an artist says, 'I play here one day and there the next, and this I do until I drop dead, since I'm a poor man and must earn money.'"[44] On the other hand, a sudden drop in income can be paralyzingly traumatic. When the funds from the generous subvention provided him by Nadezhda von Meck failed to arrive as expected, Tchaikovsky was so upset that "work was out of the question."[45]

For higher income and wealth levels, the evidence is clearer: market-oriented effort tended to be reduced as composers achieved a comfortable level of affluence. Joseph Haydn turned out prodigious volumes of work as a hired Kapellmeister with the Esterházy family and in response to the economic opportunities of two visits to London. But having amassed a fortune in London, he reduced the pace at which he composed, taking the better part of two years to perfect his oratorio *Die Schöpfung* (The Creation). Explaining his modest economic aspirations, he told a visitor:[46]

> I have my own comfortable house, three or four courses at dinner, a good glass of wine, I can dress well, and when I want to drive out, a hired coach is good enough for me.

After his operas had yielded substantial wealth, Gioachino Rossini ceased composing for pay at the age of thirty-seven. He explained to a visiting Richard Wagner in 1860:[47]

> I had no children. Had I some, I doubtless should have continued to work. But, to tell you the truth, after having labored for 15 years during that so-called very lazy period and having composed 40 operas, I felt the need of rest, and returned to Bologna to live in peace.

On the same theme, Gaetano Donizetti observed:[48]

> There are ways of earning a living in a thousand places, but I, used to little, to desiring little, cannot at all adapt myself to earning money. I am not Rossini and haven't his fortune, but when a man has enough to live on and to amuse himself enough, I think that he ought to retire and be satisfied.

At the time, at age forty-one, Donizetti had written more than 50 operas. In the remaining decade of his life, he wrote 13. Similarly, at a relatively early stage (1846) of his career, Giuseppe Verdi lamented:[49]

> They enjoy themselves; I work from eight o'clock in the morning until twelve o'clock at night and kill myself with work. What a perfidious destiny is mine.

In the same year he wrote to a friend, "Perhaps one morning I shall awake a millionaire. What a lovely, full-sounding word. How empty by contrast are the words fame, glory, talent, etc."[50] But after his successes allowed him to accumulate substantial assets, he relaxed his pace of composition, devoted increasing blocks of time to leisure in his villa at Busetto (along with political and philanthropic activities), and averaged only one new opera per decade during the last three decades of his life. As he wrote in 1874 to his publisher-friend:[51]

> If I had wanted to be a business man, no one could have stopped me, after la Traviata [1853], from writing an opera a year and making myself a fortune three times as big as I have.

But, he continued, he had other artistic intentions, wished to take more pains with the operas he wrote, and to enjoy rural life.

Turning down prestigious orchestra directorship offers and showing indifference to investment losses after becoming financially secure, the notoriously frugal Johannes Brahms wrote:[52]

> I have . . . become only too accustomed to a quite different style of life, so I have . . . grown more indifferent to many things for which one in that position must have the liveliest interest. . . . But don't make a useless scene

over the famous bankruptcy . . . for my losses — ridiculous! You must know that for now I still have enough to live on.

Conversely, Brahms's suggestion that his friend Clara Schumann cut back her strenuous concertizing tours was rejected vigorously, in part because Clara had the responsibility to educate seven children. "You actually seem to imagine," she wrote, "that I really have enough money and travel merely for my own pleasure. . . . This is hardly the point at which I should retire from public appearances."[53]

Inherited wealth could also affect composers' market-oriented behavior, although the number of cases is too small to support generalizations. As the son of a prosperous banker, Giacomo Meyerbeer refused to accept fees for his early Italian operas.[54] Another banker's son, Felix Mendelssohn, worked hard through much of his career, but the lack of financial need made him reticent to have his compositions published, and he labored for years to perfect them.[55]

TRADE-OFFS

In addition to determining how much effort to devote to remunerative opportunities, composers faced many trade-offs. Time spent teaching crowded out composing time. So also, except for rare individuals such as Mozart who could compose on a bouncing stagecoach, did time spent traveling to perform or supervise opera productions. Even becoming a musician, which was considered a socially inferior occupation by many, had its psychological costs. But one of the most important trade-offs composers had to make was whether to seek a relatively secure position with the church or nobility, or to accept the risks of freelance composition, performance, and teaching challenges.

Social Status Generally

During the seventeenth and eighteenth centuries, professional musicians tended to be seen by the aristocracy and even by many middle-class burghers as second-class citizens. Adam Smith wrote in 1776:[56]

> There are some very agreeable and beautiful talents of which the possession commands a certain sort of admiration; but of which the exercise for the sake of gain is considered, whether from reason or prejudice, as a sort of public prostitution. . . . The exorbitant rewards of players, opera-singers, opera-dancers, &c. are founded upon those two principles; the rarity and beauty of the talents, and the discredit of employing them in this manner.

About the status of musicians in England, the son of Carl Maria von Weber complained:[57]

> [The musician] performed, was paid, and then had to leave without being regarded as one of the guests of the house. The insolent lackeys served him differently from the "guests," and would have blushed at the idea of offering him refreshments in the drawing room. His host greeted him condescendingly and pointed out to him his place, which, in many salons, was separated by a cord from that of the guests. . . . And so, in spite of the loud and lavish applause he had received, the artist generally left the house hurt and angry, only too easily consoled by the clink of the lightly-won guineas in his pocket.

Mozart's chances of obtaining a position with the court of Archduke Ferdinand in Milan were undermined by his previous tours as a gratuity-seeking child prodigy. Writing to her son Ferdinand in 1771, Empress Maria Theresia cautioned him that "it gives one's [courtly] service a bad name when such people run about like beggars."[58] By becoming a music publisher and piano manufacturer, Muzio Clementi, frustrated when his offer of marriage to the daughter of a bourgeois French family was rejected because of his state in life, is said to have freed himself "from the opprobrium attached in England to professional musicians and embarked upon the kind of purposeful activity that was building a powerful nation and empire."[59] The degree to which musicians were accepted socially, however, varied by location as well as with the fame and social graces of the individual. In Germany, and especially in mercantile cities such as Hamburg and Bremen, social lines were said to have been drawn less rigidly than in other environments.[60] Similarly, when Claudio Monteverdi left the service of the duke of Mantua in 1613 and took up residence in Venice, mercantile center of Mediterranean Europe, he was said to have become "the social equal of anyone in Venice" and was "treated with genuine respect by everyone in the city."[61] By way of contrast, in Russia, the last major European nation to accept modern values, Modest Mussorgsky hesitated for a considerable period before deciding to leave his position as a civil servant and become a musician, since "there were still traces of that musical dilettantism which demanded anything from art rather than material gain. . . . The idea of making a milch cow of art was almost blasphemous."[62]

Servility and Dependence

The musician hired, even as Kapellmeister, in a seventeenth- or eighteenth-century noble court was one of the household servants. He ate with the servants. At which of the various ranks of servant tables he sat depended upon his relative status within the court. Among Wolfgang Mozart's many dissatisfactions with his life in the court of Prince-Archbishop Hieronymus Colloredo in Salzburg was that his meals were taken with uninteresting court retinue members — below the valets in seating order but above the cooks.[63] Musicians were expected to wear the master's livery at all times; failure to do so could be penalized with salary reductions or even (as in the case of Paganini at Parma) dismissal.[64]

Despite his role as administrator of an important court function, the composer was expected to treat the master with appropriate deference. Michael Haydn's letter of application for the position of Kapellmeister at Salzburg addressed the archbishop approximately (the English language can scarcely characterize the degree of deference) as "Your Exalted Princely Grace, etc. Most Worthy Prince of the State and Empire, etc. Most Gracious Prince and Sir Lord," figuratively prostrating himself with all submissive respect at the archbishop's feet in obediently seeking the position.[65] As Kapellmeister he, unlike Leopold and Wolfgang Mozart, was permitted to dine with the court officers — but not with the archbishop himself.

Court composers were typically subjected to strict limitations on the dissemination to others or publication of music they had written. Even when he was released from his position as Kapellmeister in the Stuttgart court, Niccolò Jommelli (1714–1774) was denied permission to take with him copies of his own musical manuscripts.[66] After he had negotiated to obtain publication rights following eighteen years of service with the Esterházy court, Joseph Haydn found it prudent to be secretive about the amount of money he received in publication fees.[67]

As Kapellmeister to Frederick the Great, Karl Heinrich Graun was required repeatedly to rewrite his compositions when they failed to please the sovereign.[68] Dealings with the lord and master often had to be intermediated through another court official. In his early years at the Esterházy court, Joseph Haydn was frequently in conflict with the prince's estates manager, Peter von Rahier, leading him, after he had left his service to the Esterházys, to write from London in 1791 to the wife of the prince's physician:[69]

> Oh, my dear gracious lady! How sweet this bit of freedom really is! I had a kind Prince, but sometimes I was forced to be dependent on base souls. I often sighed for release, and now I have it in some measure. I appreciate the good sides of all this, too, though my mind is burdened with far more work. The realization that I am no bond-servant makes ample amend for all my toils.

Composers were subject to dismissal at the whim of the lord and, until feudal reforms spread during the time of the Napoleonic Wars, could not leave their positions without permission as long as their employer lived. Georg Philipp Telemann was initially enthusiastic about the opportunities for composition under noble patronage. He wrote that "if there is anything in the world which encourages a man to improve upon his skills, it is life at Court. Here one seeks to earn the favor of great men and the courtesy of noble ones . . ."[70] However, after being discharged in an economy move from the court at Sorau and other unfavorable experiences at the court in Eisenach, he spent the rest of his professional career in the free mercantile cities of Frankfurt am Main and Hamburg, writing that "whoever seeks life-long security must settle in a republic."[71] When Johann Sebastian Bach attempted in 1717 to leave the service of the duke of Weimar for a position in Köthen, he was imprisoned for nearly four weeks before being dismissed. His son C.P.E. Bach had to claim illness to be granted a discharge from the orchestra of Frederick the Great and take the better-paying position vacated at Hamburg by Telemann's death.[72] J. S. Bach's contemporary George Frideric Handel was offered a position at the royal court in Berlin (under Frederick I), but was advised by friends to decline it:[73]

> For they well knew, that if he once engag'd in the King's service, he must remain in it, whether he liked it, or not; that if he continued to please, it would be reason for not parting with him; and that if he happened to displease, his ruin would be the certain consequence.

As events ensued, the royal orchestra was disbanded when Frederick I died and his son (Frederick William I, the so-called Soldier King, father of Frederick the Great) became sovereign in 1713. Thus, Handel would have lost his job or been summarily transferred to the orchestra of the margrave of Brandenburg (eight years before J. S. Bach sent to the margrave his six Brandenburg Concertos, only to have them lie unread in a cabinet for decades). It is well known that when Mozart asked in 1781 to leave the service of Prince-Archbishop Colloredo, he was physically booted out of the Vienna chambers of the archbishop's aide, Graf Karl Josef Arco.[74] Two years later, contemplating a visit to his father in Salzburg, Mozart worried that he might be arrested for violating his employment contract.[75]

Freedom of movement was little better when composers were employed by the church. Complicated negotiations were required before Johann Pachelbel could vacate his position as organist in Erfurt and become organist at nearby Sondershausen.[76] In 1722 Jean-Philippe Rameau was denied permission to leave his position as church organist in Clermont, but secured his release through a loud and dissonant performance and the threat to continue playing similarly if not permitted to migrate to Paris.[77]

Noble lords were free to discriminate as they pleased, subject to initial hiring-market constraints, in the salaries and working conditions they offered composers. Carl Philipp Emanuel Bach was perennially unhappy over his pay of 300 to 500 thaler (at the upper limit, £78) in the court of Frederick the Great while Karl Heinrich Graun and Johann Quantz were paid 2,000 thaler each and leading opera singers were paid 4,000 to 6,000 thaler.[78] Among other things, Frederick frowned on intermarriage among his employees. When composer Johann Friedrich Agricola married one of the court singers, their joint salary was reduced to 1,000 thaler; his alone had been 1,500 thaler before the marriage.[79] The son of a court chancellor was imprisoned for several months when he proposed to marry one of Frederick's singer favorites; the two were then banished permanently from Berlin when they eloped after the young man's release from prison.[80] When Napoleon pointed out to Luigi Cherubini a flaw he perceived in one of Cherubini's compositions, Cherubini is said to have replied, "Your Majesty knows no more about it than I know about a battle." All Cherubini's imperial subsidies were thereupon eliminated.[81]

As we have seen in J. S. Bach's reasons for leaving Köthen, composers were sometimes dissatisfied with nobles' lack of appreciation for their music. Franz Schubert wrote about his position with the Esterházy family in Hungary, "There is not a soul here with a genuine interest in music except, perhaps, now and then (if I am not mistaken) the Countess."[82] Similarly, of his residence at the Detmold court in 1857, Johannes Brahms wrote:[83]

> Yesterday morning . . . I had to accompany the Prince in his singing. I don't exactly wish for this to happen often. . . . There is a complete desert of musical friends here, with the exception of a few ladies.

And on a later visit in 1858, he wrote, "Half my tenure here is over, thank God."[84]

To be sure, when a composer's bargaining position was strong, it was possible to overcome the more onerous working-condition constraints and even to some degree the social stigma. Joseph Haydn's fame throughout Europe eventually let him enjoy freedom to publish and a salary exceeded only by those of the Esterházy estates manager and the court physician.[85] When Haydn returned to the Esterházy court after the death of his benefactor Nikolaus I, his relationship with the new prince, Nikolaus II, was much more strained. Nikolaus addressed him initially, for example, in the formal third person: thus, "Herr Haydn will present his new quartets at tonight's festivities."[86] Through the intervention of friends, however, Haydn soon set matters straight, so conversations were held in the second person and Haydn was invited to dine at the table with the prince and his consorts rather than with court officials. The democratically inclined Beethoven refused to be constrained by courtly formalities. When attempts were made by Habsburg aides to have him show proper deference toward his student Archduke Rudolph, Beethoven told Rudolph that although he had the greatest reverence for Rudolph's person, he could not be bound by such rules. Rudolph is said to have laughed good-naturedly and gave orders to let Beethoven pursue their relationship in his own way.[87] Unhappy over interference by officials of the Stuttgart court, Beethoven's former associate Johann Nepomuk Hummel migrated to Weimar and negotiated a new contract stating that he, not the ducal intendant, would have final authority in musical matters.[88]

Fame and the ascendance of middle-class values during the nineteenth century also helped composers overcome the social stigma to which they were subjected during the eighteenth century. Building upon the experience he gained in the salons of Warsaw, Frédéric Chopin found ready acceptance in the most fashionable salons of Paris, where he regularly appeared dressed in white tie and tails.[89] Thanks not only to his popularity as a performer but also his refined manners and compelling appearance, Franz Liszt was one of the first to demand with some success that composers be treated as equals to members of the middle class and even with the nobility. His views on the matter, demanding a "new aristocracy of intelligence," were published in a Parisian journal in 1835.[90] As the culturally refined son of a wealthy banker and the grandson of a great philosopher, Felix Mendelssohn was one of the first to be accorded such status in both England and France.[91]

Even before the social status of musicians rose, employment in noble courts, despite its aggravations, also had advantages in addition to the assurance that (at the lord's pleasure) basic material needs would be satisfied. During his employment with the Esterházy court, Joseph Haydn observed, he could perfect his composition technique without fear of outside criticism, performing all kinds of musical experiments to see what pleased and what did not.[92] And despite the tedious character of his company at the court in Detmold, Brahms admitted that he had abundant time for composition with "modest but secure emoluments" and that:[93]

> Here we must once again loudly sing the praises of the art-loving little German princely courts of the 18th and 19th centuries, which encouraged the arts, while respecting the justifiable desire of the artist for freedom, both outward and spiritual.

COMPENSATION HIERARCHIES AND RISK

Those who entered music, or more precisely, music composition as a profession faced two broad kinds of risk. First, there was career risk in the degree to which one's talent—genetically acquired and assiduously honed—matched the demands of the marketplace. Second, especially for those who chose freelance forms of music provision, there were event-specific risks: was the particular performance or composition received well by the consuming public?

Compensation Norms

In career income-earning opportunities, there was throughout most of the eighteenth and nineteenth centuries a fairly clear hierarchy of pay levels. Outstanding vocal and instrumental soloists, and especially the handful who qualified for what today would be called "superstar" status, were paid best.[94]

Particularly during the first half of the eighteenth century, the most highly paid musicians, with annual incomes several times those of leading salaried Kapellmeister, were the most able castrati. Top castrati such as Farinelli, Caffarelli, and Senesino earned season fees of £1,000 to 1,500 in the best-paying London market—at the lower bound, 35 times the annual earnings of English building craftsmen—supplemented several times over by ad hoc performance fees and gifts from the nobility. But entering this select group was a risky proposition. As Patrick Barbier observes:[95]

> Castration was like a lottery from which very few emerged victorious, for while the fortunate winners would be received by the great ones of the world, the others, for whom the operation had brought no success, would have no future beyond taking their place sadly in the depths of some obscure parish church choir.

And even at the first phase of the lottery, mortality rates following castration ranged from 10 to 80 percent, depending upon the competence of the surgeon.

Prima donna sopranos sometimes earned as much as top castrati; other singers were less well paid. As in the case of castrati, relatively few made it into the top-paying ranks. And with four or five performances per week being the norm during opera seasons, vocal cord damage that ended careers prematurely was not unusual. Top singers tended to operate in a relatively footloose market, sometimes accepting contracts for a season at an opera house and sometimes employment contracts from noble courts that managed their own opera establishments. Thus, competition operated to influence pay levels. In his excellent book, John Rosselli argues that the share of total performer outlays received by the top stars escalated beginning in the 1830s, when improved transportation media made it easier to move from one venue to another.[96] This proposition, although consistent with the received theory of superstars, is less than fully supported. A century earlier top castrati and female sopranos proved quite able to communicate with and migrate to London in quest of the highest superstar fees, and George Frideric Handel embarked upon hunting trips throughout the opera-loving parts of the European continent to sign up renowned singers for his Royal Academy opera. But certainly, beginning with the spectacular Vienna debut of Niccolò Paginini in 1828, traveling superstars gained increased prominence. So powerful was the reputation of Swedish soprano Jenny Lind that she not only received an advance of $150,000 for an 1850–1851 concert tour in America (managed by P. T. Barnum), but her cooperation was sufficient to turn some public piano concerts by Clara Schumann from feared disappointment to substantial success.[97]

The salaries of Kapellmeister paled in comparison with these top performer fees. J. S. Bach's highest monetary salary (with fringe benefits) at Köthen amounted to roughly £105 per year, or nearly four times the annual earnings of a fully employed building craftsman in southern England. The best-paid Kapellmeister on the continent during the first half of the eighteenth century were said to be those employed by the king of Saxony at Dresden. Vice-Kapellmeister Johann Heinichen (1683–1729) received in 1720 nearly three times Bach's Köthen salary. The salary of Dresden Kapellmeister Antonio Lotti (1667–1740) is harder to interpret, since it was bundled with that of his star soprano wife. It amounted to nearly £2,500.[98] Joseph Haydn's peak salary with the Esterházy family before his first London visit amounted to approximately £100 per year, not counting fringe benefits such as meals, housing (including the rebuilding of Haydn's Eisenstadt residence when it burned), and the like.[99] Needless to say, back-chair fiddlers were paid much less than those who had sufficient compositional and organizational talent to be appointed Kapellmeister — somewhere in the range of 3 to 6 times less. Instrumental soloists' pay ranged between the extremes.[100]

Event-Specific Risks

For those who elected to earn their living through free-lance performance and composition activities, incomes tended to be much less steady over time than those of hired employees, depending inter alia upon event-specific contingencies. To be sure, reputation was important. Opera composers such as Rossini, Bellini, Donizetti, and Verdi could in their more mature years command composition commissions many times higher than those they received at the start of their careers, before they had established a track record for producing hits. But adding a hit to one's repertoire was a chancy thing; a substantial majority of new operas failed within a few performances. The risks were well-recognized by father Leopold Mozart in a letter home from Milan on the eve of the premiere of fourteen-year-old Wolfgang's opera *Mitradate*:[101]

> Now it all depends upon the orchestra and ultimately on the whim of the audience. Thus, much depends upon luck, as in a lottery.

The opera in fact proved to be a substantial success, precipitating an invitation back to Milan for another successful visit the following year.

Compositions might be badly received for many reasons. The composer himself might be to blame for work that failed to please or that was not completed on time. Italian opera impresarios sometimes sought police intervention to induce composers to satisfy their contractual obligations. Donizetti's 1839 contract with the Paris Opéra imposed a penalty of 15,000 francs (£588) if the composer failed to deliver his score on time.[102] Similar provisions bound the librettist and the Opéra itself for failure to perform. Hasty preparation or poor casting could mean unwarranted defeat. Verdi's opera *La traviata* (The Fallen Woman) failed miserably in its 1853 premiere at La Fenice in Venice, in no small matter because the soprano portraying consumptive Violetta weighed in at 235 pounds. Verdi's reaction was philosophic; "Time will tell," he wrote, and a year later, the essentially unrevised opera succeeded.[103] Rossini's operas are said to have experienced almost consistently disappointing premieres, in part because of insufficient rehearsal and partly because first-night audiences were from the richest strata of society who appreciated Rossini's humor less than the middle-class spectators attending later performances.[104] And bad luck could intervene. At the first performance of *Il barbiere di Siviglia* (The Barber of Seville) in 1816, don Basilio tripped and bloodied his nose, evoking whistles from the audience, after which a stray cat wandered about the stage.[105]

Competition from a second London opera company, the Opera of the Nobility, severely eroded the profitability of Handel's operas between 1733 and 1737 until the challenger disbanded following massive losses. Franz Schubert's principal subscription concert failed to have a lasting impact on his reputation in part because a competing performance by Paganini three days later captured the Viennese public's attention.[106] An 1826 benefit concert in London counted upon by a dying Carl Maria von Weber to provide for his family was sparsely attended because a well-known tenor held a competing recital at the same time and because an important horse race was being run at Epsom.[107] After a packed premiere, the second performance of Beethoven's Ninth Symphony and *Missa solemnis* was poorly attended because it was scheduled for noon on a beautiful May day and the Viennese public preferred to stroll outdoors rather than to be crowded into a public hall.[108] A smallpox epidemic led to cancellation of benefit concerts scheduled by the Mozarts on their first visit to Vienna in 1767. Similarly, Frédéric Chopin's first public concert in Paris was only one-third full because of a cholera scare. Another Chopin concert scheduled in 1848 had to be cancelled because of the revolutionary events of the time.

For composers who sought the particularly handsome commissions attainable by scoring an opera, success ratios were affected by employment status, the composer's degree of financial security, and the composer's innate literary taste. Employed as house composer for Vienna's Italian opera, Antonio Salieri was more or less compelled to take any libretto chosen by the opera management and compose to it. This undoubtedly contributed to the numerous failures he experienced.[109] As a mature freelancer, on the other hand, Mozart could and did review carefully every text put before him and chose to compose only the most promising ones.[110] This plus Mozart's inherent genius undoubtedly accounts for the high success rate, both at the time and especially in the long run, of his operas.[111] Salieri's benefactor Christoph Willibald Gluck acquired substantial wealth through his marriage at age thirty-six, and as a result, Alfred Einstein reports, he could choose his librettos with care and declined to compose works that "did not correspond to his taste and character."[112] Freelancer Beethoven was also selective; in one year he turned down twelve libretto possibilities, confining his efforts mainly to a single opera, *Fidelio*, that after several disappointments achieved financial success in 1814 and remains an important staple in the modern repertoire.[113] Most of the leading nineteenth-century freelance Italian composers were forced by financial necessity to take on virtually every libretto offered them. Donizetti, for example, was said to have been caught up in "a self-inflicted producing schedule that made it absolutely necessary for him to set bad librettos rather than no librettos at all."[114] Donizetti, Rossini, and Verdi all become more selective as their fortunes grew. Vincenzo Bellini was more discriminating from the outset. It is not clear whether this reflected a conscious strategy choice by Bellini or because he had the good fortune to be teamed with Italy's most able librettist of the time, Felice Romani.[115] Both Johann Strauss Jr. and César Franck were poorly read in literature generally and as an apparent consequence, both accepted deficient operetta or opera libretti, leading to many failures.[116]

Of the many exogenous events that affected the fortunes of individual performance events, war and peace had perhaps the strongest systematic effect. Mozart's fortunes deteriorated during the late 1780s in part because of opposition cabals, but they were nothing new. The main negative influence was Austria's entry in 1788 into a war against the Ottoman Empire, inducing many of the wealthy individuals who had been his audience to join the forces at the front or to flee to their country estates, and through heavy taxation limiting the purchasing power of those who remained in Vienna. Mozart's rival Salieri was also adversely affected by the cancellation of a completed opera whose proposed setting was in Austria's wartime ally, Russia.[117] The 1805 premiere of Beethoven's opera *Leonore* (later, *Fidelio*) had the misfortune of being scheduled seven days after the entry of French occupation troops into Vienna, scattering what would normally have been Beethoven's natural audience. An 1808 benefit concert featuring the Fifth and Sixth symphonies was financially unsuccessful in part because of wartime audience depletion, but also because of competition from a benefit concert for widows and orphans.[118]

If war was bad for freelance concert attendance, the onset of peace was beneficial. By far the largest net proceeds from Beethoven's various benefit concerts were realized in 1814, when Vienna was rejoicing over the departure of French forces and the city was crowded with wealthy foreign dignitaries for the war-ending Congress of Vienna.[119] Similarly, the Parisian revolution of 1830 unleashed a surge of democratic sentiments with which Paganini's unique approach to performance had powerful resonance. The asserted "triumph of the bourgeoisie" led, among other things, to a spectacularly successful ten-concert booking for Paganini at the Paris Opéra.[120]

Risk-Alleviation Institutions

The risks taken by musicians and composers were in part hedged through a diversity of institutions that helped those who found themselves in difficult financial straits.

For those who had been employed over a substantial period by the nobility or church, pensions were normally provided — sometimes at full, sometimes reduced, salary.[121] Pension support was not an unimportant matter; fully 333 of the 646 composers in our statistical sample lived to be 66 years of age or older. Joseph Haydn was treated especially well by his former employers, the Esterházys. Not only was Haydn's pension increased during the inflation of 1806, but Prince Nikolaus II also undertook to pay Haydn's physician and pharmacy bills.[122] The treatment of composers' widows was more irregular. Some received pensions of much less than their husband's previous salary. Anna Magdalena Bach petitioned the Leipzig City Council for the customary half-year's salary of her husband in 1750.[123] She died later in poverty. A destitute Constanze Mozart successfully petitioned the Austrian emperor for the widow's pension (260 florins per year, or £27) normally accorded imperial employees, even though her husband had not served the ten years required to warrant such support.[124] On the other hand, the king of Saxony doubled the annual pension of roughly £25 paid to the widow of Carl Maria von Weber after he recognized how well-regarded the composer was in other parts of Europe.[125]

For musicians who lacked pension support or who were otherwise indisposed financially, the principal backstops, other than occasional acts of individual charity, were special benefit concerts and in a few places, notably London and Vienna, organizations that raised funds to support indigent musicians. In London, for example, the Society of Musicians conducted a grand annual concert for the benefit of needy musicians between 1739 and 1784. The amounts granted by the Society to individual musicians were typically small—£25 per year in 1784 and £50 per year in 1794.[126] Handel left £1,000 to the Society upon his death in 1759. In Vienna, the Tonkünstler-Sozietät (Society of Musicians) was founded in 1772 to aid indigent musicians and their widows. It held regular fundraising concerts during the Christmas and Lenten seasons. Joseph Haydn organized several performances of *The Creation* and *Die Jahreszeiten* (The Seasons) for the benefit of the Society.[127] Curiously, Mozart's widow Constanze received no support from the Society, allegedly because her husband had failed to produce the birth certificate necessary for membership.[128] The work of collective organizations like these was supplemented by similar privately supported charities. As the end of his life approached, Giuseppe Verdi left 775,000 francs (£30,500) for the construction and maintenance of a home for retired Italian musicians. The widow of Gioachino Rossini donated 200,000 francs (£7,850) to a Parisian welfare organization dedicated to supporting musicians.

Composers' Economic Fortunes: Quantitative Evidence

The typical composer, we have seen, was interested in earning a decent living but faced many economic hazards. How well overall did composers fare? Especially for those who engaged in freelance activities, income varied too much from year to year to estimate in any meaningful way averages for groups of composers.[129] Here, utilizing the sample of 50 composers on whom at least one full-length biography was read, we rely on two proxies: home ownership and net worth of the composer's estate at the time of death.

The best contemporary survey of life in Vienna at the time of Mozart is that of Johann Pezzl.[130] Pezzl's account implies that the typical non-noble Viennese rented rather than owning his or her own home. Was this true for composers too? For 38 of the composers in our select sample of 50, it was possible to glean evidence on house ownership. At some stage during their careers 18 of the 38 owned a home; some, such as Rossini and Johann Strauss Jr., owned multiple homes. It would appear that the composers in our select sample had acquired at least one symbol of middle-class affluence more successfully than the average urban resident.

An alternative approach consistent with existing data sources is to ascertain the value of the estate composers left at the time of their deaths. Implementation poses a range of difficulties. For one, for many composers, and especially for those born during the first century of our sample span, the evidence is not available, or at least, it was lacking in the biographies consulted.

Second, formal estate valuations, then as now, tended to undervalue items with no clear market value, undoubtedly in part to minimize death taxes. Johann Sebastian Bach's estate inventory in 1750 included a Stainer violin—at the time, a type widely preferred over violins from Cremona—whose value was reported to be 8 Reichsthaler, or a bit less than £2.[131] In 1791, a Stainer violin was auctioned off in London for £137; nearer in time to Bach's death, in 1756, an excellent violin of Cremona provenance brought £38 in London.[132] Either Bach's violin was tremendously undervalued in the estate inventory, or there was a massive failure of arbitrage to equalize the prices of comparable objects across distant geographic markets. No value was attached to the trove of priceless musical manuscripts left by Bach. Bach's heirs had only modest financial success disposing of his manuscripts, but forty-plus years later, Constanze Mozart shrewdly brought in substantial sums selling her husband's musical manuscripts, whose official estate valuation cannot have exceeded £2.[133]

Third, then as now, some individuals gave away substantial fractions of their assets in anticipation of death, and what was given did not appear in the postmortem estate assessments. As noted earlier, Giuseppe Verdi donated 775,000 francs (approximately £30,500) to endow a home for retired musicians. This plus the estimated value of his Busetto villa had to be included to obtain a reasonable estimate of Verdi's end-of-life fortune. The case of Niccolò Paganini is more difficult. After his performance career ended and his health deteriorated, Paganini embarked upon an orgy of gifts and investments, some of which proved in hindsight to be unwise, such as an estate in Parma for 300,000 lire (£9,900) on which he failed to obtain clear title; a second palazzo for 33,000 lire; and an investment that ultimately mounted to 100,000 francs (£3,300) in an ill-conceived Parisian casino scheme. He also made a loan to his banker of 217,000 lire; created trust funds for his two sisters totalling 125,000 lire; and gave 20,000 francs to Hector Berlioz.[134] Even though Paganini was forced to borrow funds and sell valuables to cover his cash needs during the last two years of his life, his net worth is estimated here to include at face value his gifts and investments on the assumption that, absent the shadow of death, Paganini would not have been so profligate. The reader may of course disagree.

A fourth problem arises in stating the various net worth estimates in some common monetary denominator. The pound sterling, one of the most stable European currencies, is taken as the standard. As one sees in the appendix to chapter 1, exchange rates fluctuated widely over time, and they are at best estimated with imprecision. Rampant inflation and currency devaluation made it especially difficult to convert Viennese estate values from the time of the Napoleonic wars. For five such cases, we benefit from the careful 1795 purchasing-power adjustments made by Julia Moore.[135] In addition to changing with inflation, wage and asset values tended to increase over the two centuries covered by our sample because of rising prosperity attributable to feudal reforms and the industrial revolution. To obtain a relatively constant benchmark, our final estimates take monetary estate values current around the time of death and divide them by an index of the nominal wages received by building craftsmen in the south of England, with the benchmark year set as 1790.[136] The final estimates therefore attempt not only to strip away localized inflation but also to adjust estate values for changes in the compensation of an "average" skilled English worker. Since, as we saw in the appendix to chapter 1, the inflation-adjusted earnings of such workers nearly trebled between 1800 and 1895, our figures tend to underestimate the real purchasing power of assets for later periods.

The results for the 23 composers on whom data of acceptable quality were available are summarized in table 4.1 in descending order of estate values adjusted for English building craftsmens' earnings. There are, not surprisingly, huge differences among the various composers. Despite having retired from active opera composition at the age of thirty-seven and living the life of a gentleman thereafter, Rossini heads the list. Muzio Clementi, who enlarged an already appreciable fortune from piano teaching by founding a firm that published sheet music and later manufactured pianos, fared second best despite an 1807 piano factory fire on which insurance coverage was deficient by some £15,000. From the narratives on his declining revenues, high expenses, and accumulating debts, it should be no surprise that Wolfgang Amadeus Mozart trails the list, with seldom-employed Franz Schubert in second to last place.

The wealthiest 10 percent (by count, 2) of the composers together accounted for 44.4 percent of the 23 composers' estate wealth; the wealthiest 20 percent (5 composers), 80.3 percent. For 13 other composers, it was possible to make qualitative judgments about estate sizes,

TABLE 4.1
VALUE OF 23 COMPOSERS' ESTATES AT OR NEAR TIME OF DEATH

			Estate Value	
Composer	Born	Own House?	£ at Time of Death	Craftsmen-Wage-Adjusted £
Gioachino Rossini	1792	Yes	97,580	47,071
Muzio Clementi	1752	Unknown	45,664	29,472
G. F. Handel	1685	Yes	21,000	26,630
Niccolò Paganini	1782	Yes	30,284	19,935
Giuseppe Verdi	1813	Yes	39,400	15,766
Johannes Brahms	1833	No	24,295	9,955
Carl Czerny	1791	Unknown	10,000	5,690
Gaetano Donizetti	1797	Yes	7,831	4,976
Franz Liszt	1811	No	8,266	3,534
J. P. Rameau	1683	Unknown	1,905	2,353
J. N. Hummel	1778	Yes	2,928	1,880
Antonio Salieri	1750	Yes	1,893	1,773
Vincenzo Bellini	1801	No	1,563	1,006
F. J. Haydn	1732	Yes	950	890
Robert Schumann	1810	No	1,540	880
Ludwig van Beethoven	1770	No	612	573
Leopold Mozart	1719	No	224	232
César Franck	1822	Unknown	393	166
J. S. Bach	1685	No	30	39
Michael Haydn	1737	No	33	24
Johann Vanhal	1739	No	10	9
Franz Schubert	1797	No	−14	−13
W. A. Mozart	1756	No	−99	−93

with the categories being "substantial," "modest," "small," "nil," and "negative." Assuming extremely crudely the "substantial" estates to be valued at the upper 20 percentile point of the adjusted value distribution in table 4.1, the "moderate" estates at the median, the "small" estates at the 75th percentile, and "negative" estates to have an adjusted value of −30, one finds that the wealthiest 10 percent of composers accounted for 52.8 percent of total estate assets, and the wealthiest 20 percent of composers held 72.5 percent of estate assets.

These net worth estimates come from a triply biased sample. To enter our large sample, a composer had to have some of his music listed in the *Schwann* catalogue for Fall 1996. Second, the sample selected for reading of full-length biographies was biased toward the more productive composers, as indicated by the length of *Schwann* catalogue listings. Indeed, it includes all the top 26 *Schwann* catalogue composers.

Third, to enter table 4.1, the composer's life had to be interesting enough for biographers to have included detailed information on surviving estate values. Thus, by and large, the composers recorded in table 4.1 are "winners" in the judgment of posterity, even if not at the cash register. To the extent that musical output honored by posterity yielded immediate economic benefits — a point to which we return — one might expect the sampled composers mostly to have done well economically, which means that those in the intermediate ranks of the table 4.1 distribution may have fared better than would a completely random selection of composers.

This conjecture can be tested thanks to the painstaking research of Julia Moore.[137] Using Viennese estate valuation archives, she obtained net estate value estimates for a total of 69 Kapellmeister, freelance composers, and ordinary court musicians who died in a period spanning the heyday of Mozart and Beethoven. All were adjusted by Moore to constant 1795 purchasing-power levels. For the 42 freelance composers and Kapellmeister, the top-ranked 10 percent accounted for 64.0 percent of total composer net worth and the top 20 percent for 92.9 percent. The shares of the leaders are higher than for our more select samples of 23 or 36 composers, all prominent enough to survive and enter the *Schwann* listings. When the list is augmented with instrumentalists who lacked court leadership positions,[138] but who played in court orchestras, one finds that the top 10 percent accounted for 86.5 percent of the 69 musicians' terminal net worth and the top 20 percent for 98.9 percent of the net worth. This increase in concentration occurs because the back-chair musicians were almost uniformly less wealthy than the freelance composers and Kapellmeister (the formers' average estate net worth was only 5 percent that of the latter), but their addition to the count meant that a larger number of wealthy individuals would be included in the top 10 and 20 percent tallies. The less selective the sample, the higher is the share of some given fraction of wealth leaders.

Distributions such as these, in which the top-ranked members account for the lion's share of total sample wealth or other quantitative attributes, are known as skew distributions. They are typical of all such economic outcome distributions, whether the focus be individual wealth, popular motion picture or record receipts, or the share of stock market portfolio value attributable after a substantial holding period to the most successful high-technology enterprises.[139] For the United States as a whole, the top 10 percent of all families, ranked in descending order of net worth in 1998, accounted for 53.3 percent of total family net worth; the top 25 percent for 79.7 percent.[140]

Economists have long speculated about the reasons for these skew wealth distributions. There are three main categories of explanation, in all of which some kind of uncertainty plays a key role. The most popular, which seems largely irrelevant to the fortunes of composers, is that wealth is accumulated through year-by-year investment, with investors who enjoy a run of luck doing better than those who are unlucky (or inept). Second, there may be "path dependence" in the fortunes of a composer. Those who succeed at an early stage of their careers in attracting public or noble patrons' enthusiasm and becoming superstars gain through a kind of self-reinforcing snowball effect fortunes disproportionate to those lacking such auspicious beginnings.[141] This explanation undoubtedly has some relevance in explaining the skew distribution of composer wealth. Finally, the more-or-less God-given distribution of talent and ability to market oneself successfully to the public is undoubtedly distributed unequally. Some are endowed with better ability to thrive in job markets, freelance composition, or performance markets than others. There is evidence that such differences in inherent opportunity — difficult or impossible to identify in advance — help explain the outcomes of high-technology investments,[142] and it would not be unreasonable to believe that an analogous sampling process was at work in determining the fortunes of composers.

We advance from this speculative realm to ask whether we can identify systematic variables that affected composers' success in accumulating terminal wealth, as measured in the rightmost column of table 4.1. Four plausible explanatory variables could be quantified: the year of the composer's birth, the number of years lived, whether the composer engaged in substantial freelance composition or performance, and the composers' musical output, as measured by the length of listings in the 1996 *Schwann Opus* catalogue. Among the variables, only the one measuring the years lived by a composer was statistically significant: the longer a composer's life, the higher adjusted wealth was, other things being equal.[143] Wealth tended to be higher for composers born in later periods, even though the wealth values were adjusted (in later years, downward) to reflect increasing building craftsmen earnings over time. Composers who plunged into freelance activities fared slightly but insignificantly better than those who earned their living mainly through employment with the nobility or the church. Being judged well by posterity, as evidenced by the length of *Schwann* catalogue listings, was *negatively* but weakly correlated with contemporary wealth accumulation, other things being equal. In other words, financial success during a composer's lifetime did not project systematically into reputational success over a longer historical perspective. Leopold Mozart advised his son that he should chart his career recognizing that what really mattered was to become "a famous Kapellmeister about whom posterity will read in books."[144] Certainly Wolfgang achieved that, even if not a substantial net worth during his lifetime. Yet if the regression results can be extrapolated, both Mozart and Franz Schubert might have accumulated more wealth if they had been granted the gift of a longer life.[145]

Fashion and Public Relations

To say that the fortunes of composers depended entirely on chance variations in natural talent and accidents of the fates would be to go too far. How composers used their talent and how they responded to their opportunities were also important.

Changing Tastes

Especially important was composers' adaptability to the changing tastes of music patrons and other aficionados. A few days before he was booted out of Graf Arco's Vienna chambers, marking the end of his servitude to Prince-Archbishop Colloredo, Mozart was warned by Graf Arco:[146]

> Believe me, you let yourself be blinded here. Here [in Vienna] the fame of a person is short-lived. At the beginning one hears all sorts of praise and earns a great deal of money—that is true—but how long? After some months the Viennese want something new.

Mozart acknowledged to his father that there was wisdom in this warning, but he argued that the fickleness of the Viennese applied more to theater compositions (such as opera) than to the piano music at which Mozart excelled. And when he had accumulated fame and fortune with his compositions, he would in any event leave Vienna if the public tired of him. Mozart was certainly aware that composers had to be sensitive to audience tastes. After Leopold warned him in 1780 to write not only for the music-appreciating public but also for the unmusical, of whom there were 100 for each ten true connoisseurs, Wolfgang assured his father that in his opera *Idomeneo* there was music for every species of listener.[147] Similarly, describing his strategy in composing three piano concertos whose scores were offered for sale by subscription in 1783, Mozart wrote that "the concertos strike a balance between being too difficult and too light—they are brilliant—pleasant for the ears, naturally, without falling into emptiness—every now and then only the experts are gratified, but the great unwashed must also be satisfied without knowing why."[148] In this he may have been following the example of his early mentor Johann Christian Bach, who aimed the various movements of his London symphonies at diverse segments of the audience, targeting the finales toward those of the least refined taste.[149] Whether Mozart continued to follow these early principles is questionable. During the late 1780s, as his economic fortunes began to worsen, he advised his live-in student Johann Nepomuk Hummel:[150]

> Go as far as you can, my son, avoid the everyday tinkling and hurdy-gurdy playing, the nail-smith hammering, the powerful claptrap and thrashing about with hands and fingers, that God have mercy, mindless critics call music. Remain true to your own feelings, my Hansl, it will never lead you astray.

It seems clear that in his later Vienna years Mozart's music was sometimes too sublime for the tastes of Vienna listeners. But ascertaining the reasons for the decline in his economic fortunes is more complex. The war with Turkey certainly had an impact, as did the cabals that had been operating against Mozart from the time of his 1767 Vienna visit, as did nobles' resentment over Mozart's unfavorable portrayal of their foibles in *Figaro* and *Don Giovanni*.

The typical music patron's tastes during much of the eighteenth century and the early nineteenth century were far narrower and more fickle than those of twentieth-century classical music lovers. In opera, for example, patrons demanded several new operas each season, and old successes were rarely repeated in subsequent seasons unless the music was extensively rewritten, often with title changes. Only in the second half of the nineteenth century did repertory opera—the performance of established classics without substantial change—become commonplace. On the instrumental side, Johann Sebastian Bach's polyphonics and innovative progressions displeased the average churchgoer of his time, leading to complaints by the Arnstadt church consistory about Bach's making "many curious variationes in the chorale, and mingled many strange tones in it, and for the fact that the Congregation has been confused by it."[151] In a 1730 essay on important German composers, Georg Philipp Telemann failed even to mention J. S. Bach, apparently because Bach's complex contrapuntal music was considered old-fashioned.[152] Beethoven's early symphonies, notably the Third (*Eroica*) and Fifth, were perceived by the Viennese public and the press as too avant-garde and dissonant. But by the third decade of the nineteenth century, Beethoven's works had been overshadowed in popularity by the operas of Rossini, who, in Beethoven's own evaluation, "suits the frivolous and sensuous spirit of the times."[153] Similarly, Beethoven said in 1822 to a visitor about his once-popular piano solo pieces, "They went out of fashion here long ago, and [in Vienna] fashion is everything."[154] Rejecting the advice of his family members to compose music less refined and more suited to a larger public, César Franck persisted in writ-

ing his now-revered Symphony in D Minor (motto), presented to an
"ice cold" Paris Conservatory audience in 1889.[155]

To be sure, not all music lovers' tastes were narrow and mercurial. In
London during the closing decades of the eighteenth century, a minority
of concertgoers were devotees of the Concert of Ancient Music, which
performed the works of Johann Sebastian Bach and restored George
Frideric Handel to prominence, leading eventually to large-scale Handel
Commemoration concerts beginning in 1784 and continuing into the
1790s.[156] In Vienna, small groups met on Sundays beginning in the
1780s at the home of Baron Gottfried van Swieten and in other venues
arranged by him to perform and hear the nearly forgotten works of J. S.
Bach, C.P.E. Bach, and Handel.[157] Among the participants were Mozart
and Beethoven, whose often declared admiration for Bach and Handel
stemmed at least in part from those sessions.

Adaptation

Some composers adapted flexibly to perceived changes in public tastes.
The most notable success story is that of Handel. By the 1730s, it became clear that London operagoers were tiring of operas presented in
Italian. The situation was complicated by the existence of two separate
companies competing to present star-studded Italian operas, and Handel, as impresario and principal composer for the older company, tee-
tered on the brink of bankruptcy. But Handel saw a possible solution,
introducing in 1732 an English-language oratorio *Esther*. When its success proved durable, he followed with a series of English language oratorios, including *Alexander's Feast, Israel in Egypt, Messiah, Samson*,
and *Judas Maccabaeus*, not all of which were financially successful
(*Messiah* was much more successful initially in Dublin than in London),
but which together restored Handel's bank balances. Similarly, during
the 1780s, when Joseph Haydn began composing symphonies for an
audience beyond the Esterházy court, he adopted more expansive orchestration and changed his style in other ways to appeal to broader
groups.[158] Even so, after his oratorio *The Creation* was received with
great enthusiasm in 1799 by the Viennese, his later oratorio, *The Seasons*, was performed to half-full performance halls. His biographers observe that "the fickle Viennese were turning away from their darling."[159]
In her early 1840s Paris concerts, Clara Schumann found most listeners
to be "frivolous and superficial." She saved for the final periods of musical soirees, when only the connoisseurs remained, more serious works,
including the compositions of her husband Robert.[160] Many composers,
including Clementi, Haydn, Beethoven, Carl Maria von Weber, and
Brahms, responded to popular tastes by departing from their normal

styles and orchestrating popular pieces (for instance, Beethoven's "easy and pleasant" Scottish and Irish song settings[161]) that brought substantial honoraria from publishers.

Others adapted less well. Vivaldi's plunge into debt as a result of operas he produced in Ferrara during the 1730s was attributable in part to changes in operatic taste toward a bel canto style he shunned.[162] Jean-Phillipe Rameau lamented late in life, "Music is perishing; taste is changing at every moment. I should not know how to manage it if I had to work as I did in the past."[163] Rossini's cessation of opera writing for pay was attributable not only to satisfaction with the fortune he had accumulated and a desire for leisure, but also by the recognition that audiences now preferred more serious works over his florid rococo style, and he was unable and unwilling to cater to the changing demand.[164] Verdi, who continued writing operas at a less frenzied pace into his final years, was more philosophical:[165]

> When an artist allows himself to have two or three successes while young, still under thirty, he can be sure that the public will then grow tired of him. . . . If the artist has the strength to stand up to this turn of the tide [and abuse by the public] and go ahead on his own path, he'll be safe by the time he's forty. Then the public no longer has contempt for him but puts on its grand airs, keeping a gun cocked, ready at any time to let him have a good burst of shot.

Writing in her diary, Clara Schumann observed sadly that the then-famous composer Ignaz Moscheles had outlived the reception for his works, and that "gradually the enthusiasm for him evaporates, and that must cause him pain."[166]

Militaristic Themes

A powerful means of gratifying contemporary musical tastes was the composition of patriotic anthems in time of war. The change in Handel's economic fortunes is clearly traceable to the 1740s. During this period he composed two major works with explicit patriotic appeal: his stirring *Dettingen Te Deum*, written to honor England's June 1743 victory at Dettingen, Germany, over the hated French; and *Judas Maccabaeus*, an oratorio commemorating the famous ancient Hebrew general, written as the forces of King George II prepared to defeat in April 1746 a rebellion by Stuart pretenders to the British throne. A Handel biographer asserts that *Judas Maccabaeus*, which enjoyed fifty performances during his lifetime, "turned Handel into a national institution, henceforth unassailable" with a "public that lived through the Spanish and Austrian wars and the Stuart rebellion . . . eager to hear Britain praised."[167] How much of Handel's subsequent wealth accumulation, despite occasional setbacks, was attributable to these popularity-entrenching works and how much to his general adoption of English-language oratorios over Italian operas and his sale of tickets to the general public as well as to advance subscribers (resumed, after a hiatus, with *Judas Maccabaeus*) is impossible to determine.

Similarly, the most successful benefit concerts undertaken by Beethoven, in 1813 and 1814, combined the grandest piece of schlock ever written by Beethoven, the so-called Battle Symphony, or *Wellington's Victory*, with the magnificent Seventh Symphony. The Battle Symphony commemorated the victory of England's General Arthur Wellesley Wellington over the forces of Joseph Napoleon, brother of Napoleon Bonaparte and self-asserted King of Spain, at Vitoria, Spain, in June 1813. At the initial performances of *Wellington's Victory*, Johann Nepomuk Hummel and Giacomo Meyerbeer beat the drums and Antonio Salieri directed battle-simulating instruments in the balcony. The applause at the first concert is said to have risen to "the point of ecstacy."[168] Beethoven's amanuensis Anton Schindler wrote that this was "one of the most important moments in the life of the master, at which all the hitherto divergent voices, save those of the professional musicians, united in proclaiming him worthy of the laurel."[169] Those concerts plus a successful remounting of *Fidelio* let Beethoven earn more from public concerts in 1814 than in all the other years of his life taken together, permitting him to buy bank stock shares that comprised most of his fortune at the time of his death thirteen years later.[170]

Many other composers, such as Antonio Vivaldi, Antonio Salieri, Hector Berlioz, Robert Schumann, Bedřich Smetana, and Camille Saint-Saëns wrote music calculated to arouse public spirits in times of military or revolutionary fervor. Perhaps the most lasting successes were those of Joseph Haydn, whose 1794 London Symphony no. 100 (the *Military*) is said by his biographers to have "caught the spirit of the day in a miraculous way" and to have been "the greatest success of his whole career."[171] His "Volkslied," written in 1797, when the German-speaking portion of Europe was under attack from French forces, became the national anthem of both Austria and Germany.

Self-Promotion and Press Relations

Success in any career depends in part upon one's ability and willingness to thrust oneself forward ahead of the jostling crowd. Franz Schubert's experience defines an extreme in this respect. He was shy and self-effacing by nature, and his ability to promote himself outside his immediate circle of close friends was impaired even more when at the age of twenty-six, as he began to enjoy public recognition, he withdrew from general society for more than a year with the onset of venereal disease. His biographer questions:[172]

> Why, with the appearance of [more than 100 published items of] music, ambitious and yet so likeable, did Schubert still fail to catch the ear of Vienna, and hence of musical Europe? One can only remind oneself . . . of Schubert's inability to appear before the public in some executive capacity. . . . It is . . . impossible to reconcile the externals of Schubert's being with the internal fire of creative energy which transformed him when he worked.

Frédéric Chopin was nearly as mild-mannered as Schubert, and for him the stare of large crowds at concerts was intimidating and paralyzing.[173] But like Schubert, he fared well in small, intimate groups. When an acquaintance from Poland, Prince Walenty Radziwill, introduced him into the salon of Paris's leading banker, Baron James de Rothschild, and from his regular subsequent appearances in the best Parisian salons, he became the most popular musician in Paris for providing one-on-one piano lessons to affluent Parisians and for performing his music before small groups. Two years after migrating to Paris, Chopin reported to a Warsaw friend:[174]

> I've been led into the best company, sit between ambassadors, princes, ministers, and I don't know through what miracle; for I haven't been personally pushy.

On the strength of his immensely popular operas and then his self-effacing humor, Gioachino Rossini is said to have induced Parisians to fight for the privilege of attending his soirees.[175] While serving as a humble church organist, Camille Saint-Saëns was taken once to a Rossini soiree and asked to perform. Rossini was characteristically skeptical of the proclaimed prodigies paraded before him, but recognizing Saint-Saëns's genuine talent, he invited him back repeatedly and brought him to the notice of music-loving Parisian society.[176] The moral is that one's career as a successful composer can be fostered by being accepted into the best circles, and for that, one needs the right combination of talent, self-promotion, or when one is reluctant to blow one's own horn, enthusiastic backers.

Relations with the press could also have an important bearing on composers' acceptance, especially during the nineteenth century, as a more vigorous press covering musical matters emerged. As a journalist himself who was critical of contemporary trends in Parisian music, Hector Berlioz aroused the antipathy of the Paris Opéra authorities, fellow musicians, and journalists. Consequently, except in the closing years of his life, his works tended to elicit lukewarm or even negative reviews from the local press. His reception was much more positive on concert tours to Germany, Prague, Austria, Russia, and England, where there was no latent hostility.[177] César Franck's early acceptance as composer and piano performer was inhibited inter alia by the persistent opposition of a leading Parisian newspaper critic.[178]

The success of Johannes Brahms in Vienna was aided in part by strong support from Vienna's best-known music critic, Eduard Hanslick. Clara Schumann gave Brahms a copy of Hanslick's book, *Vom musikalistischen Schönen* (On Beauty in Music). He reported back to Clara in 1856 that "I wanted to read it, but paging through it I found so many dumb things that I put it aside."[179] Brahms made his first trip to Vienna in 1862, and in 1863, he was offered the directorship of the Vienna Singakademie. He must have come into contact with Hanslick in the process, for in 1863 he wrote to Hanslick accepting the offer and adding:[180]

> I must still express my great thanks for your outstanding book about *Beauty in Music*, to which I owe most delectable hours, enlightenment, yes, a kind of tranquility. . . . For one who understands his craft there is work to do everywhere in our art and science, and I wish that we may soon be as handsomely enlightened about other matters.

Whether Brahms had changed his mind about Hanslick's contribution or whether he was strategically cultivating an important potential backer is unclear. What we do know is that in subsequent years, Brahms and Hanslick became the closest of friends, among other things sharing vacation locales and birthday celebrations. And Hanslick's favorable reviews certainly contributed to the acceptance of Brahms's music. That the friendship was eventually sincere is revealed in a much later letter about Hanslick to Clara Schumann:[181]

> I can't help it, I know few people to whom I feel as sincerely drawn as to him. I consider it very fine and very rare to be as simply good, well-meaning, honest, truly modest, and everything else I know him to be. . . . That he is uncommonly competent in his field I am entitled to say, the more so since we have very different outlooks — however, I demand and expect of him nothing that's unjustifiable.

The proclaimed attitude of Brahms's contemporary, Giuseppe Verdi, toward the musical press was much less amicable:[182]

> I write my operas as well as I can, and let things go their way without ever trying to influence public opinion in the slightest. . . . Nowadays, what an apparatus accompanies each opera! . . . Journalists . . . all must carry their stone to the edifice of publicity, to build up a framework of

wretched gossip which adds nothing to the merit of an opera, but merely obscures its real value. This is deplorable, deeply deplorable!

Whether Verdi's aloofness vis-à-vis the press was offset by the promotional efforts of his able managers, Giovanni and later Tito Ricordi, who published a house newspaper and engaged in other promotional activities, remains unclear.[183]

CONCLUSION

Composers experienced widely varying economic outcomes in their pursuit of music as a profession. They were subject to a broad spectrum of risks, from the hereditary and environmental variables that determined how much talent and energy they brought to their pursuits to event-specific risks determining how well particular strategies, decisions, and undertakings turned out. That much seems clear. Now we advance onto highly speculative ground.

It is possible, as I have argued elsewhere with respect to modern high-technology investments, that the skew distribution of potential rewards confronting composers provided a more or less ideal motivational system to induce striving toward fame and wealth.[184] Unless their affairs were managed particularly badly, those who were gifted enough to be composers could at least be reasonably certain of employment, living conditions as comfortable as those enjoyed by less affluent members of the middle classes during the eighteenth and nineteenth centuries, and the sheer pleasure of making music. But if their efforts to excel in performance or freelance composition were unusually effective, they might achieve, in Samuel Johnson's apt phrase, riches beyond the dreams of avarice. As economist Joseph A. Schumpeter observed of businessmen, not composers:[185]

> Spectacular prizes much greater than would have been necessary to call forth the particular effort are thrown to a small minority of winners, thus propelling much more efficaciously than a more equal and more "just" distribution would, the activity of that large majority of businessmen who receive in return very modest compensation or nothing or less than nothing, and yet do their utmost because they have the big prizes before their eyes and overrate their chances of doing equally well.

Few composers, to be sure, succeeded in gaining spectacular prizes. The payoffs were like those in a lottery. It is interesting in this respect that many of the more ambitious composers, such as Mozart, Paganini, Rossini, and Robert Schumann, are known to have been frequent participants in the public lotteries of their day.[186] But in those instances, except in the case of Paganini, who had to pawn his violins to cover early gambling debts, they were betting small sums against the remote prospect of a sizable payoff, whereas in the lottery of career decisions, their whole standard of living was at risk. The conjecture may therefore be false, but we leave it here as a tantalizing possibility.

THE GEOGRAPHY OF COMPOSER

SUPPLY AND DEMAND

ALL BUT 17 among the sample of 646 composers surveyed in this book were born in Europe. We turn now to a more detailed analysis of geographic birth and employment patterns.[1] We ask whether some national locations or ethnic constellations were more prolific in giving birth to composers, or in employing them, than others.

Geography could matter for many reasons. The culture of one region may have bred traditions more conducive to the performance and enjoyment of music than others. Throughout the time period emphasized here, some national clusters were more affluent than others, and hence may have been better able to provide financial support for music education and performance. There are economies of scale in some aspects of music performance. For instance, a large city is better able than small cities consistently to agglomerate audiences sufficient to sustain costly opera or symphony orchestra offerings.

Perhaps the most interesting hypothesis on how geography affected music composition blends elements of historical accident, political structure, and social relationships. Although there were fragmentary antecedents,[2] the hypothesis was first crystallized by the sociologist Norbert Elias and then by William J. Baumol, a prominent economist, and Hilda Baumol.[3]

Their argument proceeds from the historical developments traced in chapter 2, which we review briefly here. During the centuries that followed the coronation of Charlemagne as Roman emperor in A.D. 800, the secular power of the emperor (called the Holy Roman Emperor, beginning in the late twelfth century) over local kings, princes, and dukes gradually atrophied. To gain support in recurring military engagements, the emperor was forced to grant territorial and governance concessions to the rulers of individual states within the Empire, especially in what is now Germany, the Czech Republic, and northern Italy. In France, Spain, Russia, England, and Habsburg Austria (which controlled substantial parts of northern Italy), governmental power had been concentrated by military force and marriages of convenience under a centralized sovereign (with Parliament playing a restraining role in England). But already by the outset of the Thirty Years War, Germany

was divided into hundreds of local kingdoms, principalities, and dukedoms whose rulers enjoyed substantial autonomy from the emperor's
authority in secular matters.[4] The 1648 Treaty of Westphalia confirmed
this decentralization of power in what is now Germany.

The numerous local German rulers derived substantial incomes from
the farm and forest lands over which they exercised feudal domain or
outright ownership and from tariffs imposed on trade and travel across
their territories. They competed with one another for prestige by the
excellence of their court amenities.[5] Among other things, every local
court (*Hof*) worth its salt had its own orchestra or band (*Kapelle* or
Harmonie), and the more affluent courts maintained opera houses. This
competition in conspicuous courtly consumption is said to have encouraged a flowering of music composition. Thus, sociologist Elias argued in
1991:[6]

> In France and England the decisive musical positions were concentrated
> in the capitals, Paris and London, as a result of state centralisation. A high-
> ranking musician in these countries therefore had no chance of escape if he
> fell out with his princely employer. There were no competing courts that
> could rival the king's in power, wealth and prestige, and that could have
> given refuge to, for example, a French musician who had fallen from favor.
> But in Germany and Italy there were dozens of courts and cities competing
> for prestige, and thus for musicians. It is no exaggeration to trace the ex-
> traordinary productivity of court music in the territories of the former Ger-
> man empire among other things to this figuration — to the rivalry for pres-
> tige of the many courts and the correspondingly high number of musical
> posts.

Apparently unaware of Elias's work, Baumol and Baumol advanced a
quite similar argument in 1994:[7]

> Obviously, economic and political conditions cannot create talent, but
> they certainly can either inhibit it or provide opportunities for its exercise.
> Our main hypothesis is intended to narrow the pertinent geography — to
> account for the striking level of composing activity emanating from Ger-
> many and Italy. This hypothesis suggests that the political division of the
> Holy Roman Empire and the Habsburg possessions into many petty states
> worked to produce the circumstances (notably substantial demand and a
> profusion of jobs) that help to explain the profusion of musical produc-
> tivity.

From these hypotheses we should expect a disproportionate number of
composers to emerge from, and work in, territories that comprised the
fragments of the Holy Roman Empire. We differentiate here between
"strong" and "weak" forms of the hypothesis, the strong form empha-

sizing Germany alone, where political fragmentation was greatest, and the weak form encompassing the four main Empire remnants (defined by 1992 borders) — Germany, Austria, Czechoslovakia, and Italy. The effects should be observed at least until the closing decades of the eighteenth century, when noble houses apparently tired of their costly competition for prestige, or the early nineteenth century, when the feudal system collapsed in western Europe as a result of economic reforms and changes precipitated by the Napoleonic wars.[8]

The lavish support of musical activities by noble courts does not *necessarily* imply, however, that the choice of music as a profession received special stimulus in the geographic regions with many dukedoms and principalities. As we have seen in chapter 4, there were substantial disadvantages as well as advantages in being employed as a court musician. Most court musicians had to endure onerous servile relationships as underlings of the feudal lord. They were subject to dismissal at the lord's whim, could not leave their positions for a better one without the master's consent, and might find their freedom to compose what suited their creative instincts and to publish it elsewhere constrained by the master's contrary preferences. And even as the golden age of court music reached its zenith during the eighteenth century, the Industrial Revolution and its commercial precursors were beginning to materialize, propagating a prosperous and growing middle class that demanded the cultural amenities of music performance and education. These prosperity-increasing developments were initially clustered at locations other than those dominated by noble courts, and so the courts were by no means the only places where would-be composers could apply their talents — to be sure, as we have seen in chapter 4, with more risk for freelance activity in market-oriented environments. It is an open question, therefore, whether music composition was nurtured best in locations characterized by a proliferation of noble courts. We address it in this chapter.

BIRTH LOCATIONS

Our main approach will be an analysis of the birthplace and work location information coded for the 646 composers included in our large sample, whose derivation is discussed in chapter 1. We begin with figure 5.1, which shows the number of composers born in diverse national territories, as those territories were defined in 1992 — thus, after the reunification of East and West Germany, but before the breakup of Czechoslovakia.[9] In some cases, the geographic assignments could not be carried out mechanically, but required an element of subjective judgment.

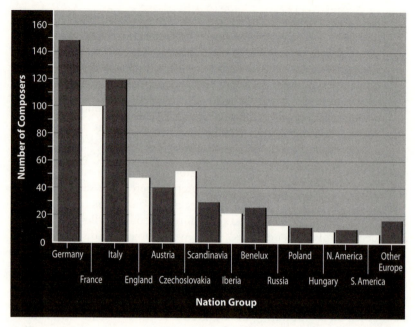

FIGURE 5.1 Number of Composers Born in Nations and National Groups, 1650–1849

For Germany in particular, 12 composers were born in territories that housed numerous ethnic Germans at the time, but which have since become part of what in 1992 was Czechoslovakia (Sudetenland), Poland (including Breslau and Danzig), and Russia (Königsberg). On the basis of family ethnicity, 11 of the 12 were classified to Germany rather than to the nations occupying the more recent boundaries. In some cases, because exact population matches could not be effected, such composers had to be removed from analyses that relate composer births to population (but not from figure 5.1). Similarly, composers born in cities that drifted from one part of eighteenth-century Austria to another national jurisdiction—for instance, Pressburg, which was the Habsburg capital of Hungary but is now Bratislava, in Slovakia—were assigned to national categories on the basis of family ethnicity, adding 2 composers of debatable origin to the Austrian count, 1 to Hungary, and 1 to Czechoslovakia. Even though he was born in Bohemia during a temporary visit to the family's original homeland, Anton Stamitz was classified as German in birth, since his family's permanent residence at the time was Mannheim.

Germany is seen to have given birth to the largest number of composers, at 148, followed by Italy at 119, France at 101, what was in 1992 Czechoslovakia 52, and England (including Scotland and Wales but not Ireland) 47. For the nations that are not included in figure 5.1 or that are consolidated into larger regional groups, the 200-year birth tallies are as follows:

Sweden	17	Ireland	4
Denmark	7	Romania	2
Norway	3	Yugoslavia	1
Finland	2	Liechtenstein	1
Spain	17	Lithuania	1
Portugal	4	Estonia	1
Belgium	16	United States	9
Netherlands	9	Canada	1
Switzerland	4	Latin America	7

To be sure, the nations covered here were of widely varying size. A better test of the competing courts hypothesis is achieved by analyzing the number of composers born per million resident inhabitants. National population estimates (necessarily crude for the earlier portion of our 200-year span) were obtained for 50-year intervals and interpolated linearly to individual years within those intervals.[10] The composer birth counts for the principal nations, excluding composers born in areas outside the 1992 national boundaries, were related to birth-year-matched national population estimates. Figure 5.2 summarizes the results.

Consistent with a broad interpretation of the competing courts hypothesis, composer births per million inhabitants were highest in the four main remnants of the Holy Roman Empire. Germany, however, with the largest profusion of independent principalities and dukedoms, ranks only third with an average tally of 8.52 per million, trailing Austria with 12.62 and Czechoslovakia with 9.22. Adding ethnics born in lands outside 1992 national borders, which imposes a bias because adjustments could not be made for the excluded populations, does not change the ranking: Germany rises to 9.20 and Czechoslovakia to 9.40.

Since the nobles of Austria and Czechoslovakia were more subservient to imperial power than those of Germany, the data provide less than complete support for the competing independent courts hypothesis, although the courts in Austria and, somewhat less clearly, Czechoslovakia did compete with one another for cultural prominence. Interpreting the hypothesis for Czechoslovakia is complicated by the fact that the families of many leading Bohemian courts tended to spend the high social seasons at their town houses in Vienna.

It is also possible that national cultures differed in the role music played in everyday life, that is, outside the scope of noble establish-

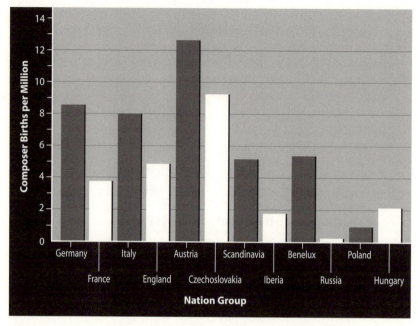

FIGURE 5.2 Number of Composers Born per Million Population

ments. Czechoslovakia's strong performance is consistent with John Clapham's observation that even small villages in Bohemia had local bands and that village schoolmasters were expected to teach singing and violin to their pupils.[11] As Hector Berlioz observed from his travels across Europe, "I must say however — since it is a matter of public notoriety — that the Bohemians are the best musicians in Europe, and that the love and feeling for music are universal in all classes of society."[12] The trailing performance of Russia at the other extreme is attributable to the abject poverty of the huge number of serfs (inflating the denominator of composers-per-million ratios) and to the fact that a Russian nationalist school of music composition emerged, under the leadership of Mikhail Glinka (1804–1857) and then Mily Balakirev (1837–1910), only in the nineteenth century.

Further insight comes from calculating composer counts per million population by 50-year intervals, as shown for the leading national origins in figure 5.3. Two influences underlie the trends evident there: rising population counts, as shown in chapter 2's figure 2.1, and an upward trend in the number of composers born. The broad balance of these two tendencies, one affecting the numerator and one the denominator of the figure 5.3 data, is revealed by the following summary:

Time Period	Total Composer Births	Cases with Matched Population Data	Births per Million
1650–1699	141	138	10.82
1700–1749	148	143	13.22
1750–1799	168	160	11.71
1800–1849	189	174	9.01

The tabulation of births per million is for only 615 composers on whom matched population data were available.[13] For 1650–1699 to 1700–1749, growth in the number of composer births was more rapid than population growth. The 1700–1749 birth cohort reaches a peak that parallels the heyday of court music support during the mid-eighteenth century. After that the trends reverse, with declining composer counts per million population.

In figure 5.3 we see, consistent with the competing courts hypothesis, that Germany's position as a birthplace of composers faded following the Napoleonic wars, which undermined many noble courts. Relative birth rates also fell sharply in Czechoslovakia in the post-Napoleonic period but not in its imperial master, Austria, which, contrary to the competing courts hypothesis, experienced high composer birth rates along

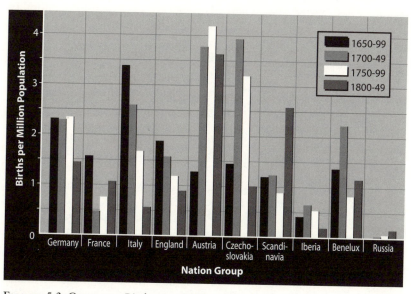

FIGURE 5.3 Composer Births per Million Population, by 50-Year Birth-Date Period

with a centralization of governmental power under Emperor Franz II and his foreign affairs minister, Klemens von Metternich. The decline in relative birth rates began earlier in Italy, England, and Iberia. France, on the other hand, experienced its golden age during the reign of King Louis XIV, after whose death the number of composers born (relative to an increasing population) declined sharply and then rose gradually. Late-developing Scandinavia and Russia achieved their strongest growth during the nineteenth century.

Viewed in their entirety, the birth data exhibit weak consistency with the competing courts hypothesis, but several anomalies blur the relationships.

EMPLOYMENT

Since the competing courts hypothesis is at bottom a statement about employment opportunities, which are assumed to influence young people's decisions to pursue a career in music, we must also examine the pattern of composer employment by nation. Analysis of national employment patterns is necessary because, during the period covered by our sample, composers were quite mobile geographically. A young person might embrace musical activities professionally not because employment was available locally, but because it was known that attractive opportunities existed somewhere else. Indeed, the geographic mobility of composers in the eighteenth and nineteenth centuries, to be investigated more fully in chapter 6, would astonish modern-day Europeans. Of the 646 composers in our sample, 30 percent died in national territories other than those in which they were born. And of the sampled composers on whom data were available, 45 percent worked at least two years in a nation other than the one in which they spent the plurality of their working lives.

To explore the geography of composers' employment, data were collected on the number of years composers spent from age twenty to their death in each of the leading European nations or nation groups, again assuming 1992 boundaries. Visits of less than two years' duration were viewed as temporary, as on a concert tour, and were not tallied. The fraction of each composer's total working life spent in relevant nations was computed, and the fractions were summed by nation to obtain a tally of "equivalent working lives" or full-time equivalents (FTEs) attracted to each nation.

Figure 5.4 summarizes the results for the entire 1650–1849 birthdate sample. Two quantities are graphed: the raw number of composers who worked at least two years in any given nation, and the full-time equiva-

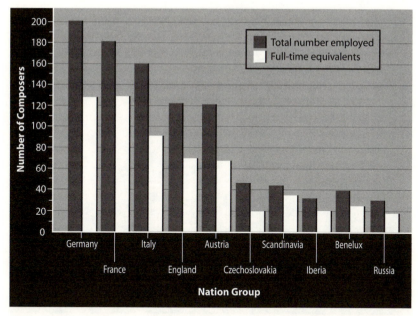

FIGURE 5.4 Number of Composers Employed by Nation and National Groups

lents linked to each nation. The differences between the two reflect how long on average a composer remained at a given work location. The Scandinavian nations exhibit the strongest holding power, with equivalent working lives averaging 80.9 percent of the number of persons employed. France is second with a 71.1 percent average. Czechoslovakia had the least holding power, at 41.4 percent; Italy the second least at 56.9 percent; and England (whose climate alienated many visiting composers) the third least at 57.3 percent.

Germany, with its many competing courts, attracted the largest absolute number of composers but emerged in a virtual dead heat with France, whose government was centralized, in terms of equivalent composer working lives. Italy, England, and Austria follow.

Again, however, it is instructive to relate these employment counts to the widely varying populations in the employing nations. To do this, equivalent working life sums were divided by national average population counts, lagging the population count for each composer by 35 years from his or her birth date to match opportunities more closely with the peak of most composers' work lives.[14] The results for the full 200-year sample are presented in figure 5.5.

Austria stands head and shoulders above the other nations and national groups, with 20.93 equivalent composer working lives per mil-

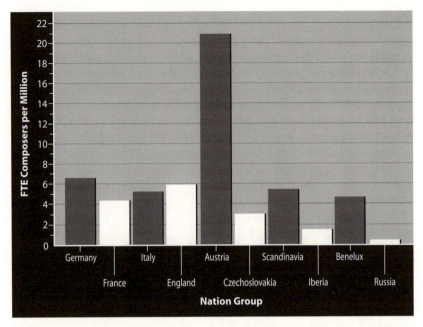

FIGURE 5.5 Number of FTE Composers Employed per Million Population

lion population. Germany is second with 6.57 FTEs, or less than a third of the Austrian figure, but its average differs little from that of England (5.86) and the Scandinavian nations (5.39), whose governance structures were much more centralized than those of the Holy Roman Empire fragments. Thus, the availability of performance and composition opportunities in numerous competing courts did not distinguish Germany from nations with quite different, typically more centralized, court musical employment structures.

Figure 5.6 offers additional insight by breaking the FTE employment counts down into four 50-year composer birth intervals. The averages for nations are uniformly lower than those in figure 5.5 because figure 5.5 sums employment over a full 200-year period whereas figure 5.6 uses four shorter intervals. Austria continues to occupy a dominant position, although less so during the first and last 50-year periods. Vienna's musical culture was invigorated by the ascent of Leopold I to the emperor's throne in 1658[15], when the 35 year age marker used in matching population with employment data would have been achieved by composers born too early to be included in our sample. Consistent with claims that Mozart represented a kind of turning point, composer employment in Austria peaked during the second half of the eighteenth century and then declined following the depletion of governmental

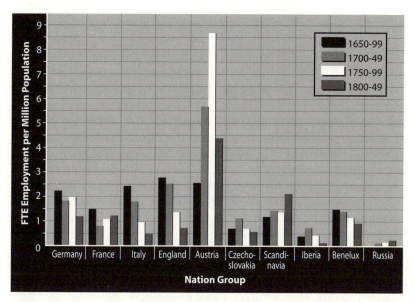

FIGURE 5.6 Employment of Composers, by 50-Year Birth Date Period

funds during the Napoleonic wars and the gradual reform of feudal institutions. As with the birth statistics of figure 5.4, Germany exhibited a sharp decline in composer employment during the 1800–1849 period, after the French invasions disrupted feudal court structures. The Iberian nations, Spain and Portugal, experienced precipitous drops after 1750 as their worldwide empires disintegrated and they failed to join the northern European nations in the rising prosperity brought by the In- dustrial Revolution. The Scandinavian nations on the other hand at- tracted rising numbers of composers as their governments' policies shifted from military adventures to economic development. The composer em- ployment patterns in England, birthplace of the Industrial Revolution, are inversely related to its rapidly rising prosperity—a phenomenon in- consistent with the hypothesis that increasing affluence among the mid- dle class had a particularly stimulating impact on the demand for music.

From the evidence examined thus far, it would appear that the influ- ences affecting the employment of composers (relative to population) are more complex than can be accommodated by simple unicausal hy- potheses such as the competing courts hypothesis or the growing mid- dle-class demand hypothesis. Before we proceed further in our attempt to unravel the puzzle, one additional plausible link must be identified. Composers may be attracted to a nation not so much because of its overall prosperity or the availability of decentralized work opportunities as by the concentration of demand in one or a few large magnet cities, whose citizens are much more affluent than the average resident of the nation as a whole.

Magnet Cities

Table 5.1 presents an opening wedge into this "magnet cities" hypothesis. It arrays, in descending order of estimated 1750 population, the 14 largest cities of Europe.[16] In all years, London and Paris tower over all the rest. The presence of a German city, Berlin, only in 14th place as of 1750 provides the mirror image of the competing courts hypothesis: Until its rapid industrialization began during the nineteenth century, Germany was fragmented into numerous small cities, hundreds of which were the seats of feudal courts.

London and Paris are universally acknowledged as the most important magnets to composers during the eighteenth and early nineteenth centuries. It was to London that George Frideric Handel migrated in 1710 and Joseph Haydn traveled in 1790 to seek their fortunes. Rossini's seven months in England during 1824 laid the basis for his own personal wealth.[17] On a trip to London in 1847, Giuseppe Verdi com-

TABLE 5.1
Europe's Largest Cities, Ranked by 1750 Population

City	Estimated Population (Thousands)			
	1700	1750	1800	1850
London	550	676	861	2,230
Paris	530	560	547	1,314
Naples	207	324	430	416
Amsterdam	172	219	201	225
Lisbon	188	213	231	259
Vienna	105	169	291	426
Moscow	130	161	238	374
Rome	149	158	153	171
Venice	144	158	146	141
St. Petersburg	n.a.*	138	220	502
Dublin	80	125	165	253
Milan	124	123	135	193
Madrid	110	123	170	263
Berlin	24	113	172	446

Source: Chandler and Fox (1974).
*Established only in 1703.

plained about the miserable weather, but wrote, "And they pay so much money! Oh, if I could stay here a couple of years, I should like to carry off a sackful of this blessed money."[18] Lacking the personality to perform successfully before the large audiences one could attract in London, Frédéric Chopin had a more negative experience, writing a year before his death that the English love art because it is a luxury, but a person had to be a machine to present all the concerts they desired.[19] If he were younger (and implicitly, in better health), he continued, he would become a machine and present concerts in every corner.

Paris was also a magnet not only to musicians from the opportunity-poor provinces of France, but also to foreign composers aspiring to improve their financial well-being. Brought to Paris by Marie Antoinette to reform French opera, Christoph Willibald Gluck earned opera fees in Paris far above those to which he was accustomed in Vienna.[20] He advised one of his opera-writing successors, Niccolò Piccinni (1728–1800) "to think of nothing in Paris except making money."[21] Visiting Mannheim in 1777, a youthful Mozart was advised by a well-traveled acquaintance that "Paris is the only place where a person can gain both money and fame."[22] As the debate over where Mozart should travel next continued, his father provided an answer by mail:[23]

> To Switzerland? To Holland? During the summer there you'll find not a soul, and in winter one earns in Berne or Zurich exactly enough so that one does not starve; otherwise there is nothing. And Holland presently has things other than music to consider,[24] and half of your receipts would go to [an Amsterdam music dealer] and covering concert costs. And what would that do for your fame? That is something for small lights, for half-composers, for scribblers, for [names of three long-forgotten composers]. Name me one great composer who improves his honor by taking such a demeaning step. — Get on your way to Paris! And quickly . . . From Paris the reputation and name of a greatly talented person travel throughout the whole world.

Offering composition honoraria much larger than those customary in Italy, plus an incremental payment for subsequent repetitions of a successful opera, the Paris Opéra attracted the leading Italian opera composers of the nineteenth century such as Rossini, Bellini, Donizetti, and Verdi.

Determining what other cities qualify as magnets is more problematic. Despite its superior income per capita, Amsterdam is ruled out by its relatively small population, especially at the later time benchmarks. There is also reason to believe that its wealthy burghers had much more zeal for making money than listening to music. On an 1853 concert tour, for example, Clara and Robert Schumann noted that even though

Clara performed to a full house, the Amsterdam public was "colder" than audiences in the other cities they had visited.[25]

As the music-loving focal point of the Austrian empire and home to nobles, well-heeled government functionaries, and prosperous merchants, Vienna, the sixth-largest European city in 1750 and the fourth-largest in 1800, is the strongest contender for magnet city status.

Then, during the nineteenth century, two new candidates emerged. Russia was a cultural wasteland until German-born Catherine the Great began her systematic encouragement. The Irish composer and pianist John Field (1782–1837) settled there in 1803, giving lessons among others to Mikhail Glinka, founder of a new Russian composing tradition. The concentration of nobles and government officials in St. Petersburg and Moscow and a growing hunger for western culture then attracted many important performers and composers, including Hector Berlioz, Franz Liszt, Clara Schumann, Richard Wagner, and Johann Strauss Jr., for shorter but lucrative visits.

In the second half of the nineteenth century, as steamships made travel more reliable, rapidly growing New York City (1850 population, excluding Brooklyn, Queens, and Staten Island, 515,500) became another magnet. The New York Philharmonic Society began a regular concert series in 1842. The Schumanns weighed the pros and cons of a trip to the United States in 1842, but in the end decided it would remove them for too long a period from their first child.[26] Felix Mendelssohn was offered $5,000 in 1845 to conduct the New York Philharmonic Orchestra, but turned the offer down.[27] In 1850 soprano Jenny Lind received from P. T. Barnum an advance of $150,000 against the first several concerts of a U.S. tour that eventually included 93 performances. Her first appearance, in New York City September 11, 1850, drew an audience of 7,000. During the 1870s Franz Liszt received two offers of £20,000 to £24,000 for performing in the United States, but chose not to make the trip.[28] More positive responses were elicited from Pyotr Ilyich Tchaikovsky, who received $2,500 (£520) for conducting four times at Carnegie Hall in New York and recorded his great pleasure from occasional dining with Andrew Carnegie; and Antonin Dvořák, whose initial contract on a two-year U.S. visit between 1892 and 1894 paid him $15,000 (£4,000) per year.[29]

A Quantitative Test

We have accumulated three main hypotheses contending to explain differences in the employment of composers per million inhabitants across the various nations of Europe: the competing noble courts hypothesis, the rising middle-class prosperity hypothesis, and the magnet cities hypothesis. For ten of the nations and national groups covered by figure 5.6, sufficient data could be assembled to attempt a crude quantitative test.

For our measure of affluence, we use estimates of gross domestic product per capita (adjusted to constant 1990 dollar terms) compiled by Angus Maddison.[30] The data are subject to all the hazards of historical backcasting in the absence of systematic national income statistics. In addition, Maddison provides estimates only for 1700, 1820, 1850, and 1870. The 1700 estimates had to be used as measures of GDP per capita for both the first (1650–1699) and second (1700–1749) composer birth date periods. The 1820 estimates were used for the third 50-year period and the 1850 estimates (interpolated in some cases) for the 1800–1849 birth date cohort.

England (with London), France (with Paris), and Austria (with Vienna) were assumed to have magnet cities throughout the 200 years over which composers' birth dates were sampled. Russia was assumed to have magnet cities (St. Petersburg and Moscow) only for the 1750–1799 and 1800–1849 composer birth date cohorts.

The competing noble courts hypothesis is tested in two ways. The strictest (strong form) construction of the argument by Elias and the Baumols implies that only Germany, with its hundreds of independent courts, qualifies. A looser (weak form) construction ignores imperial oversight from Vienna and includes the four main remnants of the Holy Roman Empire — Germany, Italy, Austria, and Czechoslovakia — which had numerous local kingdoms (in Italy, Naples and Savoy), principalities, and dukedoms, many supporting musical activities. Given the adverse impact of the Napoleonic wars and feudal reform, the strong and weak noble courts hypotheses are assumed to apply only for the first three 50-year composer birthdate periods, but not for 1800–1849.

The dependent variable in regression analyses is the measure of equivalent working lives plotted in figure 5.6. It is defined for four 50-year composer birth-date intervals across 10 nations or national clusters. Thus, there are 40 observations on each of the diverse variables.

A test embodying the strong form of the competing courts hypothesis, with Germany alone as the nation whose courts promoted composer employment, yielded meager results, with no explanatory variable — court, magnet city, or GDP — being statistically significant by conventional standards.[31] The picture changes dramatically when the broader (weak form) Holy Roman Empire competing courts hypothesis is tested.[32] All three variables have coefficient signs consistent with the underlying hypotheses, and two variables are statistically significant at the 99-percent confidence level. The strongest explanatory variable is the measure designating Holy Roman Empire remnant courts. But nations also employed more full-time equivalent composers per million population when they had a magnet city and (more weakly correlated) when their estimated gross domestic product per capita was higher. Thus, there is support for all three explanatory hypotheses when all three are taken into account simultaneously.

THE BALANCE OF TRADE

We advance now a further step. We have seen that many composers were geographically mobile, being born in one national territory but working and sometimes even dying in a different territory. The inducements to and implications of their mobility will be explored further in chapter 6. But here we utilize our birthplace and employment-locus data to measure the balance-of-trade in composers, that is, the extent to which some nations tended on balance to export composers and others tended to import them. Our balance of trade index is the ratio of full-time equivalent working lives attributed to a nation divided by the number of composers born in a nation. The higher the index, the more a nation tended to be a net importer of composers; the lower, the more composers to whom it gave birth found working conditions more attractive in other nations. A value of 1.0 implies that a nation employed on average as many composers as it bred.

The data for the full 200-year sample period are arrayed in figure 5.7. Austria, with its magnet city Vienna as the locus of numerous Kapelle-supporting noble residences, many owned by families whose feudal domains lay in other parts of the Austrian empire, was on balance the strongest net importer of composers. Czechoslovakia, with what many observers claimed was a particularly strong native musical culture,[33] was the leading net exporter of composers. Its largest city, Prague, had a population of only 58,000 in 1750, and its wealthiest feudal magnates tended to spend the high cultural season at their Vienna town houses. Nearly tied for second place as net talent importers were England, with its wealthy magnet city London beckoning to composers born on the continent, and Russia, whose nobles and government officials were eager to absorb western culture following the lead of Empress Catherine the Great, but which developed a strong local composing tradition only toward the middle of the nineteenth century. The three most vigorous net exporters after Czechoslovakia — Hungary, Poland, and Italy — were nations whose modern economic development lagged relative to that of the more northwesterly European countries.

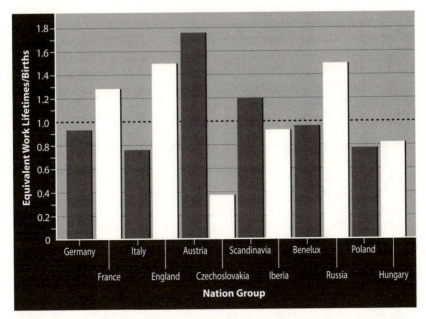

FIGURE 5.7 Balance of Trade in Composers by Nation

BIRTHS AND WORK LOCATIONS WITHIN GERMANY

Germany is viewed by proponents of the competing independent courts hypothesis as providing the most abundant array of job opportunities for would-be composers. But Germany's governmental structure was by no means homogeneous. Some parts of Germany had a vast proliferation of local courts, mostly in small towns; others had local governmental structures in which titled nobility played little or no role. The so-called "free cities" — those that during the Middle Ages escaped from or avoided local control by nobles or prelates with secular governmental power, obtained special privileges from the emperor to act independently of the Holy Roman Empire in economic and liturgical matters, and established governments representative of prominent, wealthy local burghers (called the *Patriziat*) — might be expected to project quite different incentives for the choice of and location in a musical career.[34] Here we address two questions: (1) Were fewer composers born per million population in the free cities, as defined here, compared to the other parts of Germany? And (2) were fewer composers employed in free cities, relative to their population, than in the other parts of Germany?

As we have seen in chapter 4, employment in noble courts carried the disadvantages of servility, restrictions on job mobility and publication rights, and autocratic control of the musical agenda. The free cities, as we shall identify them here, tended to be the home of prosperous merchants and craftsmen, many of whom appreciated music as much as their noble counterparts.[35] Their governing bodies were typically multi-member councils, so the employment tenure of a composer such as Georg Philipp Telemann (in Frankfurt and Hamburg) or Johann Sebastian Bach (in Leipzig) was determined through a more or less democratic process of give and take, with the possibility that minorities might block hasty decisions, and not through the capricious whim of a monolithic noble lord. As Telemann observed later in his life, "whoever seeks life-long security must settle in a republic."[36] To be sure, being a composer in a free, business-oriented, city, was not without its drawbacks. As Felix Mendelssohn observed, comparing the quiet life of musicians at the royal court in Stuttgart with the situation in Frankfurt am Main:[37]

> In Frankfurt everything is more upstanding, businesslike, and more metropolitan, but less fun; may the devil take the republics, they're simply not suited for music. They are altogether stingy, asking first what it costs, and don't have the least bit of flair.

Or as a disappointed Johannes Brahms complained to his Hamburg-resident father in 1869, after failing for the second time to win the Hamburg Senate's approval of his candidacy to become conductor of the Hamburg Philharmonic orchestra, "Vienna is too important to exchange with Hamburg, where everyone has his eye on business; Vienna, where you find understanding and recognition to allow you to work and create."[38]

Determining which cities in Germany to classify as "free" was not unproblematic. Two eminent German historians were consulted but were unable to provide unambiguous advice, except to read the histories of plausible candidate cities. This was done. Evaluating candidates by the free-city criteria articulated earlier, the following list of free cities was obtained:

Augsburg
Bremen
Cologne
Frankfurt am Main
Hamburg (excluding Altona)
Kiel
Leipzig
Lübeck

Nürnberg
Ulm
Worms

The treatment of Worms was questionable because parts of the town area were governed by burghers and parts by a bishop, but since no sampled composers were born in or worked there, to include it causes no upward bias on the free-city averages. Danzig (now Gdansk) was a strong candidate for inclusion, but the lack of matched population data and the absence of any sampled composer births there dictated its exclusion. Some other possible candidates may have been missed, but they could only be quite small, and their misclassification would add a modest amount of statistical noise to the quantitative results.

It would be an overstatement to insist that these free cities were entirely free of noble control. Johann Sebastian Bach's appointment as Cantor of the Thomasschule was nominally the responsibility of the Leipzig city council, but when the council failed to resolve Bach's disputes with the school's administration satisfactorily, Bach appealed successfully to the king of Saxony.[39] The royal government in Dresden also imposed upon the Leipzig city council its own preferred choice as Bach's replacement.[40] When Leipzig's Breitkopf & Härtel music publishing firm sought in 1816 to close part of its operations and dismiss some employees, it had to petition the king for permission, who in turn conveyed his consent to the Leipzig city council.[41] When Frederick the Great of Prussia was angered in 1751 because his guest Voltaire fled Potsdam after a dispute over affixing Frederick's imprimatur without approval to a published pamphlet, Frederick's agents prevailed upon the mayor of "free" Frankfurt am Main to keep Voltaire under house arrest for two weeks until the Frankfurt city council intervened to authorize his release.[42] Nevertheless, governmental decision making in the free cities was clearly more pluralistic than in authoritarian noble courts. And for those who earned their living through freelance activity directed toward prosperous burghers, the structure of government was less relevant.

Linking population data to the cities, free and otherwise, was equally problematic. Population estimates are available at roughly 50-year intervals for some 31 German cities, including all the cities listed above.[43] But these include only counts of inhabitants within city boundaries, which sometimes expanded over time. City dwellers typically drew most of their food and other raw materials from outside the city, so the population of the city alone cannot be treated as a self-sustaining body. Until Germany was unified during the mid-nineteenth century, data on the division of population between farming and city occupations were not collected. However, for the generally comparable territories of Austria (in 1790) and Bohemia (in 1756), 75 percent and 78 percent of the economically active population, respectively, were attached to agriculture.[44] From this and parallel statistics for the United States in 1820, France in 1697, Italy in 1700, and England in 1801, it is estimated conservatively that the typical city dweller derived food and other raw materials from four rural persons.[45] Thus, to arrive at the relevant population for free cities, the recorded population is multiplied by 5.0.[46] To the extent that this estimate errs, the bias is on the high side, because agricultural productivity rose rapidly during the nineteenth century, so that a given farmer could feed more mouths, and because the Hanseatic cities derived substantial portions of their food through trade with Eastern Baltic lands. The population for the remainder of Germany was calculated as the interpolated national population from periodic estimates (assuming 1992 boundaries) less the estimated free-city populations. Special upward population-base adjustments were made for composers who were born or worked in parts of Germany that were neither free cities nor within Germany's 1992 boundaries.

One further consideration developed in chapter 2 needs to be reiterated. The Napoleonic wars brought substantial changes to the political structure of Germany. Carrying with them legal reforms in the relationship between feudal lords and their peasants, French forces invaded the east bank of the Rhine in 1796 and, after interruptions in the early 1800s, completed their sweep through the rest of Germany with the battle of Ulm in 1805 and the battle of Jena in 1806. By 1805 at the latest, a young German contemplating a career in music could rightly be apprehensive about the chances of employment in noble courts. After Napoleon's armies withdrew following the battle of Leipzig in 1813, nobles who had fled their estates returned, but land reform (already underway in some parts of Germany before the Napoleonic invasion) and the elimination of laws undergirding feudal obligations continued.[47] Granting their former peasants clear tenure on some land in exchange for the elimination of servile duties on other tracts of land, nobles often found it necessary to become serious farm managers rather than mere rent collectors. Accumulated debts also forced many nobles to dismiss or downsize their orchestras. Thus, the environment had changed, and one might expect budding composers' incentives to seek and retain employment in the courts to have been attenuated. We therefore investigate whether there was a change in birth and employment patterns for composers who were born after 1785, drawing the dividing line at those who were eleven years of age when the French invaded Mainz and Stuttgart and twenty years old when Napoleon defeated Austrian forces at Ulm.

Figure 5.8 summarizes the evidence on the birthplace origins of 143

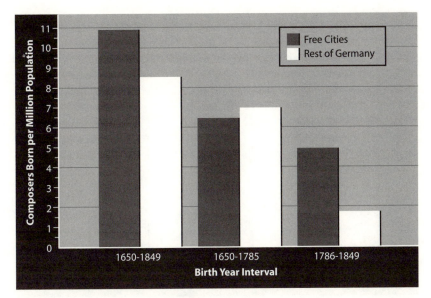

FIGURE 5.8 Birth Locations of German Composers

German composers. Over the full span of two centuries, 22 composers were found to be born in free cities, as defined here (which on average had 12.4 percent of the total population), and 121 in other parts of Germany. The number of composers born per million average population in the free cities was 10.93; the number in other parts of Germany 8.58. The difference is statistically significant at the 95 percent confidence level.[48]

When the data are broken down into two time periods, for composers born between 1650 and 1785 and those born thereafter, a more complex picture emerges, as shown in the middle and right-hand bar clusters of figure 5.8. In the earlier period, when the remnants of the feudal system were strongest, composer births per million population were slightly lower in the free cities: 6.49, as compared with 6.98 in the rest of Germany. In the later period, there is a striking difference: 4.99 births per million in the free cities compared to 1.79 in the rest of Germany. (The average composer counts per million population are lower in the later period because it covers only 65 years, compared to 135 years for the pre-1785 period.)

Figure 5.9 turns to the employment side of the picture. In total, 199 of the 646 sample composers were found to have worked at least part of their careers in Germany, devoting 111.7 full-career equivalent lifetimes to their German tenures.[49] Of these, 17.0 FTEs were spent in free

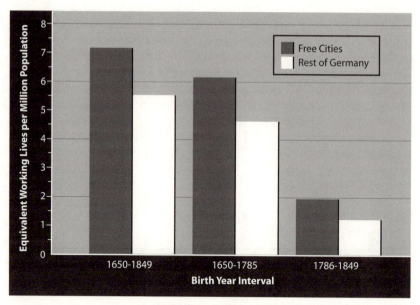

FIGURE 5.9 Work Locations of German Composers

cities (with 12.3 percent of the average population count) and 94.7 in other parts of Germany. For all composers born between 1650 and 1849 and employed in Germany, full-career-equivalent employment in free cities was 7.14 per million population (estimated at the included composers' thirty-fifth birthdays), compared to 5.52 for career-equivalent employment per million in other parts of Germany. This surprising result, at odds with the competing courts hypothesis, is statistically significant at the 95 percent confidence level.[50] It would appear that employment opportunities in the free cities — for example, in freelance activities, in the churches, and in city-sponsored orchestras — were more abundant on average relative to resident population than opportunities in the regions populated by noble courts or lacking both local courts and bourgeois governance. Since the free cities were for the most part prosperous centers of commerce and finance, private wealth would appear to have been an effective substitute for noble patronage as a basis of employment through which composers could earn their bread.

The middle and right-hand bar groupings in figure 5.9 show that the tendency for free cities to employ more composers per million resident population than the rest of Germany persists both before and after the Napoleonic invasions. In the birth date period before 1786, for which we found nearly equal court versus free-city stimuli to young local inhabitants' choice of musical careers, the ratio of free-city to rest-of-

Germany employment per million was 1.34 to 1; for the later period, during which the free cities generated a disproportionate number of composer births, the ratio rose to 1.57 to 1.[51] Although the difference between periods is modest, it is consistent with the evidence presented in chapters 2 and 3, showing the retrenchment of noble courts and, owing to growing prosperity, the increase of freelance composition activities during the nineteenth century.

We address the data one more time to inquire whether employment patterns were the same for German-born as compared to immigrant composers. Among the 199 individuals working for at least two years in Germany, 143 were born within the 1992 boundaries of Germany or belonged to German-ethnic families in lost territories, and 56 were foreign-born. Their career-equivalent employment experiences in Germany were as follows:

	Equivalent Working Lives	Equivalent Working Lives per Million Population
German-born composers		
Employment in free cities	14.94	6.52
Employment elsewhere	71.05	4.06
Foreign-born composers		
Employment in free cities	2.10	0.76
Employment elsewhere	23.62	1.45

For German-born composers, the results mirror figure 5.9 but are stronger; employment per million average population in free cities was 1.61 times that of other German areas. For foreign-born composers, however, the ratio reverses. They were employed more intensely per million population outside the free cities. For foreign-born composers, the principal employment-finding mechanisms were either being discovered by a German nobleman visiting some other country or traveling to Germany and inquiring at the most obvious locus of opportunity — a noble court. German-born composers, on the other hand, enjoyed a richer network — they could find work as an organist or Kapellmeister in a local church, or pursue the freelance opportunities their talent and relationships with countrymen opened up, in addition to seeking employment through the courtly recruitment systems. And in numbers disproportionate to the resident population, they opted to work in a free city rather than in the parts of Germany where the noble courts were dominant.

These results offer little support for the hypothesis that noble courts competing for prestige provided *uniquely* favorable inducements to musical career choices in Germany. The most one can do to rationalize them is to suggest that when prestige competition among courts was in

full flower, the abundance of musical employment opportunities provided a generalized stimulus to musical careers, recognized by young
people in free and noble areas alike and exploitable by migration to
localities, near or far, in which jobs were available. After the Napoleonic invasions, the retrenchment of noble courts may have sent particularly discouraging signals to young people who were born and raised
in their shadow.

THE GEOGRAPHY OF OCCUPATIONAL CHOICES

Chapter 3 analyzed patterns over time in the choice of career paths
among freelance performance and composing, employment with a noble
court, and employment with the church, among others. Here we return
to the occupational choice question and ask how geography matters.
We again use multiple regression analysis to disentangle the relationships. We focus on explaining three different measures, indicating
(1) whether a member of our 646-composer sample engaged in primary
or secondary freelance composition and/or performance; (2) whether a
composer had primary or secondary employment and/or support from a
noble court; and (3) whether the composer experienced primary or secondary church employment. Explanatory variables include the year of
the composer's birth and indexes (based upon the information underlying figure 5.4) measuring the fraction of a composer's working life (beginning with age 20) spent in each of six national territories — Germany,
France, Italy, Austria, England, and what in 1992 was Czechoslovakia.
     Regression equations for each of the three occupational variables
(freelance, court, and church) are presented in an end note.[52] For all
three regressions, the birth date variable is highly significant statistically
and has a sign consistent with the results reported in chapter 3. There
was an upward trend over time in the incidence of freelance activity, but
the time trends in court and church employment were downward.
     In the regression equation explaining differences in freelance activity,
the strongest propensity toward freelance activity is found for Italy,
where, as we have seen in chapter 2, opera writing was a favored outlet
for composers' creative energies and most operas were organized in
such a way that composers worked as freelance agents. The second
strongest tendency was for England, a bastion of freelance musical activity, and the third strongest for France — a puzzling result that may be
attributable to the organization of opera along lines similar to the Italian pattern.
     Not surprisingly, the strongest positive tendencies toward noble court
employment are found in Germany, to which the competing courts hy-

pothesis applies most closely, and Austria, with a substantial imperial musical establishment and numerous lesser Kapelle-sustaining courts. None of the other nations exhibited significantly different court employment patterns.

Germany and France deviated most noticeably from other nations in terms of church employment, with significantly fewer composers deriving their living in that way. Italy shows the highest relative incidence of church employment, but its coefficient does not differ significantly from the values estimated for other nations.

CONCLUSION

To sum up, the competing noble courts hypothesis receives mixed support from the data on 646 composers. A proliferation of courts offered visible job opportunities and apparently contributed to the choice of music as a career for young people in Europe. But the strong form of the hypothesis—that Germany, with its preponderance of independent courts attributable to the breakup of the Holy Roman Empire, was especially conducive to composers' careers—is not supported. The more politically centralized Austrian environment dominated in this respect, and Italy, another territory forming the core of the Holy Roman Empire, was nearly as active as Germany in giving birth to composers relative to its population. Austria also dominated Germany in the employment of composers per million population. And within Germany, composers chose free cities disproportionately relative to those cities' population as places in which to pursue their profession. A lack of large magnet cities is one probable reason why Germany could not pull beyond its population weight. On the balance of employment choices within Germany, it remains uncertain how much we should attribute to the economic pull of the free cities, foreshadowing the broader growth of prosperous middle-class demand for the output of composers, and how much to composers' desire to shun the servility of the courts and to make their way in a freer, more market-oriented environment.

Chapter 6

CHANGES IN TRANSPORTATION AND

COMPOSERS' MOBILITY

MANY COMPOSERS, we learned in the previous chapter, worked in more than one national territory. Both to change jobs and to perform at venues away from home, travel was necessary. Accompanying the Industrial Revolution were several revolutions in transportation methods that had a noticeable impact on composers' working lives. We analyze those changes here.

THE TRANSPORT REVOLUTIONS

Much of composers' intercity and even international travel was done by land. During the eighteenth century, the condition of the typical road was abysmal. Economic historians Clough and Cole describe the situation as follows:[1]

> The traditional European road of the early eighteenth century was little more than a track across the land, comparable to the poorest dirt roads. In winter, if there was no frost, these roads became boggy with mud; and if there was frost, they were quagmires when the frost came out . . . The result was that travel by carriage was extremely slow, expensive, dangerous, and judging from the remarks of travelers, extraordinarily irritating. A trip at five miles an hour is referred to as "winged expedition."

Clough and Cole observe that the quality of the roads, although almost uniformly bad, tended to worsen as one traveled to the east from England, France, and the Low Countries. France and Italy benefited to some extent from the remnants of the old Roman road system. In France from 1720 until the revolution, peasants were required to spend thirty days per year improving the roads; after that, Napoleon placed priority on maintaining good trunk roads to sustain military mobility. The extensive decentralization of governmental authority was a serious barrier to similar efforts in Germany. In Russia, conditions were even worse. A person who traveled in 1718 from Moscow to St. Petersburg reported that it was necessary to improvise floats to cross twenty rivers that had neither bridges nor ferries.[2] Travel by sled, when the rivers and ground were frozen, was greatly preferable to travel by coach during warmer seasons.

Travel Conditions

Given the primitive state of the roads, travel in Mozart's time was slow, exhausting, and costly. On his journey home from Paris in 1778, Mozart was advised that he might travel from Paris to Strasbourg, a distance of approximately 400 kilometers as the crow flies, in five days by "diligence" or express post coach. However, he ended up in a slower coach that retained the same team of horses and required at least ten days — to be sure, with costly overnight stops at inns along the way.[3] In September 1790, Mozart hired his own coach to travel from Vienna to Frankfurt am Main, where he offered freelance concerts in connection with the coronation of Leopold II as emperor of the Holy Roman Empire. The trip, roughly 635 kilometers, as the crow flies, took six days, with only three overnight breaks for rest.[4] Assuming a generous eight hours for each overnight stop (departures on other Mozart trips occurred as early as 4:00 A.M.), Mozart's average over-the-road speed, including as part of travel time stops to change horses and the like, was approximately 5.87 kilometers per hour, or 3.6 miles per hour.

Recognizing these travel times under favorable conditions, it is less surprising that in 1705 Johann Sebastian Bach *walked* all the way from Arnstadt, where he was employed as church organist, to study with Dietrich Buxtehude at Lübeck[5] — a distance of nearly 400 kilometers, as measured on 1990s German road maps. A youth in good physical condition can walk at the average speed Mozart achieved on his Frankfurt coach trip, although to be sure, he would require more rest breaks than a stagecoach able to change horses at regular intervals. Walking was a reasonable alternative for those who lacked adequate finances.

Traveling by stagecoach was also physically debilitating. On an overnight trip in 1780 from Salzburg to Munich to present his opera *Idomeneo*, Mozart reported to his father that no one was able to sleep — the bouncing was enough to drive the soul out of one's body.[6] Halfway through the trip in what must have been an unusually badly upholstered coach, Mozart believed that he would not bring his "fire-red" backside to Munich in one piece; on two laps of the route, he braced himself with his arms on the seat and his behind in the air. As late as 1846, lacking other alternatives, Hector Berlioz found it necessary to travel from the Russian border to St. Petersburg by closed sled, undergoing "tortures, the very existence of which I had never suspected, for four weary days and as many terrible nights."[7]

Even within larger cities, travel was time-consuming and unpleasant.

On his visit to spatially vast Paris in 1778, Mozart found his ability to earn money severely constrained by the distances between his residence and the homes of potential students or composition patrons. "By foot," he wrote, "it is generally too far — or too littered with excrement. Traveling by coach within Paris is unbelievably dirty, and one can have the honor of paying out 4 to 5 livres [for transportation] without much result."[8] Moving to Paris in the 1830s, Vincento Bellini chose his residence more astutely. He lived in suburban Puteaux, seven kilometers from the city center. A horse-drawn omnibus departed for central Paris every ten minutes, taking half an hour for the trip.[9] But even during the late nineteenth century, after intraurban trains became available, Gabriel Fauré averaged three hours per day traveling to his various students — a burden that sapped his energy for composing and depressed him.[10]

When water transportation was available, as it was, for example, to composers traveling between Naples or Rome and the northwest cities of Italy, it was often preferable to passage on eighteenth-century roads. Germany, in particular, might have benefited from its abundance of internal waterways. But its fragmented governmental structure permitted local *Raubritter* (robber barons) to set up numerous toll-collection stations, each attempting to extract from travelers a profit-maximizing toll. Over the 85-kilometer stretch on the Rhine river between Mainz and Koblenz in 1780, there were 9 toll stations, and from Koblenz to the Dutch border, there were 16 more.[11] Two decades later, there were 33 toll-collection stations on the Main river between Mainz and Bamberg and 14 on the Elbe between Hamburg and Magdeburg.[12] The proliferation of tolls discouraged most of the traffic that otherwise would have used the rivers. The situation was not fully remedied until the 1830s.

Journeys on the open seas in eighteenth- and early nineteenth-century sailing vessels had their own hazards. Passage across the English Channel posed well-known difficulties. In 1829, the twenty-year-old Felix Mendelssohn traveled by ship from Hamburg to London. The trip lasted four days and was memorialized by Mendelssohn as "very long and not pleasant."[13] Delays occurred because of fog, head winds, mechanical problems, and congestion on the Thames. Everyone on the ship, he wrote, was seasick during the Channel passage. Two years later, as Hector Berlioz was sailing from Marseilles to Livorno to begin his Prix de Rome tenure, a sudden storm heeled the ship over to a near-foundering angle, throwing the captain down from the ship's helm. As Berlioz prepared to die, salvation came only when a Venetian seaman assumed the helm and ordered the crew to trim the sails.[14] After difficult trips by land to and within Russia in 1844, Robert and Clara Schumann debated whether to return to Germany from St. Petersburg by land or sea. Clara won the argument, and they sailed—into a fierce Baltic sea storm that came up so suddenly that the ship's sails could not be trimmed in time to avoid the terrifying shattering of one mast.[15]

The Improvements

The nineteenth century saw major improvements in virtually all modes of transportation. On land, private turnpike companies received franchises to build and maintain improved roads in England beginning in the late eighteenth century. Greatly improved road-building techniques, using as a foundation small stones laid over large stones, were then developed by John McAdam and Thomas Telford. After experimental work, McAdam began constructing roads using his new methods in 1815. By 1829, Felix Mendelssohn could report that the trip between London and Edinburgh—a straight-line distance of about 530 kilometers—could be made by mail coach in three days.[16]

A much more important step, however, was the development of railway trains propelled by steam locomotives. Although there were primitive predecessors, the era of railway-building was heralded by the completion of a link between Liverpool and Manchester, over which in 1830 George Stephenson's *Rocket* achieved an average speed of 31 miles (50 kilometers) per hour.[17] By August 1848, Frédéric Chopin was able to travel by rail from London to Edinburgh in 12 hours.[18] The new technology spread quickly to the European continent. Figure 6.1 shows how the completion of rail lines progressed in six major European nations.[19] Germany followed the United Kingdom in track laying, with a notable acceleration during the mid-1840s. One of the first links, between Leipzig and Dresden, was completed in 1839;[20] connections from Leipzig to Berlin followed in 1840. France led Germany briefly but then followed close behind from the 1840s on. Italy, with fragmented governments, lower per capita income, and superior coastal ship alternatives, was much slower to follow, and over the vast expanse of even poorer Russia, acceleration of railway building occurred only in the late 1860s.

Steam power and then the construction of iron-bottom vessels also brought major improvements to domestic and international water transportation. Robert Fulton demonstrated an experimental steam-driven boat in Paris during 1803. His *Clermont* began to navigate the Hudson River between New York City and Albany in 1807. By 1815, a steam-driven ship began regular service between Liverpool and Glasgow. During the late 1830s several British companies began the construction and operation of steam-driven paddlewheel vessels for regular transatlantic service. Significant further improvements followed with more reliable,

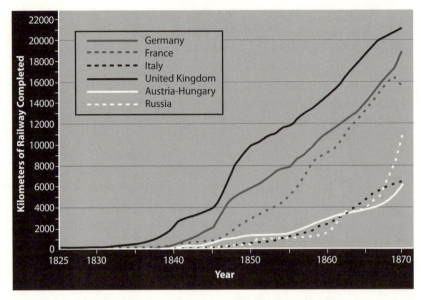

FIGURE 6.1 Growth of Rail Networks in Major European Nations

faster, screw-propelled iron-bottom vessels in the 1850s and ships driven by compound steam engines in the 1860s.

How Composers Were Affected

These new transportation developments greatly reduced the time composers needed to travel a given distance in pursuing their trade and brought into the realm of practicality trips that during the eighteenth century would have been inconceivable. In November of 1843, Clara Schumann presented a series of piano concerts in Dresden. During her three-week stay in Dresden, she made two trips home to Leipzig (280 kilometers round trip) — one to attend the rehearsal of her husband's oratorio *Peri* and one motivated by homesickness.[21] At eighteenth-century stagecoach speeds, each segment would have taken nearly a full day and night. After an 1884 concert trip that carried him to Weimar, Dresden, Leipzig, Breslau, Cologne, Frankfurt, Karlsruhe, the Hague, Rotterdam, and Amsterdam, Edvard Grieg decided to alter his plans and travel to Rome for winter holidays.[22] A year later he wrote that "a happy Norwegian artist (N.B. one who really loves his fatherland) will never be found till all can strap on their wings and make off like the birds in presto time wherever they feel inclined."[23] Between 1861 and 1893, Pyotr Ilyich Tchaikovsky undertook 20 major trips outside the boundaries of Russia, Finland, and Poland, some to satisfy professional commitments, some for holidays, and some to visit friends:[24] 4 were to England, 12 to France, 5 to Italy, and 1 to the United States, among other destinations. Camille Saint-Saëns was even more peripatetic.[25] Between 1871 and 1893, he ventured from Paris to London every year to perform his works. He vacationed regularly in Algeria. In 1890–1891, he traveled to what is now called Sri Lanka, and in 1895, to Vietnam, composing an oratorio while at sea. He made two trips to South America and in 1906, on the first of his two journeys to the United States, he visited New York, Chicago, Philadelphia, Washington, and Chicago, adding San Francisco on a 1915 trip.

Not all composers viewed the new transportation possibilities positively. On his first train ride between Antwerp and Brussels in 1836, Gioachino Rossini was so unnerved that, during the remaining thirty-two years of his life, he never again traveled by train.[26] Johann Strauss Jr. had a similar fear of railways, but overcame it in 1854 to accept a lucrative concert invitation from the vicinity of St. Petersburg.[27] On a winter rail trip to Russia during the 1860s, Giuseppe Verdi and his wife found themselves shivering in an unheated rail car; the wine they brought with them froze.[28] On a Rhine steamboat taken by Robert Schumann in 1830, the ship caught fire, triggering anxieties and morbid dreams.[29] However, he overcame the fears engendered by this and his equally traumatic Baltic sea voyage, among other things traveling up the Rhine to Switzerland in 1851 on what was said to be the best vacation ever for the Schumanns.[30]

A Quantitative Perspective

In chapter 5, we learned that 30 percent of the composers in our sample of 646 died in a national territory other than the one in which they were born, and 45 percent worked at least two years in a nation other than the one in which they spent the plurality of their working lives. One might expect these statistics to be affected by the changes in transportation that increased composers' mobility. Now we probe the 646-member sample data more deeply to identify the effects.

Figure 6.2 plots by 50-year birth-date intervals the percentage of composers who died in a national territory other than their birthplace. We see a sharp rise from the first to the second time period and, more surprisingly, a marked drop—from 37.5 percent to 23.8 percent—for the cohort born between 1800 and 1849, who presumably benefited most from the transportation revolutions of the nineteenth century.

For further insight, we use the data on the geographic locations at which composers resided and worked beginning at age twenty, computing an index known as a numbers equivalent.[31] It is defined as $1 / [\Sigma F_i^2]$, where F_i is the fraction of a composer's working (and retired) life spent

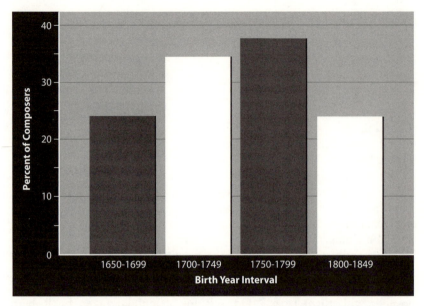

FIGURE 6.2 Percent of Composers Born in One Nation Who Died in Another

in the ith nation. It rises nonlinearly, the more nations in which a composer worked, but it falls, the more composers concentrated their work effort at one or a very few locations and spent only small fractions of their working lives in other venues. If a composer's whole life was spent in one nation, the value would be 1.0. If the composer's working life was divided equally between two nations, the value would be $1 / [.5^2 + .5^2] = 1 / .5 = 2.0$. If the composer worked in two locations, spending 87 percent of the time from age twenty onward at one location and 13 percent at the other, the numbers-equivalent index would be $1 / [.87^2 + .13^2] = 1.292$. Again, the more unequal the fractions are for a given number of nations, the lower the numbers-equivalent index is. The average numbers-equivalent value for all 646 composers was in fact 1.283, which suggests that our 87 percent — 13 percent example provides useful insight into the way average composers divided their working lives. But there is considerable variation among the composers. Of the 646 composers, 55 percent resided in only one nation from age twenty on (ignoring stays abroad of less than two years). Forty-eight composers, or 7.4 percent, had numbers-equivalent values in excess of 2.0. The composer with the most widely scattered working life (and a numbers equivalent of 4.35) was Manuel Garcia (1775–1832), born in Spain and residing from age twenty on for two years or more in Spain, France, Italy, England, the United States, and Mexico.

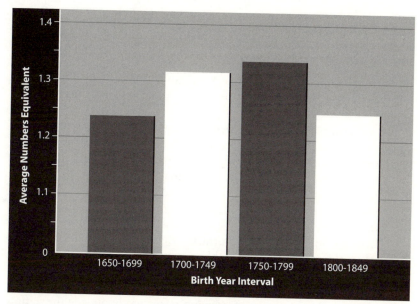

FIGURE 6.3 Numbers Equivalents for Nations in Which Composers Lived from Age 20

Figure 6.3 plots the average numbers-equivalent values for each of the four half-century birth-date intervals. The picture is strikingly similar to that of figure 6.2. The equivalent number of national territories in which composers resided and worked rises sharply from the first to the second interval, with a peak at 1.337 for composers born between 1750 and 1799. It then drops sharply, to an average value of 1.245, for composers born during the nineteenth century. It seems that our birth versus death and fraction-of-working-lives indexes, which were intended to measure mobility, show mobility to be *declining* just when transportation media were radically improved. An apparent paradox demands explanation.

The probable answer is that, with much faster and more economical means of travel at their disposal, composers born during the nineteenth century could choose to live wherever they wished and, if need be, travel to other venues where the opportunities to earn commissions or performance fees were most attractive. For composers born in earlier half-century intervals, the benefit / cost ratio for short trips was much less favorable, slanting choices toward longer visits or even extended residence in the nations presenting the richest opportunities.

Support for this interpretation comes through multiple regression analysis. We seek to explain whether composers died in a nation other than the one in which they were born, or alternatively, the numbers equivalent indexes whose average values are plotted in figure 6.3. Among the four 50-year intervals within which sample composers were born, explanatory variables distinguish whether a composer engaged in substantial (primary or secondary) freelance composing activity, and whether a composer engaged in substantial freelance performance activity.

The resulting least squares regression equations are presented in an end note.[32] In the first two of four distinct analyses, variables differentiating time periods are consistent with the patterns shown in figures 6.2 and 6.3, although only the indicated decline in the numbers-equivalent index for composers born between 1800 and 1849 is statistically significant. The coefficients reflecting substantial freelance composing and performance activity are both positive and statistically significant. The largest effects are for freelance performers. Relative to composers whose primary employment was with noble courts, churches, or other institutions, composers who engaged in substantial freelance activity, and especially those who were freelance performers, tended to work in a wider diversity of nations and to die more frequently outside the nation in which they were born. In the third and fourth analyses, additional shift variables permit the freelance composition and performance variables to have effects different for composers born during the nineteenth century than for composers born between 1650 and 1799. This modification largely nullifies the impact of variables characterizing differences among half-century time intervals. What this means is that most of the decline in presumed mobility indexes shown by figures 6.2 and 6.3 was associated with increasing freelance activity. Freelance artists were much more mobile than other composers, and as freelance activity increased over time, what otherwise appears to have been an increase in mobility from the first to the second 50-year birth period and a decline from the third to the fourth period in fact stemmed from increases in the extent of freelance activity along with changes in transportation media. Mobility appears in figures 6.2 and 6.3 to be low for composers born between 1650 and 1699 because there were very few freelance artists in that cohort. Measured mobility appears to have fallen during the fourth time period because the freelance artists who were most mobile could tap distant opportunities through short trips, rather than having to relocate in foreign markets for periods of two years or more.

Other Effects

Improved transportation costs also benefited composers by making it easier for them to hedge against the risks of nonacceptance in a particular locality, availing themselves of more receptive audiences elsewhere. Mozart remarked on more than one occasion that if the Viennese tired of his music, he would seek his fortune outside Vienna.[33] But when his luck turned in the late 1780s, the prospective rewards from employment possibilities elsewhere or a risky freelance trip to England were outweighed by the high costs of uprooting his family and moving them, or alternatively, leaving them behind temporarily. When queried whether his extensive travel might be harmful to his health, Mozart's cousin-in-law, Carl Maria von Weber, asked in reply, how else he could find an arena in which to practice his art? He saw no alternative to continuing his search.[34] Felix Mendelssohn wrote in 1732 that when the people of Germany no longer appreciated him, going abroad, where it was easier to be received, remained a possibility. However, he hoped it would not be necessary to leave the place where he felt most at home.[35] The music of Johannes Brahms often encountered hostile receptions, but with good railway connections, Brahms simply moved on to another city and sooner or later found appreciative audiences and favorable reviews.

The received theory of superstars implies that when the costs of transportation fall, competition for top talent is less limited geographically and hence becomes more intense, raising the salary differential between ordinary talent and superstars.[36] Among the 50 composers whose biographies were researched in depth, many took advantage of easier land and sea transportation during the nineteenth century to embrace lucrative opportunities outside their home territories. It is also clear, however, that even in the eighteenth century, superstar pay differentials existed. And despite the monetary and psychic costs of travel, those whose talent was in high demand were willing to travel to the ends of Europe to reap the rewards. Our data are insufficient to determine whether fee and other compensation differentials increased during the nineteenth century, as the theory predicts. The most that can be said is that, for the 23 composers on whom estate values at death could be estimated,[37] there was no statistically significant adjusted net worth difference between the 6 composers born between 1800 and 1849 and the 17 born earlier.

As we have seen, composers traveled a lot. In their travels, they met and interacted with other composers. Although our research did not pursue the question systematically, it seems clear that networks of composers emerged out of these contacts. It would be an interesting dissertation project in sociology to trace those networks and identify their foci. Some tentative observations can be offered to help initiate such research. During the early eighteenth century, significant networks had their focal points at the palace of Cardinal Pietro Ottoboni (1667–1740) in Rome; with the distinguished group employed by the royal

court at Dresden, including Johann David Heinichen (1683–1729) and
Johann Hasse (1699–1783); and with Johann Sebastian Bach, whose
four composer sons fanned out through much of musical Europe. During the second half of the eighteenth century, networks might be traced
to Padre Giovanni Battista Martini (1706–1784) at Bologna and (toward the turn of the century) Antonio Salieri and librettist and imperial
prefect Gottfried van Swieten (1733–1803) in Vienna. At the middle of
the nineteenth century, important focal points included Franz Liszt;
Robert Schumann (who, as publisher of a musical criticism journal, met
the many composers attracted by Leipzig's Gewandhaus); and the soprano Pauline Viardot (1821–1910), who traveled widely and maintained an active salon in Paris. It is not much of an exaggeration to
propose that, after second-order connections are taken into account,
every composer of note in Europe knew everyone else active at the time.

THE BURDEN OF TRAVEL COSTS

For composers who traveled extensively, the costs of travel could significantly affect the net receipts from trips. Although he could well afford
the best available facilities, Franz Liszt typically traveled second-class —
for instance, on a trip to Russia in 1867, in crowded, ill-lighted, poorly
heated rail cars.[38] Johannes Brahms had similar ability to pay and similarly modest requirements. In 1887 he was joined by his publisher Fritz
Simrock on a trip to Venice. Coordinating travel arrangements by mail,
he asked Simrock before the journey, "Are you traveling first class? It's
all the same to me, I just don't want to pay for first class and then come
to you in second."[39] On his extensive tours, Niccolò Paganini had a
strategy for saving money and finding the ambience he desired: he would
book his first night at the best hotel in the city where he was performing
and then find a less expensive, more comfortably middle-class guest
house.[40] Robert and Clara Schumann, on the other hand, always stayed
at the best hostelry in town when they traveled.[41] It is perhaps no coincidence that the three composers whom we know to have scrimped on
travel costs all had substantial net worth at the time of their deaths. See
table 4.1 above.

Mozart's travel expenditures, on the other hand, were often lavish,
and it would not be unreasonable to argue that they were in part responsible for his ultimately impoverished state. On a trip from Vienna
to Pressburg in 1762, the Mozart family bought their own two-horse
coach. They retained it for subsequent trips, including one to Paris in
1763, as a consequence incurring many unplanned expenditures when

wheels broke or replacement horses were difficult to obtain.[42] They still had it when Wolfgang and his mother embarked in 1778 upon a trip that eventually brought them to Paris (where Frau Mozart died) by way of Mannheim. Having accumulated sizeable losses by the time of their planned departure from Mannheim to Paris, they tried to sell the coach for 60 to 70 florins (£6–7), but had to settle for selling it to a coach operator (*Mietkutscher*) for 40 florins, which was deducted from the 11 Louis d'or (105 florins = £10.68, or 31 percent of an English building craftsman's annual full-time earnings) charged by the same individual for transportation to Paris.[43] By the time Mozart reached Strasbourg on the trip home, the losses against which his father had made advances by borrowing had mounted to 863 florins.[44] On his 1790 trip to Frankfurt am Main for the coronation of Leopold II as Holy Roman Emperor, Mozart rented his own private coach, as he had done on earlier trips.[45] How much he paid is unknown, but it must have been considerably more than public coach transportation would have cost. His freelance concerts in Frankfurt were a financial disappointment. As his Frankfurt trip drew to a close, he pawned all the furniture in his Vienna apartment to borrow 1,000 florins—the most dramatic symptom of his growing indebtedness.[46]

Joseph Haydn was more fortunate than Mozart when he made his second journey to London in 1794. His friend and (later) librettist Gottfried van Swieten loaned him his personal coach.[47] Beethoven, on the other hand, contemplated in 1817 a similar invitation to London, for which a travel advance of £105 was promised. Because of his failing hearing, however, he required at least one person and preferably three (a physician, a friend, and a servant) to accompany him, and because the travel advance was insufficient to cover such high expenses, the trip fell through.[48] The cost of Hector Berlioz's 1843 trip to Germany, mostly by stagecoach, was said in the composer's memoirs to be "ruinous" because of difficult traveling-companion requirements—although in Berlioz's case, the companions were musical scores weighing 500 pounds for his contemplated concerts.[49] He made the trips nevertheless and achieved substantial successes in Leipzig, Dresden, and Braunschweig.

CONCLUSION

Transportation costs are an aspect of composers' economic lives to which scholars have devoted little attention. But as we have seen, their impact can be quite important. The transportation media revolutions of the nineteenth century increased the speed and reduced both the financial and psychic costs of travel for composers. The consequence was a substantial increase in composers' mobility, greater ability to reduce the risks of unreceptive audiences at a single locale, and if the analysis here is correct, the possibility of having one's cake and eating it — that is, living where one prefers but also traveling to tap rich performance and composition opportunities away from home.

Chapter 7

THE ECONOMICS OF MUSIC PUBLISHING

THE GROWTH of demand for printed sheet music, first from religious establishments and the nobility and then from the instrument-playing public, underlay the emergence of a music-publishing industry and augmented the sources from which composers could derive earnings through their work. In this chapter we review the industry's origins, survey the various publication technologies and their costs, and then analyze how the evolution of property rights affected publishers and their relationships, financial and otherwise, with composers.

THE EMERGENCE OF AN INDUSTRY

Printing with movable metal type, attributed to experiments by Johannes Gutenberg between 1430 and 1448, led to the emergence of vibrant publishing industries in the principal cities and towns of western Europe, Italy, and England. The industry's growth was spurred at first by the demand for printed religious indulgences and then, beginning in the 1520s, by the Protestant reformation, whose leaders encouraged individual reading of religious texts and group singing during church services. Numerous firms, some specializing in religious texts and others in musical works per se, arose throughout Europe to meet these demands and the demand for treatises explaining the principles of music notation, composition, and performance.

Consistent with research on the evolution of modern industries,[1] most of the early music-publishing firms were short-lived. Some entrepreneurs nevertheless managed to pass their franchises to successive generations and, when appropriate heirs were lacking, to maintain continuity by selling out to new owners. Among the large number of early music-publishing enterprises mentioned by Donald Krummel,[2] 11 founded before the year 1650 managed to survive at least into the second half of the seventeenth century and in some cases into the eighteenth century. Their average survival duration was 86 years. The most long-lived was LeRoy & Ballard of Paris, which enjoyed through much of its existence a royal monopoly privilege for the printing of music in France. Of these early survivors, 6 were located in German cities, 4 in Italy, 1 (LeRoy & Ballard) in France, and 1 in what is now Austria.

The earliest music publishing house to survive into the twenty-first century was Breitkopf & Härtel, which began as a Leipzig book publisher but diversified into music publishing during the 1740s, among other things on the strength of important technological innovations. Its contributions will be prominent in subsequent analyses. The separation of Germany into two sectors after World War II precipitated a move of the company's headquarters to Wiesbaden. The firm's eastern remnants were reabsorbed following German reunification in 1990. The second-oldest long-term survivor is the firm founded in 1770 by Bernhard Schott (1748–1809) in Mainz, Germany, which continues to do business as Musikverlag Schott. The most durable Italian firm is Casa Ricordi, Giuseppe Verdi's principal publisher, which was founded in Milan by Giovanni Ricordi (1785–1853) around 1808, survived for more than a century under family ownership, and continues under altered ownership arrangements. Ricordi and Schott are the only two-century survivors to retain headquarters at their original home base. The most complex history among the long-term survivors exists for what is now called the C. F. Peters Corporation, with head offices in Frankfurt, London, and New York. Its founder, Franz Anton Hoffmeister (1754–1812), began publishing musical works in Vienna during 1784. In 1800 he sold his Vienna operations and moved to Leipzig to join Ambrosius Kühnel in forming the Bureau de Musique, which in turn was acquired by Carl Friedrich Peters (1779–1827) in 1814. Doing business under the Peters name, the firm survived numerous subsequent ownership changes. A similarly convoluted history links the publishing firm founded by Nicolaus Simrock (1751–1832) in Bonn during 1793 and its survival now as the Benjamin-Rahter-Simrock organization. Music publishing was also undertaken in colonial America, but the oldest still-surviving firm, G. Schirmer, Inc., was founded only in 1848, remaining intermittently under Schirmer family management between 1854 and 1957.

Among others, some well-known composers were attracted into the business of music publishing. Announcing in 1786 that he would become his own publisher, Ignaz Pleyel (1757–1831) complained in an advertisement seeking subscriptions that:[3]

> The disagreeable emphasis, the often mutilated renditions of my works, which up to now robbed me completely of the fruits of my labor . . . all these reasons persuade me to become my own publisher and manager of the public good in the future.

The compositions Pleyel advertised were in the end published by a third party, but between 1795 and 1834, the house of Pleyel was one of the leading music publishers in Paris. In 1805 it expanded into the production of pianofortes — a business continued until it was acquired by a German firm in 1971. Muzio Clementi, one of the most brilliant piano performers of his era, entered music publishing with a London partner in 1798, shortly thereafter diversifying, like Pleyel, into piano production. After a spectacularly successful round of performances throughout northern Europe, Niccolò Paganini hovered on the brink of opening a music publishing house in Italy, but became immersed in other financial speculations and did not take the step.[4] These were the most famous among a larger number of cases. Altogether, among the 646 composers on whom systematic biographical information was collected for this book, 12 were professional music publishers during at least part of their careers, 11 of them (including Pleyel and Clementi) pursuing publishing as a primary or secondary occupation and 1 as a tertiary occupation.[5]

From the industry's early beginnings, music publishers reached out to composers and consumers beyond their national borders. Concertos by Tomaso Albinoni were printed by the prominent Amsterdam publisher Estienne Roger (1665–1722), first in pirated and later in approved editions. Roger, who had sales agents in London, Cologne, Berlin, Leipzig, Brussels, and Hamburg,[6] also published pirated versions of early compositions by Arcangelo Corelli and an authorized version of Corelli's Concerti Grossi op. 6. Most of Corelli's publishing commissions traveled 300 kilometers north from Rome to Bologna, his home town and a leading center of Italian music publication.[7] Sonatas by Domenico Scarlatti were published by London houses in both official and pirated versions. By 1816, the Breitkopf & Härtel firm had sales agents in 16 cities considered by the firm to be German (including three lost by Germany following World War II) plus 17 foreign cities.[8] Through agents, mail orders, and acquisitions made when wealthy music lovers traveled abroad, musical manuscripts circulated substantial distances throughout Europe. One of the finest portraits by Francisco Goya, painted around 1795 and hanging now in Madrid's Museo del Prado, shows José Álvarez de Toledo, the duke of Alba, holding a musical composition by Joseph Haydn.

For Breitkopf & Härtel (B&H) detailed data are available on the sales made by its diverse agents between 1816 and 1818, after the firm recovered from a severe slump during the Napoleonic wars.[9] The highest sales (2,500 Saxonian thaler = £550) were by its Berlin agent; the lowest by agents in the small towns of Göttingen and Greifswald. Economic analyses of interregional and international trade use a "gravity model" to explain how exports vary with the purchasing power of a demand locus and with distance from the production site, with which transportation costs are roughly correlated. For 26 cities on which B&H agent sales figures were reported, population estimates were also available.[10] The larger the population of a city, the higher one might expect the sales through agents in that city to be. The distance as the crow flies from Leipzig to sales outlets (which was often different from the distance stagecoaches traveled) was measured in kilometers. The resulting "gravity" regression equation is reported in an end note.[11] It reveals a strong positive relationship between population in an urban demand locus and agent sales in that area. The relationship between sales and distance was positive, contrary to the gravity model prediction, but far from statistically significant. Evidently, even though transportation was slow and difficult at the time, shipping costs were sufficiently modest relative to high-value, compact, and light music publications that they did not appreciably impair sales. Replication of the analysis for 11 cities considered by Breitkopf & Härtel to be within Germany yielded a strong positive relationship between sales and population and a negative but statistically insignificant coefficient on the distance variable, suggesting again the unimportance of distance within the geographic boundaries of early nineteenth-century Germany.

TECHNOLOGICAL INNOVATIONS

The earliest mechanical printing of music was done using pre-Gutenberg fixed-block plates of wood or metal onto which the notes, staves, and text were carved. Adapting Gutenberg's movable-type invention to the printing of music was much more difficult than printing simple letter text.[12] Unlike the letters in a line of text, the notes of a musical piece can occupy nine different vertical positions within the standard five-line staff and at least as many more above and below it. Further complexity is added by ties among the notes, dots, changing key signatures, phrase markings, and all the other accoutrements needed to express musical ideas in print and by the fact that two or three notes in a scale might be played simultaneously. At first only very primitive notation, for instance, for Gregorian chants and simple songs, could be printed using movable type. Gradually the methods were improved. Notable among the pioneers in the transition to more complex notation using movable type was the Italian Ottaviano dei Petrucci, who perfected his techniques in Venice between 1490 and 1511. His early printed masterpieces required three different impressions, the first to print the linear staves, the second to print the notes, and the third to print text and special marks. Polyphony was handled by printing parts side by side. Needless to say, considerable precision in positioning paper sheets on the press bed was required to make everything fit together. Later improvements made it possible to print music with only a single impression, each type element containing a note or marking in the proper position relative to the five staff lines. A disadvantage was that the side-by-side elements were difficult to align horizontally.

Although movable type was the principal basis of music printing during most of the two centuries following Petrucci's work, the technique became less and less well suited for the complex instrumental works toward which both composers and connoisseurs of music were turning. The solution to this problem was a transition, beginning in the late sixteenth century, to the printing of music from engraved copper or (less expensive) pewter plates. The technique spread through Europe slowly, but by the end of the seventeenth century, it had become the dominant publication method.

To engrave music, one began with a copper or pewter plate rolled to a smooth flat surface. A skilled engraver scored the staff lines on the plate. In the early years of engraved music, the engraver then used a sharp instrument to score the various clefs, notes, key signatures, markings, and the like in the appropriate places on the staves—working to create in effect a mirror image of the manuscript. As the technique evolved by the end of the seventeenth century, hard metal punches were fabricated with the diverse note and marking shapes so that the requisite notation could be tapped onto the plate—a process much faster than hand-engraving each symbol. On average, it took a skilled engraver six to eight hours to complete a single plate, which typically contained two pages of music to be printed.[13] After running of a proof sheet, proofreading, and (the composer hoped) correction, the plate was locked onto a flatbed press, inked, and wiped to remove ink from all but the engraved crevices. A sheet of paper was laid upon the plate and pressure was applied to transfer ink from the crevices to the paper—up to about 1813, by screwing a platen down upon the paper and plate, but after that time, through a much faster lever mechanism. The platen was then removed and the operation was repeated, with a typical cycle on old-design screw-type presses occupying a journeyman printer and his apprentice four to five minutes or one to two minutes with post-1820 flatbed press technologies. The sheets were allowed to dry and were then printed again on the reverse side. Because the wiping stage caused abrasion, plates had to be retouched and sometimes repunched every 100 to 200 cycles. With proper maintenance, a pewter plate could be used to make a few thousand impressions, a copper plate far more. For music set using movable type, the wiping stage was needed less often, speeding up the process slightly and permitting longer runs from the original block of type.

Movable type enjoyed a partial renaissance thanks to improvements made by a principal of the Breitkopf & Härtel firm, Johann Gottlob

Immanuel Breitkopf, during the 1750s. He devised a complex set of some 232 tiny staff, note, and marking elements, each one-fifth staff in height, that could be assembled not staff by staff, as with traditional methods, but into a mosaic or matrix.[14] When the elements were properly set by a highly skilled craftsman, it was possible to print complex musical notation with accuracy and neatness approaching the standards achieved through engraving. The matrix of set type, like engraved plates, could be stored when a run was completed in order to permit additional runs when demand conditions warranted. Printing using Breitkopf's movable type method was less costly than higher-quality engraving, and so his firm was able to make sheet music available at prices better suited to achieving substantial sales volumes. However, in addition to having somewhat inferior print quality, it was less flexible than engraving, hindering the issue of significantly revised editions.[15]

From the early years of the nineteenth century, lithographic methods began to challenge more traditional type set and engraved methods as a means of printing music. The original inventions were made by a Bavarian playwright, Aloys Senefelder (1771–1834). After various unsuccessful trials, Senefelder developed a method of impressing the staff lines and notes with a waxy ink onto a smoothly polished stone plate. After the stone was treated with other chemicals, printing inks adhered only to the imprinted musical notes and text and not to the rest of the plate, and when paper was pressed upon the stone, the ink was transferred to the paper. Senefelder collaborated with Franz Anton von Weber, the father of composer Carl Maria von Weber, to promote his invention among German music publishers. The senior Weber was an inveterate wheeler and dealer, constantly in debt and concocting new schemes to regain his footing.[16] In 1800 he approached the head of Breitkopf & Härtel with an offer to transfer lithographic technology to the Leipzig firm. Further inquiries revealed, however, that Weber did not know enough about the processes to make them work, and so successful use of lithography by B&H, in direct cooperation with Senefelder, was delayed until 1805.[17] Meanwhile, Senefelder established in Vienna during 1803 a new firm, the Chemische Druckerei (Chemical Printing Company) to apply his new process to music publishing.

Subsequent innovations enhanced the cost advantage of lithography over older music printing methods, especially for manuscripts with relatively modest anticipated sales. The first improvements, already in widespread use by 1820, allowed a copyist or even the composer to write the music with special ink on special paper, from which the images were transferred directly to polished and chemically treated lithographic plates for printing. The scores for Richard Wagner's *Rienze* and *Der fliegende Holländer* (The Flying Dutchman), both lithographed in 1844, and *Tannhäuser*, in 1845, were prepared by Wagner and his assistant in

this way. During the 1850s the technology of lithography was successfully merged with a newer art, photography. Photographs were made of
an original musical manuscript on special emulsions, from which the
images were transferred to treated stone or metal printing plates. Other
innovations made it possible to transfer the images to flexible plates or
sheets used on high-speed rotary presses.

Music nevertheless continued to be engraved, especially for works on
which high reproduction quality was sought. Henry Raynor argues that
the continued viability of engraving was attributable inter alia to the
growth of demand for printed music, lessening the disadvantage of high
front-end costs.[18] Lithographed music, however, continued for a long
time to be of lower quality than engraved music. This negative feature
initially led Richard Wagner to hesitate about dedicating *Lohengrin* to
Franz Liszt when Breitkopf & Härtel chose to publish it by lithograph,
although in the end, the dedication was made.[19] The use of engraving
was also constrained by the difficulty of retaining craftsmen with the
necessary skills. Lithography was chosen for *Lohengrin* in part because
engravers were in such short supply—a problem that also delayed the
publication of later Wagner operas.[20] Similarly, Fritz Simrock, the principal publisher for Johannes Brahms, urged Brahms in 1877 to establish
a clear schedule for the publication of Brahms's Second Symphony, since
"It is not always easy to have fine engravers available."[21]

In the twentieth century the advent of computer technology reduced
the cost of setting and printing music even more, but those innovations
came too late to affect the fortunes of the composers with whom we are
concerned in this volume.

THE COSTS OF ALTERNATIVE PUBLICATION METHODS

Publication of music with the principal methods in use at the beginning
of the nineteenth century entailed both front-end fixed costs, for engraving or typesetting and the metal used therefor, plus the modest costs of
making the press ready for printing; and variable costs, for paper, ink,
and the labor of two press operators. From this information alone we
know that the average cost of printed music must fall, the larger the
number of copies that are produced and hence the more widely that
fixed costs can be spread. But our insights can be advanced much far-
ther. In 1796, Gottfried Christoph Härtel secured full ownership of the
B&H printing firm from the Breitkopf family. Härtel was a remarkable
manager. Between the years 1800 and 1805 he subjected every facet of
the firm's operations to detailed quantitative scrutiny, among other
things estimating the cost of printing music in diverse quantities using
typeset and engraved methods.[22] Figure 7.1 summarizes his findings,

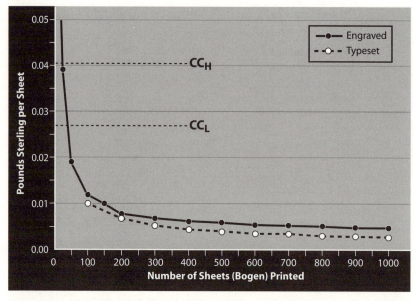

FIGURE 7.1 Cost-Volume Relationships for Engraved and Typeset Sheet Music

converted at prevailing exchange rates from Saxonian thaler to English pounds sterling.[23]

The average total cost curves for both engraved (solid line, assuming that pewter plates are used) and typeset (dashed line) music reveal as expected that for a four-page sheet (in German, *Bogen*), the average cost is greatly reduced when larger volumes are printed.[24] Solid and open circles show (with one extrapolation to be noted) the original data points computed by Härtel. When the reported average costs are multiplied by the associated quantities, the total cost curve for engraved music (not shown in figure 7.1) is found to be an almost perfect straight line, implying fixed front-end costs of £0.76 (or 4.5 days' earnings for a building craftsman in southern England at the time) per sheet and a constant marginal cost of £0.0042 (one English penny, or roughly, a building craftsman's wage for a quarter hour's work) per additional sheet printed.[25] For typeset music the total cost function is only approximately linear. For the first 100 to 200 sheets produced using movable type the incremental cost appears to have been on the order of £0.0036 per sheet, with an extrapolated front-end fixed cost of £0.63 per sheet. In the range of 800 to 1,000 sheets, marginal or incremental cost falls to £0.0021, or one-half English penny per sheet.

In 1814, after B&H had accumulated experience printing lithographically, Härtel compared the costs of lithographic printing (apparently, with notes and text inscribed directly on the stone plates) to the older methods. He found that at volumes of between 300 and 400 sheets, the average total cost per unit with lithography was 29 percent lower than the average with engraving. Three hundred copies could be printed lithographically at about the same total cost as 150 copies using engraved plates.[26] Using this information, he decided to implement a shift away from engraving and typesetting and toward lithographic printing, especially for cheap fast-selling works. To the extent that B&H continued to publish new engraved works, that is, those at the top of the quality scale, they would be made using old melted-down pewter; no new pewter was to be purchased. Lithography, however, must have proved disappointing, probably on quality grounds, because the number of B&H employees engaged in lithographic work actually shrank between 1819 and 1857, and the publication of engraved music remained vigorous.[27]

These data are important not only because they illuminate the cost differences among the three main mechanical printing methods, but also because they provide a benchmark against which to compare the cost of still another publication method—the reproduction of musical manuscripts by hand copyists. Throughout the seventeenth and eighteenth centuries and well into the nineteenth century, large numbers of copyists were engaged in the preparation of finished copies from composers' original manuscripts and copies of the copies. Copyists were often unsuccessful or back-chair musical performers, and since there was no shortage of individuals seeking to supplement their meager performance income through copying, they tended to work at low rates of pay.[28] They were hired by composers and their patrons to make presentation copies and by opera companies and orchestras to copy autograph parts for the various performers. They also pursued a freelance trade copying new music for sale to third-party consumers. In Vienna during Mozart's time, for example, specialized copying shops thrived working both on commission and as purveyors of pirated manuscripts. On one occasion Joseph Haydn considered—in the end, without result—bringing a copyist named Lausch before the mayor of Vienna on charges of theft.[29] In their freelance mode the copyists provided significant competition to music publishers on sales into the general market.

Determining how the costs of laboriously copying musical manuscripts by hand compared to the cost of mechanical printing methods poses difficult but not insuperable problems. Scattered through the biographical literature on composers are numerous references to the costs they incurred having their music copied by hand for performances and for presentation to noble patrons. Information on those outlays was linked to the specific compositions of J. S. Bach, Handel, Joseph Haydn,

Beethoven, Schubert, and Robert Schumann. Because copyists competed with printers and vice versa, the relevant comparison must focus on the amount paid for a hand copy against the number of printed pages with which the copy had to compete, not the cost per page in the copyist's manuscript. To count the number of printed pages, the earliest known printed versions were used.[30]

It must be recognized too that the copying costs recorded by composers were sometimes for presentation to patrons or publishers, in which case a close comparison can be made, and sometimes for use by the musicians in a performance, in which case multiple copies would be needed for the individual performers. Thus, for the performances of his *Missa solemnis* and the Ninth Symphony in 1824, Beethoven is said to have incurred copying outlays of 800 florins W.W.[31] The initial engraved versions of these works together encompassed 526 pages. At prevailing exchange rates, the copying cost amounts to £0.0608 per printed page. In comparison, Beethoven also employed copyists to produce ten *Missa solemnis* manuscripts distributed to noble patrons. For these, his cost per copy was 60 florins W.W., or £2.40, which implies a cost of £0.0107 per printed page (based upon the original Schott version with 226 pages). Since much duplication of parts was required for the large orchestra and chorus used in the 1824 performances, copying costs per printed page were much higher for performance use than for presentation copies.

For twelve cases in which reliable composer copying cost data were found, the average copying cost per printed page ranged from £0.0049 to £0.0891, the highest value being for a performance of Beethoven's *Gloreicher Augenblick* (Glorious Moment). For another of the most costly cases, later editors express astonishment at the high cost of original hand copies and speculate that the copyist must have been compensated for additional work.[32] Eliminating from the sample four cases with copying costs of £0.0480 per printed page or more, the average copying cost was £0.0101 per comparable printed page — roughly, the pay of a contemporary English building craftsman for working 36 minutes.

This does not eliminate all ambiguities. The typical sheet (*Bogen*) for which Breitkopf & Härtel cost data exist had two pages of music on one side of the page. It would appear, although it is not absolutely certain, that the data pertain to a sheet printed on both sides.[33] Thus, the per-page copying costs estimated here must be multiplied by four to be comparable with the average printing cost data of figure 7.1. It is also not certain whether the B&H cost estimates are before or after allowances for spoilage, which amounted to approximately one-third of total print runs.[34] If the estimates are gross, the costs in figure 7.1 must be increased by roughly 50 percent, or copyist cost estimates must be reduced by one-third, to be comparable.

Taking into account the spoilage uncertainty, figure 7.1 presents two estimates of the average copying cost per printed sheet. The horizontal dotted line CC_H (the subscript H denoting a high-end estimate) assumes that the data in figure 7.1 are net of spoilage; the dotted line CC_L adjusts copying costs downward (and implicitly, printing costs upward), assuming that the Härtel cost estimates were for printed sheets before culling of spoiled items. To bring the printing cost estimates into the same range as copying costs, the average cost of engraved music at a volume of 25 sheets has been extrapolated from B&H data. For our high-end copying cost estimate CC_H, the volume above which engraving becomes less expensive than copying is on the order of 25 copies; for our more conservative estimate, the break-even point is roughly 40 copies. For compositions of limited appeal, print runs of this magnitude were not at all unusual. During the early years of the Schott publishing house, for example, initial press runs of 30 to 100 copies were said to be the rule, although runs as small as 3 to 12 copies were experienced, especially when publication was commissioned by noble patrons.[35] Thus, hand copying provided serious competition to mechanical publishers. And the hand copyists had a timing advantage, since they could bring their copies to the market quickly and skim off eager purchasers while the mechanical publishers were still laboriously engraving plates or setting type. The more limited the potential demand for replicated musical manuscripts, the greater was the advantage of copyists relative to mechanical publishers.

Still to be reconciled with this comparison is the available evidence on the prices at which copyists sold manuscripts. During Mozart's last years in Vienna, the typical price for a sheet with four pages of music front and back is said by H. C. Robbins Landon to have been 5 kreutzer, or approximately £0.0085 at prevailing exchange rates.[36] This is close to our estimates of the copying cost per printed *page*—not per four-page sheet. A printed page, however, usually contained considerably more music than the typical page written by a copyist. For 21 symphonies, piano concerti, and sonatas by Beethoven on which comparable page counts are available for both the initial printed version and autograph manuscripts or hand copies made for publishers, the average printed page corresponded to 1.56 handwritten pages, with a range from 0.77 to 2.70.[37] Even with adjustment for the average difference, the price of £0.0133 per comparable copied sheet remains well below the low-end copying cost estimate of figure 7.1, implying a break-even volume in excess of 90 printed sheets. The only other known report of copy prices comes from an 1837 Paris almanac.[38] There it is said that work could be copied for 25 centimes, or £0.0098, per 12-staff page—a value much closer to our estimates based on composers' individual experiences. For the more complex notation typical of piano, harp, and guitar compositions, the copying price was said to be doubled. The inconsistency between these Parisian data and those of Robbins Landon suggests a tentative conclusion that the Robbins Landon estimates may have been erroneous, confused perhaps by the complex relationships among pages, four-page printed sheets, and content per staff of copied as compared to printed music.

The publishers were in any event acutely aware of the competition from hand copyists. Since they enjoyed a cost advantage over copyists at higher volumes, a rational strategy for the publishers would be to discourage purchases of copyists' manuscripts by announcing prices below those at which the copyists could profitably operate.[39] The average wholesale price, net of 50 percent discounts to retail outlets, charged by Breitkopf & Härtel during the early 1800s was approximately £0.0150 per sheet — below our low-end estimate of copyists' costs, and enough to earn substantial margins on the sizable production runs B&H typically sought.[40] Although the evidence is sparse, it would not be unreasonable to infer that B&H was setting its prices with one eye on the hand-copyist competition.

Publishers also recognized that at low volumes, hand copying was an attractive in-house alternative to mechanical printing. The best evidence on this point comes from the experience of Giuseppe Verdi's publisher, Casa Ricordi. In the later years of their relationship, Giovanni Ricordi maintained a lively business distributing individual parts from Verdi operas for postpremiere performances in the many large and small opera houses scattered throughout Italy. Ricordi could of course engrave and print the music, but he also maintained a staff of hand copyists. For at least *I lombardi* (The Lombards, 1843) and perhaps also later operas, he engraved and printed the parts for the string sections and chorus, since numerous copies would be required for any performance, but had the soloist and wind instrument parts hand-copied.[41] This is exactly what a knowledgeable profit maximizer would do, given the differences in reproduction costs over alternative volume ranges.

THE EVOLUTION OF INTELLECTUAL PROPERTY RIGHTS

Music publishing and the income opportunities it provided for composers were affected by the structure of intellectual property rights available to composers and publishers. In most of Europe before the nineteenth century, composers' ability to maintain control of musical creations as if they were their own property was quite limited. Copyists sold copies of composers' works without the composer's permission, and publishers issued editions that had neither been approved nor proofread by the composer, often in markets far distant from the composer's residence but also in head-to-head competition with authorized publishers. When George Frideric Handel arrived in London in 1710, he discovered that John Walsh, who rose to dominate the London music publishing business toward the end of the seventeenth century by printing many unauthorized works, had already published some of Handel's Italian compositions.[42] When Jean-Philippe Rameau settled in Paris at the age of thirty-nine, copies of cantatas he had written ten years earlier were so widely circulated that he saw no point in having them engraved and published.[43] Unauthorized publications of Joseph Haydn's compositions were available by 1765 in London and Paris, "leaked" to publishers there by Austrian copyists.[44] In 1782, Mozart wrote to his father that he was indebted to a Baron von Riedesel, who elected to buy the manuscript for *Die Entführung aus dem Serail* (The Abduction from the Seraglio) directly from him, when the baron could have obtained it at any time for cash from a copyist.[45] And as late as 1830, Felix Mendelssohn was astonished to learn that an unauthorized transcription of his Symphony no. 1 in C Minor had been cannibalized from the officially published London version by the Probst firm of Leipzig. Despite a face-to-face confrontation, Mendelssohn could not avert Probst's action.[46] Examples could be multiplied. Because the laws were weak or even nonexistent, much of this unauthorized dissemination was perfectly legal. But then — as with twentieth-century allegations about the copying of computer software and pharmaceutical products in nations with copyright and patent laws that permit such practices — the term "piracy" was widely used to describe what was occurring. Or in Martin Luther's complaints, those who reproduced hymnals without permission were "robbers" and "thieves."[47]

Composers' Traditional Rights

Composers were not without some rights to the works they created. A body of tradition defined minimal standards of the composer's just due — for one, the right to be named as creator of a published or performed work. From at least the time of the Middle Ages, plagiarism — passing off another composer's work as one's own — was almost universally recognized to be wrong. In his magisterial survey of early traditions, Pohlmann recounts the case of a madrigal presented in 1729 by Giovanni Bononcini for performance by the Academy of Ancient Music in London.[48] Two years later it was alleged and eventually proven that the work claimed as his own by Bononcini had been published in 1705 by the Venetian Antonio Lotti. Bononcini's reputation was severely tarnished in the furor that ensued, and he left London in 1732, experiencing only modest success in attempts to reestablish himself in Paris, Lisbon, and Vienna.

It was also recognized that composers had the right to offer their works to others for performance and/or publication and to be compensated for conveying the requisite manuscripts, even if they could not prevent further use by third parties into whose hands the music fell by fair means or foul. The right to contract could cover a specific piece of music, for instance, when a composer conveyed music to an opera impresario for performance or to a publisher for printing in exchange for a fee or honorarium, or more generally, when a composer agreed to devote his composition efforts to a particular patron or employer.[49] On these two themes numerous variations could be played, with differences in bargaining power and changes over time in traditions and laws influencing the precise allocation of rights.

In Italy, we have seen in an earlier chapter, opera in the seventeenth and eighteenth centuries was organized along private-enterprise lines.[50] The wealthy individuals who contributed financially to the creation and maintenance of an opera house delegated most managerial responsibilities to an impresario, who in turn contracted with composers, librettists, performers, and other functionaries. The tradition was for the composer to surrender rights to the original music score to the impresario in exchange for his honorarium. This allowed the impresario to arrange repeat performances when and where he pleased and/or to sell publication rights. The impresario typically assigned ownership of the first copy to copyists, who could then make additional copies and sell them to other theaters. Writing to his wife from Milan in 1770, Leopold Mozart predicted good results for the (ultimately hugely successful) opera *Mitridate* by son Wolfgang from the enthusiasm with which the copyist received Mozart's original score:[51]

> The copyist is full of joy, which in Italy is a very good omen, since, when the music pleases, the copyist can sometimes make more money sending out and selling the arias than the composer received for his composition.

And in fact, the copyist refused to surrender the original score until copies had been dispatched to Lisbon, Vienna, and Parma.[52]

Gradually, this distribution of rights changed. In London, where traditions at the King's Theatre were similar to those of Italy, the courts intervened in 1788 to favor the composer over copyists.[53] In Italy changes came partly by happenstance and partly through shifts in the balance of bargaining power. When an opera impresario in Bologna refused in 1817 to return the score for an opera by German composer Simon Mayr (1763–1845), Mayr's student, the twenty-year-old Gaetano Donizetti, attended the opera three evenings in succession and wrote down for his teacher the entire score.[54] In 1821, when the owners of a Roman opera theater refused to pay Gioachino Rossini the promised honorarium for an opera with an unsuccessful premiere, Rossini retaliated by confiscating the score, justifying his action to the governor of Rome as an exercise of his "proprietary right" to the score.[55] A year later he confiscated with less provocation the score for a new opera in Venice. Although disputation over ownership rights continued for a year, Rossini had become too popular for the opera owners successfully to resist his demands. By 1823, he could communicate to a friend an inventive interpretation of his rights:[56]

> I own all my originals, being the custom and the law that after one year following the performance of any opera the author has the right to have back his manuscript score.

The balance changed decisively when publisher Giovanni Ricordi, who had started his career as a copyist and built his publishing business by buying numerous scores from the various opera houses, began serving as agent for Vincenzo Bellini and then Giuseppe Verdi.[57] The demand for those composers' operas was so compelling that the impresarios could not resist granting full score ownership rights to Ricordi and the composers—compensated, to be sure, by an implied reduction in composers' honoraria.

When composers were employed to compose for noble courts, their employment contracts normally reserved to the patron full ownership rights in the resulting musical scores. Publication or even dissemination of hand copies was typically not permitted without the patron's express permission. The case of Niccolò Jommelli (1714–1774) is perhaps extreme but revealing. Released during a budgetary crisis from the court of Duke Carl Eugen of Württemberg in 1769 after 15 years of service, he requested, and was denied, permission to take with him copies of the music he had written for the court. His petition to the duke conceded the nearly universally applicable right of patrons to retain original scores; but copies, he argued, were a different matter:[58]

> If I forego the right to my own autographs, then why must I be prohibited from having copies of them? It is very just and necessary that an author have in his power and possession, under his own eyes, an example at least of his own production and work . . . [E]ven in Stuttgart itself, as everyone knows, my compositions are being circulated and sold [for shameful commercial enterprise], compositions that now I myself am being denied and that justly are my right to have.

Jommelli's plea was unsuccessful, and he returned to his native Naples to spend the remaining five years of his life in disappointment. Two leading German authors on composers' rights assert that Joseph Haydn was similarly restricted by his contract with princes Paul Anton and then Nikolaus Esterházy I, until the death of Nikolaus in 1790.[59] Here, however, they err. It is true that Haydn was not allowed to disseminate his works without express consent (given on some occasions) under his original 1761 contract.[60] But by 1779, Haydn's fame and his importance to the Esterházy establishment's prestige had grown to the point that Nikolaus I was impelled to write a new contract substantially increasing Haydn's salary and allowing him to pursue outside publication opportunities, which he then did aggressively.[61] The balance of bargaining power had shifted.

Composers' Defenses

Aside from bargaining to enhance their rights vis-à-vis patrons and impresarios, composers used several tactics to defend themselves against the piracy of copyists and unauthorized publishers.

One way to control the piratical practices of copyists was to have them work in the composer's living quarters. Even then, Joseph Haydn lamented to a Vienna publisher, "you may be swindled all the same, because the rascals put a piece of paper a parte under the music, and thus by degrees they secretly copy the part they have in front of them."[62] Mozart found that copyists were making two copies of everything he gave them, and therefore, like Haydn, he had them work in his own apartment.[63] This is said to be one reason that he maintained living quarters more lavish than his income warranted.[64] Even so, many of his manuscripts were said by his sister to have been lost because copyists helped themselves to work stored by Mozart under his pianoforte.[65] Mozart also sought to minimize leakage by dividing the work among multiple copyists so that none had the complete composition.[66] Beethoven similarly left the last few pages out of any manuscript given a copyist.[67]

When publishers printed unauthorized versions of his works, Beethoven sometimes fought back by taking out advertisements in periodicals serving the target market area, proclaiming the editions to be pirated.[68] On another occasion, the Artaria publishing house of Vienna printed without permission his Sextet op. 29. Beethoven went to the publisher and demanded that he surrender the fifty printed copies so that corrections could be made. Obtaining the copies, he had his aide Ferdinand Ries go through each copy and deface it so that it would be unsalable.[69]

To prevent Viennese pianists from performing his piano works in competition with his own efforts, Beethoven made some of them so difficult that rival performers, characterized as "his deadly enemies," were unable to play them, permitting the public to recognize the true composer when Beethoven played.[70] When a rival company announced that it would present a cribbed version of Handel's oratorio *Esther*, Handel sought to erode their patronage by hastily staging an updated version.[71] His efforts were successful; he netted an estimated £4,000 from his five competing performances.

Handel also was quick to understand the maxim, "If you can't beat 'em, join 'em." Handel's early works were extensively pirated by John Walsh, who is said by David Hunter to have been the first English publisher "to employ unauthorized publication as a standard practice."[72] After nearly two decades in London, however, Handel designated Walsh as his principal authorized publisher, and in 1739, Handel and Walsh jointly obtained an exclusive publishing privilege from King George II covering among other works Handel's twelve Concerti Grossi op. 6.[73]

Royal Privilege Grants

Grants of privilege by royal authorities strengthened the intellectual property rights of composers, authors, and publishers during several centuries preceding the emergence of formal copyright systems. The composer (or publisher) with a privilege received the exclusive right to publish a work or set of works within the granting government's domain, usually for a limited time period, and to utilize official legal institutions in enforcing the right against infringers. The specific institutions varied widely in diverse parts of Europe, so we address separately the privilege systems in England, France, and the Holy Roman Empire.

In England, privileges were granted on mercantilistic grounds to encourage the publication of books and secure income for the crown beginning in 1529 during the reign of Henry VIII.[74] An early recipient was the composer Thomas Tallis (1505–1585). In 1556 the Stationers' Company was chartered. Its main function in the early years, curtailed later, was to screen book manuscripts for material contrary to the accepted religion—at first Catholicism under Queen Mary, then Protestantism under Queen Elizabeth. However, it also acquired responsibility for registering the books printed by members—including John Playford (1623–1686), the most successful London music publisher of his time—and ensuring that no one produced or imported unauthorized copies of those books. In effect, it served as a copyright manager. Its formal authority was abolished in 1694, precipitating new legislation to be described shortly, but the Company continued to operate without an express governmental mandate for some time thereafter, among other things serving as a registry for the works publishers claimed as their

own. Meanwhile, the crown continued to grant to authors and composers privileges of exclusivity, which in principle conferred for a four-
teen-year period (reduced from twenty-one years originally) exclusive
rights, permitting confiscation of and fines against infringing materials.
Among the composers who received one or more royal privileges between 1710 and 1770 were George Frideric Handel (in 1720 and, with
John Walsh, 1739), William Croft (in 1724), Thomas Arne (in 1741),
William Boyce (in 1745), Carl Friedrich Abel (in 1760), Johann Christian Bach (in 1763), and J. C. Fischer (in 1770).[75] Enforcing privileges
against infringers was costly and loophole-prone. When competing
companies offered modified versions of Handel's opera *Ottone* and his
oratorio *Esther*, there was little Handel could do to combat the imitators except, in the case of *Esther*, to mount his own improved version.[76]

France maintained a parallel system of privileges, some protecting
publishers and some composers. For publishers, the French approach
embraced single-firm monopolies much more readily than in England,
where monopoly privileges had been judicially condemned in Eliza-
bethan times[77] and by Parliament through the 1623 Statute of Monopolies. In 1551 the firm of LeRoy & Ballard obtained a royal privilege to
be the exclusive printer of music in France. The privilege was maintained by members of the Ballard family, with only brief lapses, for the
next two centuries. The Ballard privilege ended formally in 1790 after a
governmental commission found the company to be unprogressive and
inefficient, but the firm's monopoly was broken earlier with a 1713 legal ruling that the privilege covered only typeset music publication and
not engraved music, which was gaining favor rapidly. Privileges were
also awarded to individual composers. Among the recipients were François Couperin (1668–1733), Michel de LaBarre (1675–1743), Jean Joseph Mouret (1682–1738), Jean-Philippe Rameau (1683–1764), and
Jean-Baptiste Forqueray (1699–1782).[78]

Normally, the French privileges favored domestic composers with
close connections to the royal court. The unauthorized printing within
France of works composed abroad was commonplace. The principal
known exception is of considerable interest. During the 1730s, unauthorized editions of Georg Philipp Telemann's music, including various
trio sonatas, were published in Paris. Telemann learned of the publication when he began receiving enthusiastic letters from French music
lovers. He decided to travel from Hamburg to Paris, where in 1737 he
obtained a royal privilege to publish exclusively additional trio sonatas
and quartets.[79]

Telemann took advantage of his formal training in law at the University of Leipzig to clarify a quite different question of publishers' as distinguished from composers' intellectual property rights.[80] In 1722, a

year after he was appointed cantor of five Hamburg churches, Telemann came into conflict with the firm enjoying a privilege as official printer to the city of Hamburg. It was customary for the cantor to write passion music for Lent services and for the congregation to participate actively in the service. This required printing numerous copies of the passion text — a right claimed by the printer. Contrary to prior custom, Telemann insisted that he be compensated by the printer for his work in integrating text with music — a demand naturally enough resisted by the printer. In iterations of this dispute before the Hamburg city council, Telemann's right to receive compensation was repeatedly affirmed, first with a mandate that the printer supply Telemann with 300 free copies (which he could sell to churchgoers) and later with a money honorarium set at 100 florins annually. After Telemann's death, the right to an honorarium was retained by his successor, Carl Philipp Emanuel Bach, the son of J. S. Bach.

Exclusive publishing privileges, including many covering the publication of music, were granted in the territories comprising the Holy Roman Empire. The first known privilege appears to have been issued to a German book printer in 1469.[81] It followed earlier Venetian precedents conveying exclusive privileges to Tyrolean water drainage experts during the fourteenth and fifteenth centuries, and it preceded by only five years the Venetian statute considered to be the world's first formal invention patent law.[82] In the more northerly parts of the Empire, exclusive privileges could be issued either by the emperor or by territorial rulers within the empire.[83] Individual musical works were supposedly examined for originality and conformity to religious canons before a publication privilege was extended, and when the recipients' rights were alleged to have been infringed, complaints could be addressed to local law enforcement authorities and appealed to an imperial court (the *Reichshofrat*) in Vienna. Fines were commonly divided among the aggrieved composer, the authorities, and informers. Surveying the system as it applied to textual material as well as music, Gieseke reports that up to 1530 it was more oriented toward authors, who received roughly two-thirds of the privileges, while the balance shifted later toward a two-thirds majority for publishers.[84] Pohlmann provides extensive documentation on the large number of publication privileges awarded to music composers. Indeed, so routine was the application procedure, requiring no special political connections, and so extensive was the availability of music privileges, Pohlmann argues, that one might reasonably see in privileges the prototype of modern musical copyright.[85]

Nevertheless, especially after the Treaty of Westphalia in 1648 weakened the authority of imperial courts and enhanced the sovereignty of individual principalities and dukedoms, enforcement of the exclusive rights conveyed through privileges became much more difficult. The basic problem was that a privilege might be issued by the ruler of one small principality to a local composer or publisher, but it was likely to be ignored by more distant music printers, who energetically pirated manuscripts obtained from copyists or publishers located outside their home territories. Thus, the privileges were mainly effective only in localized markets too small in most cases to support the high fixed costs of publication. To cover those costs, export into territories where the protection was unreliable might be essential. Exports of pirated works could be as successful in this respect as exports of locally composed works, especially if prior publication experience had identified the items for which consumer demand was strongest. Thus, a mutually uncooperative equilibrium — you pirate my best works and I'll pirate yours — prevailed. And even though in principle the privileges could bar imports into the jurisdiction of issue from other territories, musical prints were small and easily concealed from customs authorities, who in any event were likely to focus their attention on more easily discovered and/or lucratively dutiable wares.

England: The First Formal Copyright Law

The first modern copyright law, the so-called Statute of Anne, was passed by the English Parliament in 1709. Its impetus came from the void left by the withdrawal of governmental support for the Stationers' Company. The law's preamble observed that persons frequently published and reprinted:[86]

> . . . books and other writings, without the consent of the authors or proprietors of such books and writings, to their very great detriment, and too often to the ruin of them and their families.

The preamble went on to state as the law's purpose "encouragement of learned men to compose and write useful books." Exclusive publication rights were granted for a period of twenty-one years on books already printed and, on books to be published in the future, for fourteen years. Penalties for violation included seizure and conversion to waste paper, plus one penny per sheet, half going to the crown and half to the plaintiff. A procedure was established for limiting the prices of published books when it was shown that prices were "too high and unreasonable." The Company of Stationers was charged with registering copyrighted books so that booksellers could ensure that they did not inadvertently carry pirated versions — a requirement waived under subsequent amendments.

At first, the new law was not assumed to cover printed music. Clarification came in a case filed by Johann Christian Bach, the youngest son of J. S. Bach. In the meantime, composers continued to seek royal privileges to protect their published works. Bach and Carl Friedrich Abel were allied in a successful series of London concerts. Both had royal privileges to publish their works; Abel's expired in 1774 and Bach's in December 1777. Disregarding their privileges, London publisher James Longman printed pirated versions of both composers' works. It was decided that Bach would be the one to file a legal challenge seeking to cover his compositions under the Statute of Anne, supplementing or replacing his privilege. David Hunter conjectures that Bach and Abel were "probably the only composers with sufficient position" to sustain costly legal proceedings.[87] This is plausible; at the time his suit was filed in March 1773, Bach's bank balance stood at nearly £4,000.[88] Not until 1777 did the case reach the court of final appeal, whereupon Lord Chief Justice Mansfield ruled in favor of Bach after hearing oral argument only from Bach's attorney:[89]

> The words of the Act of Parliament are very large: "books and other writings." It is not confined to language or letters. Music is a science; it may be written; and the mode of conveying the ideas, is by signs and marks. A person may use the copy by playing it; but he has no right to rob the author of the profit, by multiplying copies and disposing of them to his own use. . . . [W]e are of opinion, that a musical composition is a writing within the Statute of the 8th of Queen Anne.

Bach and all resident composers as a result became entitled to copyright protection under British law. Registrations of musical compositions with the Company of Stationers, still serving as a registry of works for which publishers claimed exclusive rights, increased from 35 in the decade 1770–1779 to 738 in 1780–1789 and 1,828 in the decade of the 1790s.[90] However, Bach himself benefitted imperceptibly from his victory. As the case was proceeding the Bach-Abel concert series fell upon hard times; Abel withdrew from the series; and Bach plunged into debt. When he died four and a half years after the high court's decision, creditors forced their way into his room and attempted (unsuccessfully) to seize his body for sale to medical schools.[91]

The Spread of Copyright Law

The next national copyright laws arose from the spirit of revolution. Article I, Section 8 of the U.S. Constitution, ratified in 1789, authorized the Congress "to promote the Progress of Science and useful Arts, by securing for limited Times to Authors and Inventors the exclusive Right to their respective Writings and Discoveries."[92] Implementing legislation offering copyright to U.S. citizens and permanent residents was passed in 1790.[93] After the French Revolution of 1789, royal grants of privilege were abolished. To take their place the National Assembly passed in 1793 a law establishing a formal copyright system for literary and artistic property, amended in 1810 to permit both domestic and foreign authors to obtain copyrights.[94]

Extending copyright to the rest of Europe proved to be more difficult. One initiative was taken by the music publishers themselves. The official history of Breitkopf & Härtel mentions an "honorary" accord originated among German booksellers in 1819 to respect the rights of writers and publishers against copying, but it appears to have been ineffective.[95] Earlier, in 1810, Gottfried Härtel complained to Beethoven that "under present conditions, avoiding piracy of revised editions in France, England, and Germany is impossible."[96] At a convocation of the German and Austrian music publishers and retailers in Leipzig during 1829, an agreement was concluded not to copy each others' works and, when publication was joint, to announce that fact in specified journals.[97] A central registry was created by the publishers in 1830 to indicate who had rights to particular publications. By 1903, more than 100,000 works had been registered.[98] Foreign publishers' rights were not to be purchased by German publishers, presumably to encourage respect for national spheres of influence. Individual agreements among publishers to serve as sales agents for each other in territories they would otherwise not cover undoubtedly helped suppress some piracy incentives. For example, in the reciprocal agency proposal of 1796 from Pleyel of Paris to Artaria, a leading Vienna music publisher, Ignaz Pleyel required that Artaria "promise on your word of honor not to engage any of my works, and those of which I am the owner."[99] There appears to have been little systematic research on the extent to which private understandings succeeded in suppressing musical piracy. That they did not succeed completely is shown by the continuation of piracy complaints.

In 1825 a group of well-known composers submitted to a meeting of the German Bundesversammlung (liberally translated, assembly of affiliated German states — a remnant of the Holy Roman Empire) in Frankfurt a manifesto urging the German states to rise above their disunity and enact an effective all-German copyright covenant. It was drafted by Johann Nepomuk Hummel and endorsed among others by Ludwig van Beethoven, Carl Czerny, Ludwig Spohr, Ferdinand Ries, Ignaz Moscheles, Carl Maria von Weber, Friedrich Kalkbrenner, and Johann Pixis.[100] It asserted that in the German-speaking lands too many music publishers were "getting fat by robbing without penalty their neighbors' property." This reduced the income of publishers and composers, injured composers' reputations through the propagation of badly proof-read versions, and worsened German states' balance of trade relative to nations such as France and Great Britain that granted copyright protection.

The Bundesversammlung created standing committees to study the copyright problem, and in 1837, it enacted for the guidance of member states minimum guidelines for the provision of copyright.[101] These were patterned after a copyright law enacted previously by Prussia, which in turn had evolved from the first German state copyright provisions adopted by Prussia in 1794 and adapted during the fifteen years that followed by Saxony and Baden. The other German states then passed laws consistent with the 1837 guidelines. Not until full unification occurred in 1870, however, was there a copyright law universally enforceable throughout the new German Reich. In the meantime, differences between German states made it difficult to enforce the laws.[102]

As member and permanent chair of the Bundesversammlung, Austria adopted copyright laws consistent with the 1837 guidelines. They were applicable inter alia in the territories Austria occupied in northern Italy, including Venice and the surrounding Veneto. In 1840 Austria entered into a copyright treaty with Sardinia (including Savoy), which had managed to retain its independence through most of the preceding century. With it, copyright law was unified throughout most of northern Italy and could be extended backward into Austria and Bohemia. The remainder of northern Italy came within the treaty's compass when Piedmont completed a political union with Sardinia in 1848 and the combined kingdom's capital was moved to Turin. A law applicable through all of Italy came into being only after the south and then Rome were joined with the northern states between 1861 and 1870.

The promulgation of copyright laws throughout what had been the Holy Roman Empire and Italy required major efforts toward making copyrights effective across sovereign state borders. In the meantime further internationalization occurred. At first, some nations such as England and France allowed foreigners to obtain copyrights, while others, such as the United States, did not.[103] In 1837 Prussia passed a law authorizing the issue of copyrights to the citizens of states — German or other — whose governments offered reciprocal rights to Prussian citizens. Great Britain passed a similar law in 1844 and entered into reciprocal agreements with Prussia and Saxony in 1846; France and Holland exchanged reciprocal rights in 1840; and France and Hanover followed suit in 1852.[104] By 1886, some of the industrialized world (but not yet the United States) was ready for a multilateral agreement, which led to the Berne reciprocal copyright convention of 1887. The citizens of convention signatories were to be accorded copyright equivalent to the rights of citizens in the nations where copyright was sought.

Even when the laws were permissive, seeking copyright in a foreign nation was a delicate affair. Before copyright existed in Austria, Beethoven typically strove to have his works published and when possible copyrighted in several major markets — notably, Germany or Austria, France, and England. His letters reveal many attempts to juggle the timing of publication in the various nations and his sometimes petulant reactions to British publishers' apparent complaints (few originals survive) that, contrary to promises, there was prior publication outside England.[105] There were two apparent reasons for the publishers' concern. At some unknown time after the Statute of Anne was passed, the English law was interpreted to require that for an English copyright to be issued, the *first* publication of a work had to take place in England.[106] Prior publication abroad jeopardized the satisfaction of this requirement. One might infer that Beethoven was duplicitous in playing one publisher off against the other, but a more charitable interpretation is that the difficulties of coordinating publication dates were simply too great in an era of snail-slow postal service, leisurely decision making by publishers, and long periods for engraving or typesetting before a work could be proofread and put into print. Also, the British publishers may have been concerned that copies printed first in Paris would soon thereafter appear in the London market, cannibalizing their English sales.

Not all national copyright laws allowed holders to control the performance of musical works as well as their publication in print. The law of Great Britain was amended to cover performance rights only in 1842; the United States law in 1870. Hummel's 1825 manifesto to the German Bundesversammlung asked that composers have the right to require fees for the performance of "operas and opera-like major works." Unauthorized use by third parties was to be fined at a rate ten times the originally agreed-upon honorarium.[107] A performance right, as we shall elaborate in a moment, was in fact part of the original Austrian law. Even before France enacted a modern copyright law in 1793, a royal decree issued in 1776 carried forward a century-old tradition and required that opera composers receive fees for the first 40 performances, descending from 200 livres (£8.50, or three months' earnings for an English building craftsman) for each of the first 20 performances down to 100 livres for iterations 31–40.[108] Fees were received for performances in the provinces as well as in Paris. To be sure, this allowed the Paris Opéra and the Théâtre Italien to pay lower lump-sum fees in advance to composers. The performance-fee system was retained in the French law of 1793, and so for several decades France was the only nation in which per-performance fees were regularly sought.

Deriving Economic Advantage from Copyright

Because public instrumental concerts were still mostly occasional one-off events in mid-nineteenth-century Europe, whereas successful operas were repeated many times at their original venue and then replicated in provincial theaters, the enactment of authors' performance rights had its major impact on opera. Gioachino Rossini had already ended his opera-writing career when copyright laws became effective in Italy, but he was advised to take measures to protect his earlier works and was pleased to receive 45 Napoleon d'or (£35) in 1867, a year before his death, as a windfall from the assertion of performance rights.[109]

For Giuseppe Verdi, the new intellectual property regime meant an altered approach to the business of operawriting. Up to 1840, provincial Italian theaters normally obtained opera scores at bargain prices from copyists and paid the composer nothing for their performance. Working with his agent, the publisher Giovanni Ricordi, Vincenzo Bellini sought performance fees from the smaller Italian houses, but little could be extracted because of intensive competition from pirated copies.[110] Dying at the age of thirty-four in 1835, Bellini was unable to benefit from the new copyright laws. After 1840 Verdi and agent Giovanni Ricordi (succeeded in 1853 by son Tito Ricordi, 1811–1888) enjoyed a much stronger legal position selling hand-copied and printed scores to the provincial theaters.[111] From the sale of scores for *Ernani* alone, premiered in 1844, they realized 20,000 lire (£1,000).[112]

During the late 1840s Verdi and Ricordi began to levy fees for each performance. Initially a fixed fee of 400 francs (£16, or three months' earnings for a building craftsman in southern England) was asked, with a 50-percent reduction in territories lacking a copyright law. This led theater impresarios in some of the smaller towns to ignore Verdi's copyright, obtaining their scores surreptitiously, and to lobby for the repeal of Sardinia's copyright law. In an exchange of letters during 1850, Ricordi explained to Verdi the principles of what economists now call second-degree price discrimination.[113] "It is more advantageous," he wrote, "to provide access to these scores for all theaters, adapting the price to their special means, because I obtain much more from many small theaters at the price of 300 or 250 Lire, than from ten or twelve at the price of a thousand."[114] Ricordi proposed to Verdi that each performance fee from a provincial theater be separately negotiated in accordance with ability to pay. Verdi would then receive 30 percent of the revenue from score rentals and 40 percent of score sale revenues for the first ten years of an opera's life. The arrangement was accepted, and later Verdi's share was raised to 50 percent. To enforce it, Ricordi deployed a team of field agents to oversee the use of scores by provincial theaters and prevent theft. He also retained lawyers in the larger Italian cities to handle performance contract disputes. These transaction costs, Ricordi argued, justified his retaining a majority share of the provincial theater licensing revenues. Obtaining substantial revenues from score sales and performance fees, Verdi observed that he no longer needed to be a "galley slave" and to compose at a frantic pace.[115] Between 1840 and 1849 (he was thirty-six years old in 1849), Verdi composed 14 operas. During the 1850s he composed 7, in the 1860s he produced 2, and he wrote 1 in each of the succeeding three decades.

Copyright also enhanced the attractiveness of a business pursued even without intellectual property protection—selling printed solo or small-instrumental-group reductions of operas and orchestral works. The number of opera houses that would buy or rent an opera's score could be counted in the dozens, but many thousands of families would buy individual parts for performance at home. In Vienna before copyright existed, Christoph Torricella (1715–1798) published with Mozart's co-operation a piano reduction of *The Abduction from the Seraglio*. Carl Czerny crafted piano reductions of Beethoven's *Leonore* in 1805, and Ignaz Moscheles wrote a four-hands piano reduction of its revised successor, *Fidelio*, in 1814. In 1841 a penniless Richard Wagner was offered 1,100 francs (£43) by a Paris publisher to write various reductions of Gaetano Donizetti's opera, *La Favorite*.[116] But it took the combination of copyright protection, Italians' love of opera, and the love of money shared by Ricordi and Verdi to carry the reduction enterprise to its height of sophistication. From *Rigoletto*, for example, Ricordi published hundreds of reductions for piano and voice, solo piano, four-hands piano, flute, piano and violin, piano and flute, violin, clarinet, string quartet, and much else.[117] Reductions of individual arias, cavatinas, choruses, and overtures could be bought separately, and packages including most of the opera's numbers could be bought at discounts of 20 to 50 percent. The substantial revenues obtained in this way permitted Ricordi to offer Verdi previously unprecedented sums for the publication rights to his operas—for example, 14,000 francs (£550) in 1851 for the publication rights, not including performance rental royalties, to *Rigoletto*.[118] Richard Wagner's later operas were also published in various reduction forms—in many cases, to relieve Wagner's urgent financial needs—well in advance of their first performance and the publication of full scores.[119]

COMPOSER-PUBLISHER RELATIONSHIPS

The perceived importance of income from the publication of musical works differed among composers, depending among other things upon individual tastes and how robust alternative income sources were. Beethoven is said by many authors to have been the first important composer who depended heavily upon income from the publication of his compositions. This is more true than not. Even though he received an appreciable annuity income from three noble patrons, its value was severely eroded by inflation, and he bargained especially vigorously with publishers to enhance his honoraria. At the other extreme was César Franck, who had a substantial income from teaching and his position as church organist. He seldom bargained with publishers and considered himself fortunate to be offered 100 francs (£4) for setting a poem to music.[120] His contemporary Johannes Brahms did bargain hard in his early lean years and relied heavily upon publication income to meet his modest consumption requirements. But in his later years he was sufficiently well off that he could explain to Clara Schumann in 1887 why he had neglected to collect copyright royalties in France: "I earn quite easily; and have no need at all to concern myself with sources of income."[121] Similarly, he complained to his principal publisher, Fritz Simrock (1837–1901), that the relatively high prices Simrock charged consumers for Brahms's music prevented him from achieving something important to him — the most widespread possible diffusion of his work: "[N]o one can persuade me that I would not gain more enjoyment (and you more money) from my symphonies and songs if buying them were anywhere near affordable, as are those of my colleagues [who publish with the low-price Peters firm]."[122] This is a sentiment with which most authors enjoying academic salaries can empathize.

Relations between composers and their publishers were often conflict-ridden and sometimes stormy. Although well off himself, George Frideric Handel is said to have been envious when his main publisher, John Walsh, left an estate of £30,000 at his death.[123] Arguing over the allocation of fees, Giuseppe Verdi wrote to his publisher Tito Ricordi, "In compensation for all my labor, I shall earn in twenty years from eight to ten thousand francs. And you earn the same amount while you are strolling around Lake Como."[124] Franz Schubert complained: "If only honest dealing were possible with these . . . publishers: but the wise and beneficent regulations of our Government have taken good care that the artist shall remain the eternal slave of those miserable money-grabbers."[125] Chopin is said to have regarded publishers as sharks, cheats, and liars. He used an agent to carry out unpleasant negotiations and demanded immediate compensation: "From now on, it's pay up, animal."[126]

Before he settled into a friendly and often humorful relationship with the Simrock family, Johannes Brahms wrote to a composer friend, "Publishers are miserable curs! . . . [D]o *not, absolutely not,* send your things without an honorarium."[127] But once he was at ease with Fritz Simrock, who wrote to him in 1877 that "no demand of yours is ever too high for me,"[128] he entrusted Simrock with nearly complete leeway in managing his financial affairs. On the difficulties of the composer-publisher relationship, he wrote to Simrock in 1881:[129]

That one thing [which is the cause of all my uneasiness] is the confounded relationship to money, which, unfortunately, is still customary between musicians and publishers. . . . We musicians are treated like children and incompetents, we don't in the least know for what and how payment is actually made, whether we are giving or getting, whether we rob or are being robbed.

In the same letter he went on to suggest that Simrock might be the one being robbed in publishing Brahms's works.

Publishers' Tactics

Composers were unhappy about a variety of practices pursued by their publishers. There was a widespread perception that publishers normally had the upper hand in bargaining and that they took advantage of the composers in times of weakness. For example, in 1823, when Franz Schubert was seriously ill from the first stages of syphilis and in dire need of funds, the Viennese publisher Anton Diabelli beat down the prices Schubert was asking on his opus 1–7 compositions to 320 florins (£32) for the package and again on his opus 12–14 works.[130] When a short time thereafter Diabelli asked Schubert to reimburse more for copying services than agreed upon in advance, Schubert switched to a different publisher and wrote angrily to Diabelli:[131]

During the earlier negotiations over the publication of the Waltzes I became aware of the not over-scrupulous intentions of my publishers . . . I feel that the extremely small purchase price which you paid for my earlier things, including the Fantasia for 50 florins, long ago wiped out this debt which you so unjustly put upon me.

Although he was a much more demanding bargainer than Schubert, Richard Wagner was disadvantaged in bargaining with his principal publishers: although his operas were best suited for German audiences, he had difficulty obtaining performance venues in Germany during the decade following the 1848 revolutions, when Wagner remained a fugitive from German police for his support of revolutionary causes.[132] In desperate need of funds, and having exhausted the willingness of Breitkopf & Härtel to provide supplements, he received advances in 1862 from Schott of Mainz by pledging title to all of his future musical works.[133] Even then, Schott's advances were too little to meet Wagner's requirements, leading Wagner to write in August 1862 that "It is impossible that you leave me so helpless!"[134] After further exchanges, an exasperated Franz Schott replied that "no publisher anywhere can defray your needs; that could be done only by a rich banker or a prince who has millions at his disposal."[135]

Composers also expressed anger over publishers' lack of diligence in carrying out what they considered to be agreed-upon measures. Thus, Luigi Boccherini complained bitterly over the tardiness of Ignaz Pleyel in returning his only copies of more than one hundred manuscripts Boccherini had sent to Pleyel in Paris, some of them held by Pleyel for as long as sixteen months. "I do not want to dispossess myself of my works, because a father loves his children and wants their company, be they fair or ugly, good or bad," he wrote.[136] A two-year publication delay by the Viennese publisher Tobias Haslinger (1787–1842) was the target of Frédéric Chopin's wrath.[137]

With multiple currencies in use and diverse offsets for copying, postage, and other expenses, it was often difficult to keep royalty accounts straight, leading to mutual recriminations. A dispute over the allocation of publication fees during the 1870s between Verdi and his agent-publisher Tito Ricordi was settled to Verdi's eventual satisfaction with a lump-sum payment to Verdi of 50,000 francs (£1,960).[138] With the breach healed, Verdi later loaned Ricordi 200,000 francs. But loans within the composer-publisher "family" could also be troublesome. Beethoven broke off what had previously been extraordinarily friendly relations with his Viennese publisher Sigmund Anton Steiner (1773–1838, successor to Aloys Senefelder and predecessor of Tobias Haslinger) when Steiner insisted that, in lieu of paying back accumulated loans, Beethoven give Steiner exclusive publishing rights for all his compositions. And when that demand was rejected, Steiner threatened a lawsuit to enforce repayment of the debt with interest.[139]

Aggravating the tensions between composers and publishers was the intertwining of geographic distance, the difficulty of inspecting works composers offered for publication, and risk aversion on the publisher's part.[140] Before copyright laws existed, the publisher might pirate a work sent for inspection, despite universal recognition that publishing a composition without the composer's consent violated moral even if not legal codes. And in any event, for fledgling composers it was a Hobson's choice to incur the cost of backup copies or face the risk that manuscripts would be lost in the slow and unreliable mails. Thus, for publishers located some distance from the composer's home base, the most common practice was for the composer to describe the work but not to send a copy. The publisher then faced the possibility of offering an upfront honorarium for a pig in a poke, especially for composers who had not yet established a record of delivering music that reliably met sheet-music purchasers' demands.

An example is the experience in 1826 of Franz Schubert, who had already published numerous works in Vienna, when he wrote Breitkopf & Härtel in Leipzig as follows:[141]

In the hope that my name is not wholly unknown to you, I am venturing to ask whether you would be disposed to take over at a moderate price some of my [listed] compositions, for I very much want to become as well known as possible in Germany.

Härtel replied patronizingly:[142]

Since we are totally unfamiliar with the commercial success of your works, and therefore would not be able to agree upon your desired monetary honorarium (which the publisher can determine or approve only after a successful experience), we must ask you whether, in an attempt to build a lasting relationship, you would accept a number of printed copies as compensation. We don't doubt that you will find this proposal agreeable, since for you, as for us, it is more a matter of establishing a continuing relationship than of bringing out a particular work.

Because the marginal cost of additional printed copies was small, this often-used approach reduced the publisher's front-end investment and hence the risk associated with a new publishing relationship.[143] But Schubert was too desperate for cash to accept it, so he remained with Vienna publishers and died in poverty two years later. A quarter century earlier, B&H had driven an even harder bargain with the teenage Ludwig Spohr (1784–1859), requiring that he purchase at half price 100 copies of his first violin concerto as a condition for publishing it.[144] Some composers, however, were more fortunate in their initial approaches to distant publishers. The publication of Antonín Dvořák's first works outside Prague's narrow compass, for example, was facilitated when Johannes Brahms strongly recommended them to Fritz Simrock, his principal publisher.[145]

Offering ad valorem royalties, which defer the publisher's financial commitment until a sales record can be established, was apparently uncommon during the time of Schubert.[146] However, finding "no rational way" to calculate the profitability of publishing Richard Wagner's proposed opera cycle *Der Ring des Nibelungen* (The Nibelung's Ring), Breitkopf & Härtel offered in 1856 a profit-sharing approach. After further agonizing, B&H reported that "the more we struggle with the issue, the more uncertain we become," and withdrew its offer.[147]

Breitkopf & Härtel, which had the most extensive network of sales agents among European music publishers during the early nineteenth century, was an eagerly desired outlet for composers seeking to enhance their reputations, but also a particularly difficult nut to crack. As a part of the extensive quantification undertaken when he assumed control of the company, Gottfried Härtel calculated during the early 1800s that, given his costs and standard prices, he could not afford to pay an honorarium of 3 to 4 thaler (£0.73 to 0.98) per four-page sheet unless early sales of 300 copies could be anticipated—an ambitious target for little-known composers at the time.[148] This had not deterred him from writing to Constanze Mozart in 1798, asking her to "let us know what genuine unpublished compositions of your esteemed husband are still in your hands, and eventually be so kind as to send them to us," whereupon B&H would give preference to Constanze in buying them if the same works were offered by other sources.[149] Mozart's reputation was well-established; there was little risk of disappointing sales. But in the early years of Beethoven's career, despite considerable back-and-forth corre-spondence, B&H could not bring itself to match the honoraria being offered by other publishers.[150] Only after Härtel traveled to Vienna in 1808 and met Beethoven face to face was a publishing relationship agreed upon, leading to B&H publication of the Fifth and Sixth sym-phonies, among others. However, as Beethoven escalated his honor-arium demands in 1812 because of inflation, currency reform, and the devaluation of his pension, Härtel's calculations again led to offers re-jected by the master. One might suppose that Härtel's supremely ratio-nal calculations saved him from the "winner's curse" of bidding high and paying more on average than compositions could return in an un-certain market.[151] Consequently, his firm survived while other publishers failed. But Härtel's replacement as the principal German publisher of Beethoven's late works, Schott of Mainz, was also one of the few long-term survivors. Thus, Härtel probably erred on the side of underesti-mating the benefits of having a strong Beethoven position in his portfo-lio. His successors erred even more seriously in 1865 when they had an outside consultant evaluate a sextet manuscript sent to them (by that time, under protection of personal copyright) by Johannes Brahms, sev-eral of whose earlier works they had published. When he learned what they had done, Brahms responded:[152]

> I found [your letter] to be the most hurtful, yes the most insulting thing that has happened to me. . . . Should your letter have been prompted by a possible trial of the work, then I ask by what right you might have ar-ranged this without my consent . . . since you know as well as I how little sympathy my works meet with in Leipzig. If it was occasioned by the judg-ment of a single individual, that too I must protest as an insult.

And from that time on, he published nothing more with Breitkopf & Härtel.

Composers' Strategies

Composers had their own strategies for making the best of their bar-gaining position. Unless a prior understanding to the contrary existed, it was perfectly ethical to play one publisher off against the others in tying to maximize the honorarium offered. Many did so. As Chopin instructed his agent in advance of a tough bargaining session in 1839, "If Pleyel makes any difficulties go to Schlesinger and tell him I'll give him the Ballade for France and England for 800 [francs = £31], and the [op. 40] Polonaises for France, England and Germany for 1500 (if that frightens him, suggest 1400, 1300, or even 1200)."[153] Where they drifted into the grey area of unethical behavior was when they offered advantages such as exclusivity but failed to abide by their promises, or when they claimed to possess higher bids when in fact they did not.

Joseph Haydn, for example, signed a contract with a London publisher stating that "Guilaume [William] Forster is the sole proprietor of the said works, and that I sold them to him as such."[154] In truth, he granted unlimited publication rights for the same items to Artaria of Vienna, which had a sales agent in London who attempted to sell the music in competition with Forster. When the London agent and Forster became entangled in a lawsuit, Haydn was called to give evidence during his first London concert visit. He explained that his contract with Forster was meant to apply to England only, while his contract with Artaria would have included England only if Artaria had paid a higher honorarium. While in London, Haydn wrote asking a friend in Austria to buy from Artaria copies of two works and send them to him, but not to tell Artaria why she was doing so, since he intended to sell them to a London publisher.[155]

Beethoven regularly attempted to maximize his earnings by having his compositions published more or less simultaneously in England, France, and either Austria or Germany. As we saw earlier, he came to grief on occasion when the requisite timing of release dates could not be properly coordinated. Some of his agreements were remarkably imprecise about the delineation of geographic rights, in effect saying that Breitkopf & Härtel would have exclusive rights in Germany and also throughout Europe unless it proved advantageous for Beethoven to publish with someone outside Germany.[156] In such cases, he continued, he would let B&H know and grant them some favor in the future. The posture he adopted in dealings with potential publishers was characterized in an early letter to a friend:[157]

> My compositions are bringing in a goodly sum. Also, for every work I have six, seven publishers, and if I choose, even more. They do not bargain with me: I demand and they pay.

This was braggadocio. In fact, many of his demands were refused, even when he insisted that he had another equally attractive offer in hand — which was not always true.[158]

Even though in his time of great need he had granted exclusive lifetime publication rights to the Schott firm, Richard Wagner began soliciting competitive offers once he was able to return to Germany and his operas began to gain in fame. In 1876, for example, he notified Schott that other firms had offered 9,000 and then 12,000 marks (£435–580) for his American centennial march when Schott had offered only one-fifth as much. Defending his solicitation of competitive offers, Wagner wrote to Schott, "What is a composer to do when others value his works more highly than Schott?"[159] A year earlier, Wagner had written that it was "his duty" to inform Schott that a Berlin publisher wished to take over Schott's exclusive relationship with Wagner — a threat that did not materialize into reality.[160]

An alternative strategy requiring both capital and access to appropriate marketing channels was to pay a publisher to carry out the printing on contract, but to handle the distribution and retain the profits oneself. There were two reasons for doing so: a lack of agreeable alternatives, or the belief that especially high prices could be realized by soliciting subscriptions from carefully selected individuals. During the time of the Ballard monopoly in France, François Couperin (1668–1733) received royal privileges and self-published a large number of his works. Publication opportunities were so meager in the time of Johann Sebastian Bach that most of the few works published during his lifetime, including the multipart *Clavier-Übung* (Clavier Exercise) and *The Musical Offering* (dedicated to Frederick the Great), were self-published.[161] Despite enormous expansion of the publishing industry during the following century, an unlucky Franz Schubert also fell into the first category. When local Viennese publishers refused his early offerings, a wealthy friend of Schubert paid the Diabelli firm to engrave and print a collection of songs and sell them on commission in its Vienna shop.[162]

Market segmentation was the strategy chosen by Joseph Haydn for his oratorio *The Creation*. He had the score engraved and printed by Artaria of Vienna, soliciting subscription sales in Germany at 3 ducats (£1.25) and in England at £1.50 per copy and attracting more than 400 subscribers, including King George III of England and the empress of Austria. Many subscribers took multiple copies.[163] After subscription sales had been completed, Haydn gave the engraved plates to Breitkopf & Härtel for a print run with more general distribution.[164]

Beethoven exhibited mixed motives in his self-publication efforts. His Opus 1 piano trios were printed under contract by Artaria and sold successfully by subscription in 1795 to an elite list of 123 individuals.[165] This attracted sufficient attention from publishers that he was able to negotiate favorable terms selling subsequent works for publication in the normal manner. However, when he completed what he considered his life's crowning work, the *Missa solemnis*, he solicited advance subscriptions from heads of state at a price of 50 ducats (£25) each, implying a substantial patronage contribution, and the copies were made by hand (with many errors) rather than through engraving and printing. Ten copies were sold in this way.[166] Only after subscription copy distribution ended was a printed version sold, following a competition among seven different publishers, by Schott of Mainz.

Unhappy about his experiences with publishers, Mozart in 1784 considered having his music engraved and printed under contract and then selling it by subscription, but asked his father in a letter how one controlled the number of copies printed and prevented the printer from selling more and "ruining the market."[167] Apparently, the idea was not pursued further. Previously, in 1783, he had his Piano Concertos nos. 11–13 hand-copied for sale to advance subscribers at a price of four ducats (£2). Richard Wagner borrowed money to self-publish three of his early operas before establishing a relationship with Breitkopf & Härtel.

What Publishers Wanted

Composers were in less than perfect harmony with their publishers not only over financial arrangements, but also over the type of music to be published. Composers chose what they wrote on a variety of grounds— because they preferred certain forms or were particularly good at them, to maximize the likelihood of having their works performed in public, and to enhance their impact in the music-loving world, among other things. Publishers naturally enough had to be responsive to the printed-music market. Thousands of consumers might buy an easy piano, flute, or vocal piece for performance at home, whereas the market for full scores of symphonies, concertos, and operas was intrinsically a small-numbers proposition. All else equal, publishers preferred the large-volume pieces, but in this they were sometimes at odds with their composers.

Advising his son during Wolfgang's 1778 visit to Paris, Leopold Mozart wrote:[168]

> When you have no students around, for God's sake go out of your way a bit to compose something that will enhance your fame. But short! Easy! Popular! Talk to a publisher, and see what he would most like to have— perhaps easy quartets for two violins, viola, and cello. Do you think you demean yourself writing such things? No way! When we were in London, did [Christian] Bach do other than turn out little morsels? The little piece is big, when it is light and flows naturally and is well-rooted in fundamentals. Composing in that way is harder than composing most incomprehensible artificial harmonic progressions and songs that are difficult to sing. Did Bach demean himself writing what he did? No way!

Like most headstrong 22-year-olds, Mozart paid little attention to his father's advice.

Two decades later, publisher Ignaz Pleyel (who as a composer should have known better) wrote Luigi Boccherini in Madrid, urging him to write simpler music more likely to attract the public. Boccherini responded angrily, "But remember that there is nothing worse than to tie the hands of a poor author, that is to say, to confine his ideas and imagination by subjecting him to rules." He compromised, however, by sending to Pleyel four easy quartets and two "in my style."[169] Advising Beethoven by mail in 1801 what kind of pieces he would most like to publish, Gottfried Härtel emphasized unaccompanied piano sonatas or piano sonatas with violin or viola accompaniment.[170] To a youthful Carl Maria von Weber in 1801, Härtel said he would most like to receive a piano sonata or three piano sonatas with or without violin.[171] And in the previously quoted 1826 letter to Franz Schubert, Härtel wrote suggesting as first submissions one or two pieces for solo piano or for four-hands piano.[172]

Härtel's early advice to Beethoven on preferred composition forms was probably unnecessary, for a few months before receiving Härtel's letter in 1801, Beethoven asked of another Leipzig publisher 20 ducats (£8) for his First Symphony and 20 ducats for a solo sonata. Explaining the identity of prices for works of vastly different complexity, he explained that "there is not such a demand for a septet or a symphony as for a sonata."[173]

Eighty-five years later, only the size of the market, but not its bias, had changed. Antonin Dvořák's initially harmonious relationship with publisher Fritz Simrock deteriorated into quarreling over appropriate fees. For his magnificent Seventh Symphony, Dvořák asked 6,000 marks (£291). Simrock offered only half as much, claiming that he was losing thousands of marks on symphonies and wanted shorter works with better sales potential.[174]

For Breitkopf & Härtel, the leading continental European music publisher, we have data on the distribution of its inventory by list price values as of July 1823.[175] From a richer set of categories, the data are aggregated into six broad groupings—sonatas (including sonatalike pieces, theme and variations, and solo or duet instrumental reductions); songs; orchestral works (including symphonies, concertos, overtures, etc.); choral works (with or without orchestral accompaniment); chamber works (including trios, quartets, and octets); and "other" (including operas and, mostly, a collection of Muzio Clementi's diverse works). Figure 7.2 shows how the total value of inventory was distributed across these categories. The first two categories include mainly works that could be played in the home, and that, the qualitative evidence suggests, publishers were most eager to have. They indeed comprise the major-

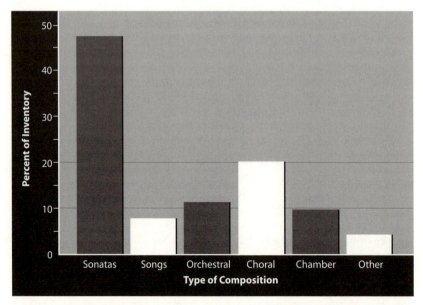

FIGURE 7.2 Distribution of Breitkopf & Härtel Inventory by Music Type, 1823

ity—together, 55 percent—of the B&H inventory holdings. Thus, although B&H published many kinds of compositions, it emphasized works with potentially large sales.

COMPOSERS' PUBLICATION HONORARIA

Thanks to the compulsive record keeping of Robert Schumann, unusually complete information survives on the honoraria received for publication rights (and for an opera, performance rights).[176] Thanks to extraordinarily careful research by Julia Moore, we also have less complete but consistent data on honoraria received by Beethoven, marred in many cases by the bundling of numerous works for sale at a single lump-sum fee.[177] From these data useful insights can be drawn on how honoraria varied with the composer's accumulated reputation and the type of work being published.

The Schumann data extend, with breaks for works not yet accepted for publication at the time of Schumann's death, from opus 18 through opus 135, which were completed between 1840 and 1852. Most entries are for discrete compositions, although for lieder, sonatas, and other sonatalike works, multiple items were often sold in a single bundle. Altogether, ninety honoraria for works could be matched to specific opus numbers, which was a requisite for the analysis that follows. Schumann, it is worth noting, appears to have shopped around for best offers at least as assiduously as Beethoven did. The available evidence reveals that he published works through 21 different publishers, with Breitkopf & Härtel holding first place, originating 21 percent of the compositions, and another Leipzig firm, Whistling, in second place at 19 percent.

Figure 7.3 shows the average honorarium Schumann received per work in seven categories, with multiwork sonata and Lieder receipts divided by the number of discrete items in the bundle. The averages are computed in Saxonian thaler, as Schumann recorded them. In 1845, approximately 7 thaler exchanged for £1 sterling. We see that compensation varied widely across the categories. By far the most lucrative works were the two characterized in figure 7.3 as operas, including a true opera, *Genoveva*, and a major oratorio, *Das Paradies und die Peri* (Paradise and the Peri). Schumann's receipts for his operas averaged 657 thaler, or the equivalent of what a fully employed English building craftsman earned in one and one-half years. Choral works — many, such as *Nachtlied* (Night Song) and *Der Rose Pilgerfahrt* (Pilgrimage of a Rose), scored for orchestra — were next most lucrative, followed by Schumann's four symphonies, with an average realization of 169 thaler (£24, or 40 percent of an English building craftsman's annual earnings) per opus. Least remunerative were individual songs and sonatas — the items consumers tended to demand in the largest quantities and for which publishers expressed a distinct preference. One's preliminary impression is that a crude labor theory of value prevailed in setting honoraria: the more work a composition required, the larger was the honorarium.

Our understanding can be expanded by using multiple regression methods to analyze the fees Schumann obtained for a work or package of works. Controlling for the type of work published, we find that Schumann's publication fee rose on average by about 0.57 thaler with each opus-number increment.[178] Since the 1840s were not a time of appreciable inflation, this means that as Schumann's reputation grew, so also did his compensation. When the same regression is estimated using logarithms of the fee variable, we find that on average, each unit increment in OPUS raised Schumann's compensation by 0.72 percent on average. Incrementing over 100 opus numbers, which is a bit less than the total range covered by the available data, leads to an approximate doubling of Schumann's honorarium, all else (such as type of work) held constant. This is a not inconsiderable reputation effect.

Beethoven's publication fees have been converted by Julia Moore to gold ducat values at prevailing exchange rates when they were not actu-

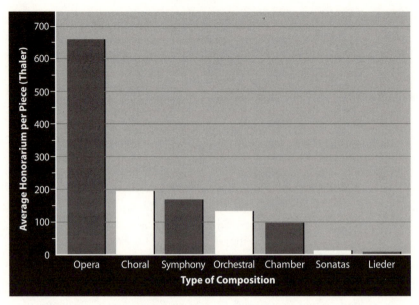

FIGURE 7.3 Publication Honoraria for Robert Schumann's Musical Works

ally paid in ducats — the currency Beethoven preferred after Vienna ex-perienced significant price inflation and florin devaluation. Data were available on ducat payments for 18 individual compositions and 42 opus-matched works purchased in a total of nine packages. Assuming despite substantial doubts that within a package, each work was of equal value, and converting thaler to ducats at a mid-period exchange ratio of 2.25 to 1, a similar analysis can be carried out, pooling 90 observations on Schumann's fees and 60 on Beethoven's. The resulting regression equation yields several additional insights.[179] First, in most respects the fee structures experienced by the two composers were simi-lar. But second, the value of an additional sonata in a Beethoven pack-age was much higher than for Schumann — 24.5 converted thaler as compared to 3.71 for Schumann. Third, when separate estimates are computed, the reputation effect for Beethoven was an increment of 1.09 thaler per opus, or twice Schumann's 0.57 coefficient. Or taking log-arithms of the fees as dependent variable, we find that each opus incre-ment raised Beethoven's compensation by 0.98 percent on average, as compared to 0.72 percent for Schumann. This difference suggests either that Beethoven's fee-earning reputation grew more rapidly than that of Schumann, or that there were inflationary effects in the Beethoven fee history that were less evident for Schumann, or perhaps both.[180]

Compensation per Published Page

As we have seen, larger works tended to receive higher honoraria than simpler and shorter pieces, despite publishers' preference for the latter because of their superior sales appeal in the home-performance market. It does not follow that publishers sent the wrong price signals to their composers. From the standpoint of an income-maximizing composer, what should matter is the compensation per unit of effort. And surely for most composers, even if not perhaps for a Mozart, writing a symphony was more work than writing a sonata of equal playing time.

If one accepts the assumption that the amount of mental and physical effort required to compose a work is roughly proportional to the number of pages the published work covers, we can advance an additional step. The assumption is hardly obvious. The printed version of a symphony contains more empty staves and hence fewer notes per page than does a two-hands piano sonata. Also, some composers, although not apparently Robert Schumann, had assistants fill in the bass lines and other orchestration. The counterargument is that getting all the parts of a symphony to function together is itself hard work, and that nearly as much mental effort is required to omit an instrumental phrase as to write it down. Lacking a clear resolution, we proceed where angels fear to tread.

For 77 of Robert Schumann's opus numbers, it was possible to make an exact match between the data on compensation and the number of pages the work covered in the original edition of Schumann's collected works, edited by Clara Schumann.[181] A complication is that, because the works for full orchestra and/or choir were more complex, they are printed on larger pages than other works. The larger-size pages were multiplied by 1.608 to make them equivalent in printed staff area to the more numerous small-page compositions. With this adjustment, the average honorarium in Saxonian thaler per page for various types of compositions was as follows, with the number of observations in parentheses:[182]

	Thaler
Symphonies (4)	1.12
Opera (1)	1.11
Oratorio (1)	1.44
Other orchestral (7)	1.80
Choir with orchestra (6)	2.24
Quartets and quintets (4)	2.79
Trios (7)	4.84
Instrumental duets (3)	5.63
Sonatas (18)	4.55
Lieder (26)	3.66

Works readily performed in one's home, such as lieder, sonatas, duets, and trios, brought on average 4.22 thaler per page, 2.43 times as much as the 1.74 thaler average for works (excluding quartets and quintets) that lent themselves only to large-group performance.[183] Although doubts remain, it would appear that publishers' honoraria per printed page reflected the superior profitability of simpler works and therefore sent price signals to composers consistent with the verbal admonitions reported previously.

CONCLUSION

As the market for published music grew, the sale of works to publishers became an increasingly important source of income to composers. The evolution of copyright from an occasional grant of royal privilege to a formal and eventually widespread system of law should in principle have enhanced composers' income from publication. The evidence from our quantitative comparison of honoraria received by Beethoven, with no copyright law in his home territory, and Robert Schumann, benefiting from nearly universal European copyright, provides at best questionable support for the hypothesis that copyright fundamentally changed composers' fortunes. From the qualitative evidence on Giuseppe Verdi, who was the first important composer to experience the new Italian copyright regime and devise strategies to derive maximum advantage, it is clear that copyright could make a substantial difference. In the case of Verdi, greater remuneration through full exploitation of the copyright system led perceptibly to a lessening of composing effort.[184]

This does not necessarily imply that copyright had a generally negative effect on the supply of compositional effort. Verdi was an extreme case of outstanding success. Most composers were less successful. But they may have derived motivation from the prospect and hope of great financial returns, demonstrated in such exceptional cases as that of Verdi.[185] The most important motivating force in the copyright system may be the demonstration effect of rare but great cases, leading young people optimistically to choose music and, with talent and luck, composition as a profession.

If this is true, one might expect abrupt changes from the absence to the presence of effective copyright to induce an increase in the number of individuals entering the composing profession, other cultural variables held equal. The data from our sample of 646 composers permit a crude test. For large and relatively homogeneous nations there were two sudden changes in the musical copyright regime comfortably within our two-century coverage span: the 1777 legal victory of J. C. Bach in England, and the enactment of a French copyright law in 1793. The hypothesis to be tested is that growth in the number of composers reaching adulthood after the emergence of copyright laws should be greater relative to a prior control period in nations providing effective musical copyright than for comparable European nations without copyright. For each of two cases, England and France, we take as the comparison group Germany, Austria, and Italy, which did not have effective copyright laws until 1837 or 1840, too late to have much influence on career choices of composers born before 1850.

For England, we use as the postcopyright period the time span from 1767 to 1849, since composers born in 1767 would have become twenty years old after ten years of experience had been accumulated under the new (post-Bach) copyright regime. For the precopyright period we select composers born from 1700 to 1752. Composers born in 1752 would have reached the age of 25 by the time of J. C. Bach's legal victory—too late in most instances to embark upon composing as a career. Using the same data as those analyzed in chapter 5, we find the average number of composers born per million population per decade in the precopyright and postcopyright birth-date periods for four nations:

Nation	(a) Pre: 1700–1752	(b) Post: 1767–1849	b / a
United Kingdom	0.348	0.140	0.40
Germany	0.493	0.361	0.73
Italy	0.527	0.186	0.35
Austria	0.713	0.678	0.95

For two of the three comparisons, the growth in the number of composers per million population in no-copyright nations was greater than for postcopyright United Kingdom; for the third, Italy, the shortfall relative to the United Kingdom is small. The hypothesis of a positive copyright effect is not supported.

Following similar reasoning, we take as the precopyright period for France 1700–1768 and as the postcopyright period 1783–1849. The comparisons are as follows:

Nation	(a) Pre: 1700–1768	(b) Post: 1783–1849	b / a
France	0.126	0.194	1.54
Germany	0.527	0.340	0.65
Italy	0.487	0.153	0.31
Austria	0.857	0.740	0.86

Here the hypothesis is supported; the growth of composer vocations was more rapid in postcopyright France than in all three comparison nations. To be sure, the change in French copyright law was only a side show in a social revolution of tumultuous impact, and even before the French law was enacted, France had the most extensive and best-enforced system of royal privileges. The most that can be said is that the evidence is suggestive, but not causally conclusive.

We conclude with a tentative verdict of "unproved." The emergence of formal copyright laws was undoubtedly important for composers as well as for their publishers. But it remains unclear whether changes in copyright law elicited systematic changes in the choice of composing as a vocation.

Chapter 8

CONCLUSION

IT IS CUSTOMARY to conclude extended works, both in instrumental music and prose, with some kind of coda or cadenza. We defer to that tradition here, recapitulating and resolving some principal themes with the least possible use of *crescendo* markings.

The overarching premise of this book is that markets matter. At least since the middle ages, there have always been markets for composers' services and their works. Everyone who has thought seriously about the problem agrees that the orientation of those markets changed over time. The dominant early paradigm entailed employment of composers by the nobility or religious establishments, with market transactions occurring mainly at the start of what might prove to be a long-term relationship. Then the emphasis changed to freelance activity typically embedded in transactions of shorter duration, such as for the composition or publication of a specific work or performance at a designated series of concerts, with greater variability of economic outcomes but also more potential for especially large financial rewards. One contribution of this book is to show that the transition was not abrupt, with Mozart's career, as some have argued, marking a turning point, but gradual and evolutionary. We have found significant traces of freelance activity among composers born during the second half of the seventeenth century, and employment by noble patrons and the church continued—to be sure, at reduced levels—for composers born during the first half of the nineteenth century. More fundamental social developments underlay these changes: the demise of the feudal system, including the support of religious establishments through revenues from feudal landholdings; and the growth of a prosperous middle class eager to perform music and hear it performed.

A more difficult question is whether one support system was better than another in encouraging composers' creative efforts. This question can be subdivided into two parts: whether the systems differed in the efficacy of incentives to embrace composing as a profession, and whether the quality of composers' creative output differed systematically with the mode in which the composers were employed. Certainly, each had advantages and disadvantages from the composer's perspective, as Joseph Haydn recognized in a 1791 letter during his first visit to London: "The realization that I am no bond-servant makes ample amend for all my toils [as a freelance composer]."[1]

The evidence assembled here provides some support for the proposition that the proliferation of court music ensembles encouraged young people to become musicians and, given sufficient talent, composers. The number of enduring composers born per million population was higher in the mid to late eighteenth century, when court music employment had its heyday, than in the nineteenth century, when the noble courts fell upon hard times while the private demand for composers' output grew. We have seen too that, after controlling for other relevant variables, the employment of composers tended to be highest relative to population in the four national territories — Austria, Germany, Italy, and Czechoslovakia — where disintegration of the Holy Roman Empire left a fragmented structure of noble courts competing for prestige. On the other hand Germany, with the most richly diversified set of independent courts, does not stand out in this respect. And composers exhibited at least as strong an attraction to musical activities in free cities (where employment with the nobility was absent) as in the rest of Germany. Thus, the evidence favoring the noble courts hypothesis is mixed.

As a crude index of the quality of composers' creations, we have used the length of *Schwann Opus* recorded-music listings. Those listings indicate how well a composer's works have held up in the minds of record-making artists and the record-buying public. They were, we have seen, at best weakly correlated with how well composers fared financially during their own lifetimes. We found that by the *Schwann* listing measure, sample members who engaged in substantial freelance composing were significantly more productive than those who did not. Those who served as court Kapellmeister or received outright court subsidies were also more productive than those who lacked such positions. The direction in which causation ran remains unclear. It does not necessarily follow that being a freelance artist or being named director of a court orchestra was conducive in its own right to creating music of enduring quality. It is equally possible that composers with the best creative talent were more likely, all else equal, to be selected for leadership positions in court orchestras and/or to perceive a balance of probable rewards over costs favorable to seeking their fortune in freelance composing. There is qualitative evidence supporting both chains of causation, so the truth is undoubtedly complex.

Although no sharp turning points are visible within the time frame spanned by our sample of composers born between 1650 and 1849, our analysis of U.S. piano production shows that such a turning point did occur during the 1920s, when radios began to broadcast music and electrical phonographs made accurate reproduction of music possible within consumers' homes. Those technological developments made music available and affordable to virtually all citizens of industrialized nations and transformed the enjoyment of music by the middle classes from what had been preponderantly a self-activated endeavor to a passive activity. Instead of making music oneself, one could listen at home to music performed by the best professionals. The consequences were radical from the standpoint of both consumers and producers of music.

For those who composed music, the changes in technology, along with the Berne copyright convention, meant that one could reach out to and derive revenue from much larger markets than was possible through the live performances and sheet music sales that dominated freelance market access during the eighteenth and nineteenth centuries. Larger markets meant larger potential revenues — indeed, for music that satisfied more or less "popular" tastes, huge potential revenues. Although there were exceptions such as John Gay in the early eighteenth century and Vienna's Strauss family during the first half of the nineteenth century, most composers of what we now call classical music were reluctant to seek mass-market audiences, if not because of an aversion to popularization per se, then because the media for reaching those audiences were so limited. But the advent of radio, phonographs, and more recently video broadcasting and high-fidelity amplification has removed those limitations, causing the supply side to bifurcate. Most composers and performers direct their efforts toward the mass markets, where rewards beyond the dreams of avarice can be realized by the relatively few who experience great success.[2] For the minority who compose or perform "serious" music, the markets are more limited in absolute magnitude and fragmented by continuing competition from recorded music written by earlier generations of composers. Even so, substantial financial rewards can be achieved by those who target their offerings to lucrative classical music niches — for instance, the advances of $15 million to $18 million paid to the Three Tenors (José Carreras, Plácido Domingo, and Luciano Pavarotti) for the 1994 (Los Angeles) and 1998 (Paris) World Cup concerts heard with amplification by large live audiences, broadcast to a billion-viewer audience through television, and recorded for postconcert album sales throughout the world.[3]

For classical music, another form of bifurcation has occurred. To the extent that performances are broadcast and/or recorded, electronic media have broadened markets and increased the demand base from which revenues can be extracted. But most performances are not broadcast or recorded. And for them, what is called Baumol's cost disease applies with a vengeance.[4]

The problem arises paradoxically from the phenomenon that has enriched the great masses of consumers and increased their ability to consume music, among other things — productivity growth. Economy-wide productivity growth raises the quantity and value of goods and services produced by any given number of workers and hence increases the real income of the average worker. As the income of workers in high-productivity-growth sectors such as manufacturing, air transportation, telecommunications, banking, and the like rises to reflect higher absolute productivity, so also must the incomes of workers in industries with lower productivity growth rates, since their employers must raise the wages they offer more or less apace to remain competitive in labor markets. The need to keep pace applies also to orchestras, opera companies, and the like, for if their wages fall too far behind the front-runners, most young people facing the choice will opt to become software writers, chemical engineers, or advertising-agency staff members rather than musicians. But presenting live performances of music is an activity in which it is especially difficult to achieve productivity growth. In 1835 it took eight talented musicians about thirty minutes to perform Mendelssohn's E-flat Octet op. 20, and it takes the same number of musicians the same amount of time to perform the octet in 2002. Absent a secondary broadcast or recordings market, which is often precluded by competition from earlier recordings, live music performance is an activity of unusually low productivity growth.[5] If the wages of musicians must rise to stay abreast of those in high productivity industries but productivity growth is minimal, the cost of a given live performance must rise relative to the cost of goods and services experiencing rapid productivity growth. Thus, live musical performances must become increasingly expensive relative to other goods and services and run a risk of pricing themselves out of all but the most well-heeled of consumers' budgets.

The solution to this contemporary "cost disease" problem is subsidy, and hence a reversion to the principal means used to support classical music during the seventeenth and eighteenth centuries. One source of subsidy — more generous on the European continent than in America — is government, which is the analogue of the noble courts that were the principal locus of political governance before the demise of feudalism. The other main source of subsidies consists of those who enjoy live performances and attend then with some frequency. They are analogous to the wealthy nobles, bankers, merchants, and barristers who provided front-end investment capital and continuing subsidies in exchange for privileged boxes from which to hear eighteenth-century operas in European cities. The main change has come from a broadening of the subsidy base, in part because there are relatively more citizens with the wealth needed to afford subsidy donations[6] and partly because radio, television, telephone, and electronic mail reduce the cost of contacting a broad base of potential subsidy providers.

Affluent patrons have always played a role in supporting live musical performances. But that role has waned and waxed over long cycles — high in the eighteenth century, especially for opera; lower as prosperity increased during the nineteenth century but before artists' wages advanced appreciably; and higher again in the twentieth and twenty-first centuries as artists' wages rise to keep pace with those of high-productivity industries, but productivity remains stagnant (again, ignoring broadcast and record opportunities). In a sense then, we have come full circle. But there is an important difference. During the eighteenth century, composers and performers were locked into onerous servile relationships with their noble subsidy-providing masters. In the twenty-first century, composers and (at least solo and first-chair) performers are the star guests at cocktail parties held to honor (and milk) wealthy patrons. Higher social status and the escape from servility, along with more generous economic rewards propelled by general productivity growth and (for a few) the vast markets reached by electronic media, have enhanced the welfare of music composers and performers. It is doubtful whether a composer as great as Mozart or Schubert could die in abject poverty today. Whether this broad-based improvement has led to a renewed era of great creativity in music composition is debatable. Since tastes differ, sidestepping that debate seems the better part of valor.

A CURRENCY CONVERSION MATRIX

IN EUROPE during the period covered by this book, keeping track of currency exchange rates was a task to which few if any were equal. Literally hundreds of currencies were in circulation. On his first extended tour to display the talents of his prodigy children, Leopold Mozart wrote from Brussels in 1763 to his landlord and friend in Salzburg:[1]

> In Coblenz and in the whole Trier area we had to learn another set of monetary accounts. There our imperial coins were useless, and one had to understand Petermäncher [a coin with an image of the apostle Peter embossed], including both heavy and light kreutzer. In Cologne and Bonn they mean nothing; there you begin with stüber and fettmännchen [literally, fat men, a half-stüber coin]. In Aachen the stüber busch and the mark appeared; and in large denominations the reichsthaler and pattacons, and also schillings and the like, along with sous in Liege. And here [in Brussels] all that is forgotten; you have to become familiar with other sous, escalins, the brabant gulden, and plaquets (each of which is worth three and one-half escalins), etc. It's unbelievable what you can lose here and there dealing in money matters.

All these currencies were encountered within a 150-kilometer radius around Liege. Since this book attempts to evaluate how composers fared in their money matters, some means of extracting order from the chaos is necessary.

Some composer biographies ignore the currency problem; some convert the values of lesser-known currencies into diverse better-known contemporary variants; and some try to leap from the value of a particular currency two centuries or more ago into present-day U.S. dollars. The third approach is hopeless. According to estimates by Angus Maddison, the real per capita income and, subject to many caveats, the purchasing power of the average European in 1998 was 15 to 20 times the counterpart value for Europeans in the year 1700.[2] In eighteenth-century Europe, there were no electric lights, no airplanes, no penicillin, no telephones, no washing machines, no air conditioning, no frozen foods, no stereophonic music players, no packaged vitamins, and very few houses with interior plumbing, to name only a few examples. Life was in a material sense incomparably different from life today. But if blessed with decent health, the average member of a (much smaller) middle class can scarcely be said to have been less happy than his or her counterpart today. Economists — or at least some economists — recognize that the level of one's income relative to one's expectations and to one's peers has more to do with happiness or its absence than absolute levels of material prosperity.[3] To place incomes and costs in perspective, one needs to know what the norms were for the society in which they existed.

It would be formidably difficult, however, to provide norms for each of the dozens of currencies that appear in this book. Some common denominator is needed. The benchmark used throughout this book is the English pound sterling, which, unlike most other currencies of two centuries ago, still exists, and which was in its time one of the most stable European currencies. To be sure, its purchasing power waxed and waned over time with macroeconomic deflation and inflation, but thanks in part to the steady presence of the Bank of England, founded in 1694, the fluctuations tended to be less violent than those of other currencies such as the Viennese florin or the Prussian thaler.

Thus, the task here is to fill a void that impedes insight by both musicologists and economic historians — the lack of systematic tables by which one can take any of a dozen or so once-popular currencies and convert them into a pound sterling common denominator for any chosen year within the span of two and one-half centuries. This was done using two kinds of sources: the extended exchange-rate time series published in historical works for a few key currencies; and the huge amount of data on ad hoc exchange rates scattered throughout the literature, and especially from the travel and publication fee records of some composers who kept good diaries and had activities extending into most parts of Europe.

Four main sources were used to establish a baseline,[4] providing exchange rates over an extended period between British pounds sterling; French ecus, livres, and later francs; German schillings, marks, Reichsthaler, and thaler. Separate series were obtained linking Italian lire, zecchini, and scudi to French and German currencies. Then exchange rates for more than 100 ad hoc transactions reported in numerous general historical works and musical biographies were linked or when necessary cross-linked to the baseline currencies. These provided at best only partial time series for the nonbaseline currencies. Minor gaps were filled by linear interpolation; major gaps are left open.

The currencies covered here were of three main types: gold-based, silver-based, and paper. Gold coins, which tended to be most stable in value, included the Louis d'or and Napoleon d'or issued in France, the Friedrich d'or of Prussia, the English guinea (= £1.05),[5] the Italian zecchini, and ducats of widely varying gold content issued in Germany,

Austria, and Italy. Only after several unsuccessful attempts to estimate uniform ducat exchange rates was it realized that Italian ducats were worth only about one-third the value of German and Austrian ducats. Silver coins included the English shilling (one-twentieth of a pound), the thaler and marks issued in diverse parts of Germany,[6] the ecu of France, florins issued originally in Italy and later Austria, and scudi of Italy. Many paper currencies were linked to gold or especially silver counterparts, but were often then debased in times of governmental fiscal stress. The most important one for our purposes was the Viennese florin, identically known as the gulden, which was issued under diverse names during the Napoleonic wars. It eventually stabilized as the florin W.W. (Wiener Währung, or Viennese standard), at a value much less than that of the silver florin C.M. (i.e., *Conventionsmünze*, a coin whose silver content had been established by convention). Fluctuations in value between the Viennese *Conventionsmünze* florin (or gulden) and the various paper florins were so tumultuous that we present here a series beginning only in 1810, after some degree of stability was achieved. For information on earlier conversion rates, one is referred to the excellent year-to-year survey by Julia Moore (1987, pp. 8–10 and 119–30). For French currency too, the Napoleonic wars wreaked such monetary havoc that we make no attempt to estimate values for the period from 1791 to 1809, after which a new medium, the franc, emerged.

The currency values, all measured in terms of the number of units of a currency required to purchase an English pound sterling, are arrayed at five-year intervals in table 1A.1.[7] Included in the table are linear interpolations of values for which no direct conversions were available. These are indicated by italics in table 1A.1.

One should not assume that the table 1A.1 conversions achieve pinpoint precision. Anyone who has traveled knows that the exchange rate one secures at a reputable bank is less favorable than the rates published for interbank transactions in financial journals, and that the rates obtained from money changers in the temple — for example, the Cambio stalls in Venice or Pisa — are even less favorable. Such market imperfections and transactions costs were more pronounced two centuries ago than they are today, so the exchange rates Leopold Mozart reported for cash transactions in Brussels could easily vary from the rates obtained through interbank bills of exchange (which he often used) by as much as 10 percent.[8] Three-step conversions — such as from florins to Louis d'or to pounds sterling — add further margins of error. The data for thaler are subject to especially great uncertainty. Circulating in Germany during the eighteenth and nineteenth centuries were several different kinds of thaler — for instance, Reichsthaler, Prussian thaler, Saxonian thaler, and Rhineland thaler (or Rheinthaler), to offer what is

TABLE 1A.1
Units of Currency Exhanging for One English Pound Sterling*

Year	French Ecu	French Livre	French Franc	Louis d'Or	German Mark	German Reichsthaler	German Thaler
1670	4.58	13.75	.	.	13.11	4.37	6.56
1675	4.19	12.58	.	.	12.29	4.10	6.15
1680	4.41	13.23	.	.	13.01	4.34	6.51
1685	4.32	12.94	.	0.87	12.58	4.29	6.44
1690	4.56	13.68	.	0.93	12.33	4.11	6.17
1695	3.97	11.92	.	0.99	10.79	3.60	5.40
1700	5.15	15.45	.	0.99	12.89	4.30	6.45
1705	5.44	16.31	.	1.00	12.29	4.10	6.14
1710	5.02	15.06	.	1.00	12.26	4.09	6.13
1715	5.72	17.17	.	0.74	13.17	4.39	6.58
1720	14.57	43.72	.	0.84	12.81	4.27	6.40
1725	6.31	18.94	.	1.19	12.73	4.24	6.36
1730	7.39	22.17	.	1.02	12.45	4.15	6.23
1735	7.69	23.07	.	0.95	13.25	4.42	6.62
1740	7.43	22.28	.	0.88	12.80	4.27	6.40
1745	7.54	22.63	.	0.97	12.83	4.28	6.41
1750	7.61	22.84	.	1.05	12.59	4.20	6.29
1755	7.75	23.26	.	1.03	12.93	4.31	6.47
1760	7.84	23.51	.	1.00	12.74	4.25	6.37
1765	7.69	23.08	.	1.05	13.00	4.33	6.50
1770	7.59	22.78	.	1.04	12.47	4.16	6.24
1775	7.82	23.45	.	1.02	12.86	4.29	6.43
1780	8.17	24.51	.	1.03	12.95	4.25	5.95
1785	8.41	25.23	.	1.05	13.19	4.20	5.48
1790	.	.	.	1.06	13.26	5.10	5.00
1795	.	.	.	0.94	12.65	6.00	4.90
1800	.	.	.	0.82	12.21	7.32	4.80
1805	.	.	.	0.89	13.07	6.88	4.70
1810	.	.	20.75	0.95	11.18	6.44	4.60
1815	.	.	21.53	1.02	11.88	6.00	4.50
1820	.	.	25.55	1.08	13.81	6.06	5.05
1825	.	.	25.21	1.05	13.84	6.11	5.61
1830	.	.	25.56	1.03	13.98	6.39	6.16
1835	.	.	25.60	1.00	13.88	6.66	6.71
1840	.	.	25.59	1.01	13.70	5.48	6.72
1845	.	.	25.39	1.14	13.86	7.41	7.00
1850	.	.	25.54	1.27	13.70	.	6.98
1855	.	.	25.47	.	13.52	.	6.97
1860	.	.	25.45	.	13.39	.	6.95
1865	.	.	25.48	.	13.63	.	6.93
1870	.	.	25.62	.	13.70	.	6.92
1875	.	.	25.49	.	20.71	.	6.90
1880	.	.	25.51	.	20.65	.	.
1885	.	.	25.44	.	20.60	.	.
1890	.	.	25.46	.	20.66	.	.
1895	.	.	25.34	.	20.58	.	.
1900	.	.	25.38	.	20.52	.	.

*Italics indicate linear interpolations for years without direct conversions.

TABLE 1A.1 *Continued*

Year	Austrian Ducat	Italian Ducat	Austrian Florin C.M.	Austrian Florin W.W.	Italian Lira	Italian Scudo	Italian Zecchino
1670	.	.	.	.	.	.	.
1675	.	.	.	.	.	.	.
1680	.	.	7.29	.	.	.	.
1685	.	.	7.47	.	.	.	.
1690	.	.	7.65	.	.	.	.
1695	.	.	7.83	.	15.25	3.72	.
1700	.	.	8.01	.	20.71	4.36	0.69
1705	2.31	.	8.18	.	26.16	5.00	1.02
1710	2.35	.	8.36	.	31.62	4.26	1.36
1715	2.39	.	8.54	.	37.08	3.52	1.69
1720	2.42	.	8.72	.	42.53	3.75	1.80
1725	2.46	.	8.90	.	47.99	3.98	1.90
1730	2.36	6.20	8.91	.	34.00	4.21	2.01
1735	2.27	6.19	8.73	.	20.00	4.44	2.11
1740	2.17	6.19	8.55	.	20.00	4.86	2.10
1745	2.08	6.18	8.36	.	20.00	5.28	2.09
1750	1.98	6.17	8.18	.	25.65	5.70	2.08
1755	1.99	6.16	8.00	.	27.32	4.92	2.07
1760	2.00	6.16	8.50	.	28.98	4.14	2.06
1765	2.13	6.15	9.17	.	27.16	4.12	2.05
1770	1.96	6.14	9.48	.	25.35	4.09	2.04
1775	2.06	6.14	9.80	.	23.53	4.07	2.03
1780	2.13	6.13	9.80	.	21.72	4.05	2.02
1785	1.98	6.12	8.91	.	19.90	4.02	2.01
1790	2.00	6.12	9.76	.	19.87	4.00	2.01
1795	2.22	6.11	9.50	.	19.83	3.97	2.00
1800	2.44	6.10	11.00	.	19.80	3.95	2.00
1805	2.03	6.09	12.70	.	22.35	3.93	2.05
1810	2.00	6.09	10.85	10.00	24.90	3.90	2.09
1815	2.00	6.08	9.00	15.00	28.37	3.88	2.14
1820	2.04	6.03	10.00	20.00	30.69	4.37	2.18
1825	2.03	6.01	11.00	25.00	33.00	4.85	2.09
1830	2.01	5.99	11.00	25.46	30.67	3.60	2.00
1835	2.00	6.01	10.00	25.91	29.39	.	2.54
1840	2.16	6.03	10.55	26.37	30.83	.	3.08
1845	2.31	6.06	10.51	.	30.24	.	.
1850	.	.	10.47	.	29.65	.	.
1855	.	.	10.42	.	29.07	.	.
1860	.	.	10.38	.	28.48	.	.
1865	.	.	10.38	.	27.89	.	.
1870	.	.	10.34	.	27.30	.	.
1875	.	.	10.30	.	26.72	.	.
1880	.	.	10.25	.	26.13	.	.
1885	.	.	10.17	.	25.54	.	.
1890	.	.	.	.	.	.	.
1895	.	.	.	.	.	.	.
1900	.	.	.	.	.	.	.

undoubtedly a less than exhaustive listing. The sources utilized are not always clear about which variant they assume; values not explicitly designated as Reichsthaler have been assumed to be plain thaler of undoubtedly varying mixtures. An analysis of the week-by-week expenditure patterns of Robert and Clara Schumann for specific goods and services (see the appendix to chapter 4) suggests that during the 1840s and early 1850s, the differences in purchasing power between Saxonian thaler and Rheinthaler were small.[9] (The Schumanns migrated to the Rhineland in 1850.) Quite generally, one should assume that the exchange rates provided in table 1A.1 are accurate to no more than plus or minus 10 percent, 80 to 90 percent of the time. This degree of accuracy appears sufficient to make tolerably well-founded comparisons. Some young scholar fluent in several languages would do a great public service extending the data to other currencies (such as for Amsterdam, Russia, and Spain) and filling in and perfecting the estimates presented in table 1A.1.

To complete the process, one needs a benchmark indicating what the average worker could expect to earn in any given year. The benchmark used here is the time series meticulously compiled by E. H. Phelps Brown and Sheila Hopkins (1955). They estimate the average money wage rates per day (or after 1847, per 10 hours) for building craftsmen (notably, carpenters and masons) and common building laborers in southern England over many centuries, including the 1650–1900 period of greatest interest here.

Their estimates, translated into annual incomes assuming a 300-day work year and interpolated linearly for years on which the authors provide no data, are presented in figure 1A.1. Nominal values—that is, raw earnings without adjustment for the cost of living—are shown by a black line for craftsmen and a gray line for laborers. One sees that a fully employed building craftsman earned about £26 in 1705, £30 in 1750, and then experienced rapid pay increases to £54 in 1808 and thereafter to £60 in 1828. Some of these increases were attributable to generalized inflation. Using parallel data compiled by Phelps Brown and Hopkins (1956), the white line ("real craftsmen") divides the wages of building craftsmen by rough estimates of changes in the cost of living, computed as a 7-year moving average, with the index for 1790 being 1.00, and higher values of the index connoting higher prices for consumable goods. Indexing 1790 = 1.00 means that the nominal and real craftsmen wage indexes coincide in 1790. Purchasing-power-adjusted wages eroded during the second half of the eighteenth century and then plunged during the Napoleonic wars (1792–1815). They then rose, surpassing their 1736 peak level only in 1832. Since similar macroeconomic forces were affecting other European nations, the English data serve tolerably well as a benchmark of what skilled and unskilled male

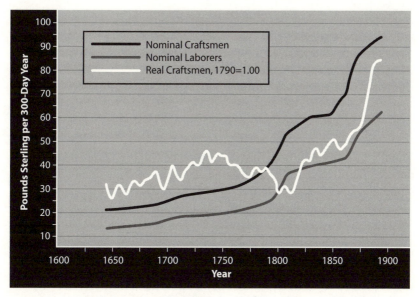

FIGURE 1A.1 Estimated Annual Wages of English Building Tradesmen (from Research by Phelps Brown and Hopkins)

urban workers could earn in other parts of Europe. Needless to say, agricultural workers and domestic servants earned less than building craftsmen and building laborers; more highly skilled workers earned more.

Composers who traveled from the European continent to England frequently remarked that the cost of living in London was much higher than what they experienced at home.[10] What this means is that the value of the pound sterling, if calculated at hypothetical exchange rates equating purchasing power in London and elsewhere, would be lower than it would be at the market exchange rates actually used to compute the series in table 1A.1. In effect, one could buy a pound sterling of equivalent purchasing power for fewer Viennese florins than the table indicates. Consequently, the person with an equivalent wage of £30 in 1750, as calculated from table 1A.1, would enjoy a somewhat higher material standard of living at home than his southern England counterpart, especially in house rents and (less clearly) the purchase of services. "Somewhat higher" is all the precision that can be mustered under the circumstances. Estimating purchasing-power parities is much more difficult than ascertaining market exchange rates, and they varied from city to city within European currency regions as well as between England and continental regions. Thus, the benchmarks in table 1A.1 are crude, but they provide much better perspective than having to deal with disparate currencies in a relational vacuum.

CONSUMPTION OUTLAYS OF ROBERT

AND CLARA SCHUMANN, 1841

Thanks to the compulsive record keeping of Robert Schumann, a fairly detailed account of the consumption spending by a moderately affluent composer-and-performer family can be reconstructed.[1] Chosen for analysis is the year 1841, which was the first calendar year following the marriage of Robert Schumann and Clara Wieck (spelled Klara in the diaries) in September 1840. Their first child, Marie, was born on September 1, 1841. The Schumanns' residence in Leipzig during that year was interrupted by only two short trips, on whose expenses no detailed records survive, although Robert's total expenditures on his trip to Weimar were recorded as 19 Saxonian thaler and on a trip to Dresden 62 thaler. Other years provide a less clear picture of normal consumption outlays because of more extended absences. No consistent attempt is made to convert thaler into the English pound sterling common denominator used in other parts of this book. In 1841 one English pound exchanged for approximately 6.75 thaler. A fully employed building craftsman in southern England at the time earned roughly £60 per year, or 405 thaler at prevailing exchange rates.

Table 4A.1 summarizes the Schumanns' 1841 consumption expenditures, rounded to the nearest thaler, and omitting money spent on the Weimar and Dresden trips and the separately tallied expenses of the journal *Die neue Zeitschrift für Musik* (The New Journal of Music), owned and edited by Robert Schumann. Some explanatory observations are warranted.

The largest single outlay category was the 6-thaler weekly allowance drawn by Clara, raised to 7 thaler following the birth of their daughter, and with frequent supplements. The uses are not itemized. Because there is no separate mention of spending for food consumed at home, except when special guests were invited to dinner, a significant fraction of the allowance must have gone toward food and other household-operation necessities. The second largest category was for meals outside the Schumann home. It was apparently customary for at least one outside meal to be taken daily; there are approximately 390 individual entries for such outlays, usually at the Gasthaus Kaffeebaum, although dinners for guests often took place at more expensive venues such as

TABLE 4A.1

Schumann Family Expenditures in 1841

Category	Thaler	Percent of Total
Clara's weekly allowance	634	33.02
Outside meals	208	10.83
Furniture	186	9.69
Rent	130	6.77
Travel	108	5.63
Bulk wine and spirits	83	4.32
Coal and wood	81	4.22
Household help	77	4.01
Gifts	75	3.91
Clothing	75	3.91
Cigars	51	2.66
Supplies, including note paper	39	2.03
Medical	24	1.25
Music copying	21	1.09
Public bath	16	0.83
Legal services	11	0.57
Entertainment	8	0.42
Insurance	7	0.36
Books and newspapers	6	0.31
Taxes	5	0.26
Other	30	1.56
Unknown	45	2.34
Total	1,920	100.00

Leipzig's Hôtel de Bavière. An exception to the nonitemization of at-home food purchases was for outlays on wine and other spirits. Some wine was bought in bulk containers, other wine in bottles. More detailed records for 1842 reveal that twelve bottles of champagne could be purchased for 14 thaler; twelve bottles of what must have been an excellent seven-year old Johannisberger wine cost 11 thaler.

Robert Schumann was an avid cigar smoker. Dividing his 1841 outlays by per-unit prices recorded on various occasions, one estimates that his consumption averaged approximately five cigars per day. For the editor of an important journal, the spending on books and newspapers seems remarkably low. The explanation is that Schumann borrowed books from and did most of his newspaper reading at a Leipzig museum-library, for which he paid a regular fee not included in the "books and newspapers" category. Also surprising at first glance are the Schumanns' modest outlays for entertainment (dinners for guests are mostly recorded under "outside meals"). Because of Robert's editorial position, admission to most public concerts and theater performances was apparently gratis. The travel expenditures explicitly recorded here include only travel within the Leipzig area, mostly for local carriage rides.

The Schumanns rented their apartment in 1841 and continued to rent in the subsequent years of their marriage. Later rentals for the space required to house an enlarged family rose to as much as 270 thaler per year. In 1840 Clara's expenditures to furnish their first apartment amounted to 1,797 thaler; thus, the 186 thaler spent on furniture in 1841 must have been for rounding-out purchases. It is interesting to see that what would today be called household insurance — apparently, covering mainly fire risks — was available in 1841, at the modest cost of 7 thaler annually. Government activities at the time were financed largely through customs duties, excise taxes, and land taxes — hence the enviably low direct-tax expenditure.

Like most middle-class families of that era, the Schumanns had considerable help to maintain their household. During the early 1840s (the explicit data for 1841 are less clear), their housekeeper received 30 thaler per year, their cook 24 thaler (dispensed with after 1846), and their child nurse 1 thaler per month — all presumably supplemented by room and board in the Schumann household along with gifts at Christmastime. Most of the household help were recruited by Schumann's brother Carl from the vicinity of their home town, Zwickau, and Carl's nearby residence in Schneeberg, where able unmarried daughters could presumably be found to work at lower wages than natives of bustling Leipzig. The wet nurse for baby Marie received 4 thaler per month beginning in September 1841. The midwife's services for delivery of Marie cost 8 thaler.

The Schumanns' recorded consumption outlays totalling 1,920 thaler (approximately £284 — 4.7 times the estimated full-time annual income of an English building craftsman) — were well in excess of their 1841 earnings. Robert's earnings from publication fees that year were 303 thaler; Clara's net from a concert in Leipzig 157 thaler. The amount of income Robert derived from the journal he edited is more difficult to ascertain. From the information available in scattered accounts, the net income could not have been more than 118 thaler. The rest of their outlays had to be financed out of their capital, which amounted to 8,493 thaler in July 1841. Of this, 4,100 thaler from his inheritance were invested by Robert's brother Carl, who paid interest on the principal totaling 202 thaler in 1841. The rest of their capital was invested in diverse government securities, paying interest of 3.5 to 5.0 percent per year. The interest payments from those investments were at most 175 thaler. Thus, without drawing down their capital, the Schumanns' current income in 1841 was on the order of 955 thaler. The Schumann budget was balanced by selling off securities, whose reported value declined from 8,493 thaler in July 1841 to 6,452 thaler in January 1842 — a decrease considerably above the deficit on the family's consumption account.[2] Anxiety concerning the excess of their consumption outlays over current income and the declining value of their financial assets led Clara Schumann to undertake more extensive concert tours in subsequent years.

Recorded expenditures on other purchases in the years immediately following 1841 supplement our sketch of what it cost to pursue a relatively affluent middle-class lifestyle in Leipzig during the 1840s. Dresses worn at Clara's public concerts cost 25 to 27 thaler. Robert's eyeglasses cost 3.83 thaler. Vests worn by Robert cost from 2 to 7 thaler; a silk vest was 4.33 thaler. A pound of tea cost 2 thaler. The legal costs incurred in a protracted lawsuit brought by Robert against his father-in-law, who had opposed the marriage to Clara, arguing that Robert was financially irresponsible and deficient in character, amounted to at least 200 thaler — about the same as an excellent grand piano purchased for Clara in 1853. Then as now, attorneys fared well from others' misery.

NOTES

1. The English translation is by the author.
2. Hildesheimer (1982), p. 19.
3. Elias (1993), p. 29. The book appeared first in German as Elias (1991).
4. Baumol and Baumol (1994a), pp. 79–80.
5. Gardner (1994), p. 48.
6. Pohlmann (1962), p. 31 (my translation). Unless otherwise indicated in the references, translations from German works are mine.
7. This summary and the one for Handel are drawn with slight revisions from Scherer (2001b).
8. A similar view is offered by Pohlmann (1962), p. 30, who names as other early freelance composers Georg Philipp Telemann and Reinhard Keiser (1674–1739). Birth and death dates for composers will be indicated only when they are not presented in table 1.1.
9. See Elias (1991), pp. 38–40; Elias (1969); and Baumol and Baumol (1994a), pp. 73–74.
10. Robbins Landon and Jones (1988), p. 240. See also Mozart (1962), vol. 3, p. 373. Collections of composers' letters without substantial interspersed editors' commentaries are cited by the name of the composer rather than that of the editor(s).
11. This argument is advanced in Cowen (1998). Unfortunately, Cowen's Chapter 4, on the evolution of musical forms, contains numerous questionable assertions.
12. Parts of what follows are drawn with revisions from Scherer (2001b).
13. Mozart (1962), vol. 2, p. 274.
14. Verdi (1971), p. 225.
15. A very few composers were found in other issues of the *Schwann Opus* and added to the sample.
16. Surian (1998), pp. 303–4.
17. See Medoff (1996); and Scherer et al. (1999).
18. Braunbehrens (1989), p. 191.
19. See Scherer (2001c). When logarithms of the observations are taken, the coefficient of skewness is found to be 1.16, which implies more inequality than the zero value associated with a log normal distribution.
20. Scherer et al. (2000), pp. 176–79.
21. Actually, 50 is an arbitrary figure, since some of the biographical references and other works consulted covered additional composers not included within the 50. Among those so excluded were two members of the Vienna Strauss family, Wilhelm Friedemann Bach (eldest son of Johann Sebastian Bach), and Alessandro Scarlatti (father of Domenico Scarlatti). Frederick the Great was

viewed principally as an employer of composers, even though he is included in the sample of 646.

CHAPTER 2

1. For an overview of causes and consequences, see Kennedy (1987).

2. See Asch (1997), p. 185; Raynor (1972), pp. 204–5; and, for a more benign view of the casualties, Steinberg (1966), pp. 2–3 and 106–16.

3. Müller (1972), pp. 13–14.

4. See Demetz (1997), pp. 227–30.

5. When the Viennese rejected a French surrender demand in May 1809, the French directed the fire of twenty howitzers upon the city. To protect his failing hearing organs, Ludwig van Beethoven is said to have covered his head with pillows to muffle the sounds. After Vienna surrendered, a dying Joseph Haydn was visited by several French officers, one of whom sang from memory an aria from Haydn's *Seasons*; and an honor guard was posted before Haydn's residence. See Forbes (1967), p. 465; and Gotwals (1963), p. 193 (from the biography by A. C. Dies). When French troops marched into Salzburg in 1800, they robbed Haydn's brother, Johann Michael, of three months' pay and a gold watch. See Croll and Vössing (1987), p. 140.

6. Raynor (1972), p. 351.

7. For example, the Viennese secret police investigated Beethoven, who professed republican tendencies. Roger Draper, "From Far Left to Far Right," *The New Leader*, November 4–18, 1991, p. 21.

8. The *Communist Manifesto*, written by Karl Marx and Friedrich Engels, was in press at the time the first revolution erupted; a French translation reached the streets of Paris by June of 1848. The revolutions, however, were directed more toward feudal institutions and governmental repression than at the kind of worker-capitalist conflict analyzed by Marx and Engels. For Marx's analysis of the governmental changes that followed in France, see his 1852 tract, "The Eighteenth Brumaire of Louis Bonaparte," in Beer (1955), pp. 46–64.

9. Fantel (1971), p. 108.

10. For a compendium of essays exploring many facets of the Enlightenment, see Delon (2001).

11. For an excellent overview, see Boorstein (1983), parts 11–13.

12. This facet of the Enlightenment is the main theme of Berlin (1956).

13. Merton (1962).

14. See especially the essays "Natural Law and the Rights of Man," "Nature," and "Social Contract" in Delon (2001).

15. From "Political Economy," originally published in Diderot's *Encyclopédie*, circa 1755. Translated and reprinted in Crocker (1969), p. 221.

16. See Blum (1978), p. 3; and Good (1984), p. 23.

17. The best single source on this set of issues is Blum (1978).

18. Again, see Blum (1978), chapter 9.

19. See the essay "Feudalism" by Thierry Bressan in Delon (2001), pp. 524–27.

20. See, e.g., Mantoux (1961), chapter 3; and Allen (1994), p. 98.

21. See Allen (1994), pp. 120–21.

22. See Aldingen (1927).

23. As Frederick wrote to Voltaire in anticipation of the second meeting, "He is an amiable and deserving prince. He likes your books and reads them as much as he can." Aldingen (1927), p. 308. See also Haslip (1977), pp. 270–73.

24. He also abolished the Jesuit order and required its members to serve as common priests at a salary of 300 florins per year, a stipend Leopold Mozart found "not so bad after all." Papa Mozart's salary at the time was 360 florins. See Mozart (1962), vol. 1, p. 494. A visit by Pope Pius VI in 1783 to reason with Joseph over his monastery policies led to the revival of Italian opera in Vienna after a five-year hiatus.

25. See Braunbehrens (1989), p. 189.

26. The best survey is Blum (1978), from which is drawn much of this chapter's discussion of reform.

27. Blum (1978), p. 356.

28. See Blum (1978), pp. 388–95; and Good (1984), pp. 74 ff.

29. On the disbanding of court orchestras in imperial Austria during the period when reforms were beginning, but without a clear inference of causation, see Moore (1987), pp. 48, 89, 94, and 562–91.

Emancipation was sufficiently adverse to the fortunes of Modest Mussorgsky's family that it was required to give up its great house in St. Petersburg, and Modest had to divert time from composition to managing the family business. Riesemann (1926), p. 72.

30. Aldingen (1927), p. 281.

31. Good (1984), p. 38.

32. All the national population data used here come from McEvedy and Jones (1978), which has the major advantage of estimating population values for national boundaries as they existed in 1975, and for which consolidation of West and East German populations is easily accomplished.

33. Despite the potato famine of the 1840s, Ireland had the most rapid 200-year growth rate of any European entity, at 0.82 percent per annum.

34. Blum (1978), p. 3.

35. Mitchell (1998), pp 145–60.

36. For a generalization, see Scherer (1999), pp. 20–21.

37. For definitive surveys, see Landes (1969 and 1998); and Mokyr (1990). On the facilitating role of the Enlightenment, see Mokyr (2002).

38. Landes (1969), pp. 13–14. Lower estimates, suggesting a 2.25-times expansion of gross domestic product per capita and annual growth averaging 0.12 percent, are offered by Maddison (2001), p. 46.

39. Crafts (1996), p. 198.

40. They are taken from Maddison (1995), pp. 194–96.

41. See Good (1984), especially pp. 13–37.

42. Because the later reconstructions differ in some cases from those originally estimated by Maddison for 1820 and because the later reconstruction includes no 1900 data, the estimates for 1700 have been adjusted to be compatible with his earlier 1820 estimates.

43. Williamson (1985), chapter 2 and pp. 200–204.

44. Williamson (1985), p. 17.

45. Lindert (1986), p. 1141.

46. Lindert (1986), p. 1137.

47. Membership in this class, whose boundaries changed over time with social conventions, was apparently by self-identification in estate reports. Usually but not always it implies possession of a family coat of arms and antecedents in the landed aristocracy. See W. A. Phillips, "Gentleman," *The Encyclopaedia Britannica*, 11th ed., vol. 11, pp. 604–6. (New York: Encyclopaedia Britannica Co., 1910).

48. Consider what Papageno intended to do when he found his true love: "Die welche mir am liebsten wär', der gebe ich gleich ein Zuckerl her" (To the one who pleases me most, I'll promptly give a sugar candy). "Luxury" is used here in the lay sense. Mokyr (1988) finds income elasticities lower than those that would characterize luxuries in the economist's technical sense.

49. Estimates for the first two periods, correcting problems in earlier data, are from Mokyr (1988, p. 75). The estimate for the early 1900s is from Mitchell (1988), pp. 709–10. U.S. sugar consumption reached an all-time high of 110 pounds per capita in 1930, declining slightly thereafter and then sharply during the 1970s as high-fructose corn syrup was substituted for sugar.

50. For a lean theoretical treatment, see Scherer (forthcoming). Pioneering earlier contributions include Schmookler (1966); Spence and Owen (1977); and Romer (1990).

51. Notably, from the work of Rosamond McGuinness extracting information from concert and sheet music advertisements in eighteenth-century London newspapers. The data are expected to be made available in compact disk form.

52. Ehrlich (1990), p. 222.

53. U.S. Bureau of the Census (1960), p. 417.

54. U.S. Bureau of the Census (1960), pp. 417 and 491.

55. Section contributed by Cyril Ehrlich in Sadie (1980), vol. 14, pp. 704–6.

56. From U.S. Bureau of the Census (1960), pp. 116–17.

57. The three-value quality index was correlated with piano shipping weight, $r = 0.735$, and with price-level-adjusted prices, $r = 0.747$, where the r values are simple two-variable correlation coefficients. Highest-quality pianos had prices 20 percent higher on average than medium-quality pianos; lowest-quality offerings (considering only pianos with 88 keys) had prices 21 percent lower on average than medium-quality pianos.

58. The variables are defined as follows:

PIANOS   Number of pianos produced in given year (in thousands).

INCOME   Average income per capita, at 1990 purchasing power levels.

PRICE   Index of quality-adjusted prices, with average = 1.00.

RADIOS   Number of U.S. households with radios (in thousands).

PHONOS   Number of U.S. households with phonographs (in thousands).

STOCK   Estimated stock of pianos in U.S. (in thousands).

SPREAD   Stock of pianos divided by number of families (in percent).

To interpret the relationships in terms of percentage changes or elasticities, logarithms (to base 10) were taken of each variable. Where N is the number of observations, multiple regressions for the full time series, first using STOCK and then SPREAD as alternative explanatory variables, were as follows:

(1) Log PIANOS = -12.25 + 4.32 log INCOME $-$ 0.195 log RADIOS
                [3.05]   [2.77]   [6.22]

    + 0.038 log PHONOS $-$ 0.378 log STOCK; R^2 = 0.901, N = 17.
     [0.42]   [0.65]

(2) Log PIANOS = -9.51 + 3.16 log INCOME $-$ 0.173 log RADIOS
              [3.19]   [3.23]   [4.77]

    -0.023 log PHONOS + 0.31 log SPREAD; R^2 = 0.899, N = 17.
     [0.24]   [0.41]

For the smaller sample on which price data were available, the corresponding regression equations were as follows:

(3) Log PIANOS = -14.79 + 2.40 log INCOME $-$ 0.777 log PRICE
              [4.22]   [1.63]   [1.32]
    $-$ 0.0056 log RADIOS $-$ 2.44 log PHONOS + 4.62 log STOCK;
     [0.08]   [2.99]   [2.59]
    R^2 = 0.887; N = 12.

(4) Log PIANOS = -7.80 + 2.75 log INCOME $-$ 0.624 log PRICE
              [1.34]   [1.82]   [0.96]
    $-$ 0.012 log RADIOS $-$ 1.10 log PHONOS + 2.98 log SPREAD;
     [0.16]   [2.62]   [2.04]
    R^2 = 0.859; N = 12.

When the price variables are excluded from these regressions, the t-ratios on INCOME rise to 2.08 and 2.05, suggesting competition between the income and price variable for explanatory power—a common problem when the number of observations is small in relation to the number of explanatory variables. In contrast to the full-sample regressions, the number of phonographs is more powerful here than the number of radios as an explanatory variable representing competitive products. Note the theoretically implausible "plus" sign on the STOCK and SPREAD variables—probably attributable to the exclusion of early observations for those variables when piano usage was much less widespread.

59. In 1929 in the U.S., 10.25 million families had radios and 10.4 million had phonographs, compared to an overestimate (because pianos were also used in nonfamily settings such as schools and places of entertainment) of 6.4 million for pianos. Purchases of phonographs experienced their most rapid growth during the 1910s, before piano purchases plummeted. In 1921 phonographs, all of the mechanical-acoustic type were found in 5.9 million homes.

60. For an excellent book-length survey, see Raynor (1972).

61. Verdi (1971), p. 247. See also pp. 233 and 249 of the same collection.

62. Raynor (1972), p. 132.

63. Raynor (1972), p. 126.

64. See, for example, Gradenwitz (1984), pp. 17ff.; and Dewitz (1933), p. 5.

65. Thus, in the Innsbruck court of Duke Sigismund of Tirol during the fifteenth century, the principal daily meal was serenaded by a Kapelle consisting of fifes, drums, and trombones. Leitner (1994), p. 39.

66. See DeNora (1991), p. 327.

67. For various views on this phenomenon, see Blum (1978), pp. 160–61; Elias (1969, 1991, and 1993); Moore (1987), especially chapter 2; DeNora (1991); and Baumol and Baumol (1994a).

68. See Abel (1978), pp. 158–61 and 179–91. For the underlying Ricardian theory and an explanation of how technological progress eventually rendered it invalid, see Scherer (1999), pp. 10–22.

69. Julia Moore (1987) lists 85 Kapellen functioning in Austria, Hungary, and Bohemia during the seventeenth and eighteenth centuries; speculates that it should be possible to identify at least 100, not counting the large number in Germany; and observes (p. 563) that "another dissertation could, and should, be written on this subject."

70. See especially Boulding (1962), chapter 2; and the work upon which Boulding builds, Richardson (1960).

71. The term is Richardson's.

72. See Baumol and Baumol (2002), who emphasize the role of both profligate spending and bad luck (e.g., untimely death, conflagration, and war losses). On the extravagant outlays of Württemberg's Duke Carl Eugen and the financial crisis that forced their curtailment, see Alt (2000), pp. 34–50.

73. Johann F. von Schönfeld, *Jahrbuch der Tonkunst von Wien und Prag* (Musical Yearbook of Vienna and Prague, 1796), excerpt translated by Moore (1987), p. 47.

74. Moore (1987), pp. 564–97. At p. 94 Moore adds two Kapellen, but for some reason ignores four others said in her detailed summary to be active. For estimates of the wealth of Kapelle-maintaining families, see Robbins Landon (1991), pp. 58, 71, 105, and 140; and Blum (1978), pp. 24–25. Blum asserts that during the 1840s, the wealthiest of the group, Prince Paul Anton Esterházy, is said to have controlled 700,000 peasants, or 6.5 percent of the Hungarian population. Since a reliable source used in chapter 5 estimates the Hungarian population at the time to be about 4.25 million, an alternative more plausible estimate is 275,000 peasants.

75. One of the contributing musicians was Vincenzo Galilei, father of the physicist Galileo. Among the most important of the Florentine precursors was *Euridice* in 1600, which provided a model upon which Monteverdi improved at Mantua. See Kelly (2000), pp. 24–25.

76. On the tensions that precipitated the move, see Raynor (1972), pp. 93–96.

77. The low estimate is from Timothy King, "Patronage and Market in the Creation of Opera before the Institution of Intellectual Property," working paper, Budapest: 2000. The high estimate is from Raynor (1972), p. 170.

78. Boyd (1986), p. 3.

79. Piperno (1998), p. 28.

80. Raynor (1972), p. 165. See also Rosselli (1984), pp. 20–46.

81. Weinstock (1963), p. 145.

82. Barbier (1996), p. 66.

83. For an illustrated history, see Salmen (1988).

84. See Raynor (1972), pp. 256–57; and Holland (1932).

85. See Raynor (1972), pp. 255–58, and McVeigh (1993), pp. 56–58.

86. Bohemia had similar traditions; see Clapham (1979), p. 9.

87. Quoted in Reich (1985), p. 123.

88. See Percy M. Young, "Collegium Musicum," in Sadie (1980), vol. 4, pp. 559–60.

89. When Telemann later migrated to Hamburg, he organized similar public concerts, held in the city opera house, inns, and a militia exercise hall. See Petzoldt (1974), pp. 64–65.

90. An engraving of a Salle Pleyel concert is included in Salmen (1988), p. 29.

91. Holoman (1989), p. 579.

92. Smith (1999), Chapter 2.

93. Presumably, count A.G. Razumovskii was the uncle of the Count Razumovsky to whom Beethoven dedicated his op. 59 quartets.

94. See Rosselli (1984), pp. 170–71.

95. See Roger Fiske, "John Gay," in Sadie (1980), vol. 7, p. 203. The work was revised in the twentieth century to create the Weill-Brecht *Threepenny Opera*.

96. See Mozart (1962), vol. 1, pp. 159–60, in which Leopold Mozart reports, "Vauxhall is something that astounded me; it is impossible to describe" (but he does proceed to do so). Salmen (1988), p. 171, includes an engraving of a Vauxhall concert.

97. McVeigh (1993), pp. 39–44. Public-garden concerts spread to Moscow in the late 1760s and to St. Petersburg in 1793, in both cases with "Vauxhall" included in the gardens' names. Smith (1999), pp. 68–69 and 74.

98. McVeigh (1993), p. 37.

99. McVeigh (1993), pp. 24–25.

100. "Beer and Opera," *The Economist*, August 11, 2001, p. 47.

101. Fantel (1971), pp. 36 ff. The number may be exaggerated; Fantel is inaccurate in other details.

102. Wierzynski (1949), p. 136.

103. Fantel (1971), pp. 194–95. Salmen (1988), pp. 135–38, provides an engraving of a Peace Festival concert and a history of other "monster" concerts.

104. Moore (1987), pp. 50, 58–59, and 62–64.

105. Moore (1987), pp. 45–46.

106. DeNora (1991), pp. 334–35.

107. DeNora (1991), pp. 340–41.

108. Lang (1966), p. 474.

109. McVeigh (1993), p. xiv.

110. McVeigh (1993), pp. 32–33.

111. McVeigh (1993), p. 41.

112. Mozart (1962), vol. 3, pp. 305–7, reproduces the original letter and provides a more legible typeset list. More detailed biographical information are found in Mozart (1962), vol. 6, pp. 167–77; and (for a smaller subset, mostly noble) Robbins Landon (1989), pp. 248–50.

113. Pezzl's *Sketch of Vienna* (1786–1790) is translated in Robbins Landon (1991); the excerpt quoted here is from pp. 80–81.

114. The seating plan with names of box holders is given in Haydn (1959), p. 307. See also McVeigh (1993), appendix A, for a listing of venues in which the Bach-Abel concerts were held.

115. Deutsch (1955), p. 91. Not included in the list is the king, who contributed £1,000 per year.

116. The wage estimates are from Phelps Brown and Hopkins (1955), p. 205. A time series is presented in the appendix to chapter 1.

117. Piperno (1998), p. 8.

118. Berlioz (1966), p. 414.

119. Marek (1972), p. 303.

120. Rosselli (1998), pp. 87–88.

121. Rosselli (2000), p. 179.

CHAPTER 3

1. McVeigh (1993), p. 196. This was at least equally true in the twentieth century. See, e.g., Caves (2000), p. 359, who reports from a survey of 494 American composers by Marianne Felton that median income from composing per se was only 1.9 percent of the composers' overall median income.

2. Robbins Landon (1988), p. 48. On the substantial fortune Hoffmann left at his death, see Moore (1987), pp. 440–41.

3. Rees (1999), p. 41.

4. Barbier (1996), pp. 202–7.

5. Despite his stinginess, which was not atypical, Frederick apparently considered Bach "the greatest of all masters." Einstein (1962), p. 150.

6. See David and Mendel (1966), p. 339.

7. Gotwals (1963), p. 34.

8. Moore (1987), p. 367; and the memoirs of Ferdinand Ries, reproduced in Noonan (1987), p. 95.

9. Beethoven (1969), vol. 2, p. 448.

10. Lang (1966), pp. 130 and 133; and Deutsch (1955), p. 817.

11. On these and other subventions, see Moore (1987), pp. 273–83; and Baumol and Baumol (2002).

12. Deathridge and Dahlhaus (1984), pp. 48–66.

13. Altmann (1911), vol. 2, pp. 77–85.

14. Garden (1973), p. 129; and Garden and Gotteri (1993).

15. Courcy (1977), vol. 2, pp. 285–88; and Berlioz (1966), pp. 226–31.

16. The line between employment and free agency is blurred, subject to all the subtleties identified by Coase (1937).

17. McVeigh (1993), p. 170.

18. Benyovszky (1934), pp. 48 and 198.

19. Benyovszky (1934), p. 105.

20. Courcy (1977), vol. 2, p. 15.

21. See Reich (1985), pp. 100, 177–78, and 279.

22. Czerny (1968), p. 23; and Wehmeyer (1983), pp. 12–13.

23. Wierzynski (1949), p. 198.

24. Avins (1997), p. 112.

25. Avins (1997), p. 260.

26. Altmann (1911), vol. 2, pp. 16, 48, 62, 160, and 190.

27. McVeigh (1993), pp. 167–75.

28. See Gärtner (1994), pp. 299–303.

29. Mozart (1962), vol. 4, p. 92.

30. Moore (1987), p. 313; and McVeigh (1993), pp. 67–69.

31. Moore (1987), p. 287.

32. Berlioz (1966), pp. 341–98.

33. A more complete picture of Berlioz's concert-organizing activity is provided in Holoman (1989), passim.

34. Berlioz (1966), pp. 352–60; and Holoman (1989), pp. 308–11. For an engraved illustration, see Salmen (1988), p. 129.

35. A later "monster concert" organized by Berlioz in 1855 drew an estimated 40,000 listeners. Holoman (1989), pp. 476–77.

36. In his *Memoirs*, Berlioz (1966) records receipts of 32,000 francs; Holoman (1989), p. 311, claims that they were 66,000 francs. Both agree on the 800 franc net to Berlioz.

37. Berlioz (1966), pp. 477–78.

38. See also Bianconi and Pestelli (1998); and Rosselli (1984).

39. For a listing, see Piperno (1998), p. 23.

40. This account is drawn from Hogwood (1984); Lang (1966); Deutsch (1955); and Raynor (1972), pp. 272–88.

41. Hogwood (1984), p. 142.

42. Heller (1997), p. 97.

43. Heller (1997), pp. 112–13.

44. See Schubert (1974), pp. 39–46; and Large (1970), pp. 19–39.

45. Moore (1987), pp. 105 and 501.

46. Plantinga (1977), pp. 152–55 and 227.

47. Czerny (1968), p. 25; and Wehmeyer (1983), p. 113.

48. Beethoven (1969), vol. 2, p. 108.

49. Mendelssohn-Bartholdy (1986), p. 132.

50. Samson (1996), pp. 85 and 126.

51. Robbins Landon and Jones (1988), p. 232.

52. Moore (1987), p. 365.

53. Moore (1987), p. 365.

54. Benyovszky (1934), p. 32.

55. Braunbehrens (1989), pp. 218 and 259.

56. Schumann (1971), vol. 2, pp. 108 and 170.

57. Mozart (1962), vol. 2, p. 264.

58. Mozart (1962), vol. 2, pp. 104, 120, and 131.

59. Mozart (1962), vol. 4, p. 108.

60. Beethoven (1969), vol. 2, p. 247.

61. Chopin (1984), p. 299.
62. Samson (1996), p. 203.
63. Monrad-Johansen (1938), p. 297.
64. Raynor (1972), p. 20.
65. Raynor (1972), pp. 50–51 and 136.
66. See Barbier (1996), pp. 36–57.
67. See the articles by several authors on "Education in Music" in Sadie (1980), vol. 6, pp. 8–21.
68. Parts of what follows are drawn with revisions from Scherer (2001b). One initially overlooked composer has been added to the sample since that article was published.
69. One set of codings for a smaller sample was completed using sources less comprehensive than the *New Grove*. Before the second phase was begun, at least one book-length biography on each of twenty leading composers was read and annotated. A second full-sample pass was then made through the *New Grove*. In a third pass, the first several volumes were recoded to ensure that coding patterns had not changed through learning by doing. Fourth and fifth passes extracted data used in later chapters, but led to a few corrections in the data presented here.
70. Because the distribution of *Schwann* lineage counts was so skew, and hence threatened to let a very few observations (notably, those for Mozart, Bach, and Beethoven) overwhelm all the others, logarithms were taken of the dependent variable OUTPUT, i.e., the number of centimeters of *Schwann* listings. A variable that is nearly normally distributed, as Log OUTPUT is, tends to be better-behaved statistically.

Used as explanatory variables were the following: YEAR for the year of the composer's birth; FREE, a dummy variable with a value of 1 if the composer engaged in primary or secondary freelance composing activity and zero otherwise; ONLYFREE, a dummy variable with a value of 1 if the composer had no primary or secondary church or court employment but engaged in freelance composing activity and zero otherwise; OPERA, a dummy variable with a value of 1 for those who composed more than one opera and zero otherwise; and ROYAL, a dummy variable with a value of 1 for those who served as court music directors and / or received subsidies from the nobility for composing, and zero otherwise. Musicians with court appointments of less stature had zero ROYAL values.

With *t*-ratios for the coefficients in subscripted parentheses, the resulting regression equation using 646 observations was:

Log OUTPUT = -2.76 + 0.0017 YEAR + 0.409 FREE
 [3.07] [3.24] [5.66]
$-$ 0.119 ONLYFREE + 0.043 OPERA + 0.263 ROYAL; $R^2 = 0.135$.
 [1.32] [0.71] [4.08]

71. This relationship fades to insignificance when the dependent variable is OUTPUT without a logarithmic transformation, largely from the overwhelming impact of the J. S. Bach, Mozart, and Beethoven observations.

CHAPTER 4

1. Surian (1998), pp. 302–4.
2. See Einstein (1962), pp. 3–5.
3. Dewitz (1933), p. 13.
4. It is difficult to be more precise in characterizing the many pursuits of Carl Maria von Weber's father.
5. A narrower definition of middle class was used by Elvidio Surian in his analysis of 81 Italian opera composers' backgrounds. He counts as lower class occupations such as carpenter, grocer, tailor, barber, blacksmith, stonemason, weaver, shoemaker, and baker. By these definitions, 12 of his composers were assigned lower-class origins; only 1 of these was a farmer. The fraction of his surveyed composers with aristocratic origins — 7 of the 81 — is considerably higher than ours.
6. See for example the university-period diary of Robert Schumann (1971), vol. 1.
7. Wolff (2000), p. 321.
8. Wolff (2000), p. 39.
9. Wolff (2000), pp. 240–42.
10. On this phenomenon, more systematic statistical research could yield interesting insights.
11. Czerny (1968), p. 15. There is no mention in the Czerny autobiography and no known evidence in the Beethoven literature as to the magnitude of fees, if any. Czerny reported that his father was too poor to afford regular schooling for him, and the lessons with Beethoven were eventually discontinued because the father sacrificed too much income from teaching while he escorted young Carl to Beethoven's residence.
12. One of Liszt's students was Martin Krause, in whose Berlin home pianist Claudio Arrau lived while receiving free lessons.
13. The dependent variable is the logarithm (to base 10) of listing centimeters in the *Schwann* catalogue. Logarithms were taken to reduce skewness and avoid overinfluence from extreme values associated with Mozart, Beethoven, Bach, and a few others. Educational categories were entered as 1–0 dummy variables; also included was the birth year. Using the variable names in figure 4.1, the estimated coefficients and their t-ratios were as follows:

Intercept	−2.069 [1.92]	Church	0.173 [1.86]
Birth year	0.001 [2.00]	School	0.110 [1.01]
Family	0.238 [3.49]	Self-taught	0.215 [1.99]
Private Lessons	0.224 [2.99]	On-job	−0.021 [0.16]
Conservatory	0.226 [2.57]	University	−0.045 [0.24]

The R^2 was a modest 0.060, with $N = 532$. A similar regression without taking logarithms of the *Schwann* listing variable yielded even weaker results, with FAMILY as the only significant explanatory variable.
14. Gärtner (1994), p. 295; and David and Mendel (1966), p. 292.
15. *Fidelio*, Act 1. See also chapter 1, p. 1.
16. See Baumol and Baumol (2002).

17. Beethoven (1969), vol. 1, pp. 39–40 (from 1801).

18. Czerny (1968), p. 47. Compare Robert Schumann's youthful introspection: "Ah, immortality! How many billion people live and how many are immortal; and who knows, whether on average out of a million humans one is immortal. . . . What will become of me? I'm too insignificant to be sought out, and too proud to seek. Plainly in a society where I can't be the first, I would rather be nothing than the second or third." Schumann (1971), vol. 1, pp. 276 and 416.

19. Weinstock (1968), pp. 274 and 334.

20. Berlioz (1966), p 486.

21. Westernhagen (1956), p. 310, recounting a conversation with Frau Wille, in whose Zurich home Wagner was temporarily residing.

22. Altmann (1912), vol. 1, pp. 144 and 178.

23. Altmann (1911), vol. 2, p. 56 (from 1862).

24. Altmann (1911), vol. 2, p. 100.

25. Alan Walker (1983), vol. 1, p. 442, asserts that Liszt's retirement decision was one of the wisest he ever made, because he "kept the legend of his playing untarnished" and avoided the competition from numerous emulators. But this conclusion seems overdrawn, because Liszt continued to concertize successfully for charitable causes.

26. Sitwell (1967), p. 305.

27. Actually, more than free. Walker (1983), vol. 2, pp. 243 and 378, observes that Liszt often gave money to his needy students — generosity that was said to be the despair of his friends.

28. Walker (1983), vol. 3, pp. 528–29.

29. Schubert (1974), p. xii (from the foreword by Ernest Newman).

30. Schubert (1974), pp. 122–23 (1826).

31. David and Mendel (1966), pp. 98–104.

32. David and Mendel (1966), p. 129 (1733).

33. David and Mendel (1966), p. 125.

34. David and Mendel (1966), p. 125. Bach did not live in the prince's palace at Köthen.

35. David and Mendel (1966), p. 430.

36. Mozart (1962), vol. 3, p. 120. A similar assertion was made from Munich in 1780. Ibid., p. 102. One must be wary of accepting Mozart's letters to his father at face value, for he wrote to please, and his father, mired in a poorly paying position at Salzburg and having invested much in Wolfgang's career development, was eager to see his son succeed economically.

37. Mozart (1962), vol. 2, p. 51 (1777). His student and youthful boarder Johann Nepomuk Hummel apparently learned the lesson well. When Hummel was offered a much higher salary as music director of the Dresden opera than the recently deceased Carl Maria von Weber (cousin of Mozart's wife) had received, Weber's wife wrote bitterly: "That's the way the world works: only the one who can make big demands is the right man for these people." Benyovszky (1934), p. 114.

38. See chapter 3, section on "Teaching."

39. Mozart (1962), vol. 5, pp. 65–114.

40. See, e.g., Hamermesh and Rees (1984), pp. 31–40.

41. That initial amounts of work performed often yield utility rather than disutility is seldom recognized in standard economics texts — a serious shortcoming.

42. See Baumol and Baumol (1994b), pp. 185–89 and 194.

43. Einstein (1972), p. 135.

44. Schumann (1971), vol. 2, p. 130.

45. Tchaikovsky (1945), p. 46. See also Garden (1973), p. 129.

46. Gotwals (1963) (from a biography by G. A. Griesinger), pp. 54–55.

47. Weinstock (1968), p. 295.

48. Weinstock (1963), p. 140.

49. Kimbell (1981), p. 180.

50. Verdi (1971), p. 35.

51. Verdi (1971), p. 194.

52. Avins (1997), pp. 492, 501, 503, 611, and 726.

53. Reich (1985), pp. 205 ff. See also p. 287, where Clara Schumann observes that "I feel a calling to reproduce great works, above all, those of Robert, as long as I have the strength to do so. . . . The practice of art is, after all, a great part of my inner self. To me, it is the very air I breathe."

54. Rosselli (1984), p. 130.

55. Marek (1972), p. 101.

56. Smith (1937), p. 107. See also Towse (1993), p. 42, quoting Venetian composer Benedetto Marcello.

57. Quoted from Max von Weber's biography of his father in Newman (1933), vol. 1, p. 157. On pp. 158–68 Newman identifies additional examples and exceptions.

58. Einstein (1962), p. 33.

59. Plantinga (1977), pp. 117 and 156.

60. Courcy (1977), p. 308 (quoting the sociologist Max Weber).

61. Raynor (1972), p. 182.

62. Riesemann (1926), p. 335.

63. Mozart (1962), vol. 3, p. 94.

64. Courcy (1977), p. 107.

65. Croll and Vössing, (1987), p. 37.

66. Raynor (1972), pp. 297 and 334.

67. Haydn (1959), pp. 30 and 38. Compare p. 77 (1788), by which time Haydn had become less cautious.

68. Helm (1960), pp. 142 ff. As early musicologist Charles Burney observed after a visit to Potsdam, "His Majesty allows no more liberty in music than he does in government." MacDonogh (1999), p. 353.

69. Haydn (1959), p. 118.

70. Petzoldt (1974), p. 23.

71. Petzoldt (1974), p. 23.

72. Helm (1960), pp. 173 ff.

73. Hogwood (1984), p. 19 (from the contemporary biography by John Mainwaring).

74. Mozart (1962), vol. 3, p. 126. Wolfgang Hildesheimer (1982, p. 17) observes, "There should be a kind of negative order of nobility for such behavior,

with a visible sign like a mark of Cain, which only the intentional good acts of descendants could erase. Though, if we examine the history of the great Habsburg houses, we must acknowledge that they accumulated their titles and possessions by acts far more shameful than a kick in a great man's rear."

75. Mozart (1962), vol. 3, p. 279.

76. Welter (1998), p. 18.

77. Girdlestone (1957), p. 6.

78. Helm (1960), pp. 110 and 173 ff.

79. Helm (1960), pp. 206 ff.

80. Helm (1960), pp. 115–17.

81. Forbes (1967), p. 960.

82. Schubert (1974), p. 42 (1818).

83. Avins (1997), pp. 158 ff.

84. Avins (1997), p. 162.

85. Robbins Landon and Jones (1988), pp. 118–19.

86. Robbins Landon and Jones (1988), pp. 298 ff.

87. Noonan (1987), p. 97.

88. Benyovszky (1934), pp. 210–15.

89. Samson (1996), pp. 9–23; and Wierzynski (1949), pp. 165, 185, and 330.

90. See Newman (1933), vol. 1, pp. 163–67.

91. Newman (1933), vol. 1, p. 116.

92. Robbins Landon and Jones (1988), p. 101.

93. Niemann (1937), p. 66 (from 1857).

94. On the modern theory, see Rosen (1981).

95. Barbier (1996), p. 29.

96. Rosselli (1984), pp. 52–78.

97. Marek (1972), p. 298; Ostwald (1985), pp. 211 and 233–34; Schumann (1971), vol. 2, pp. 411, 421, and 437, and Vol. 3, Part 2, pp. 521–22 and 783–84; and Swafford (1997), p. 144.

98. Wolff (2000), pp. 183 and 540.

99. Robbins Landon and Jones (1988), p. 118.

100. For more systematic evidence on the late eighteenth century in Vienna, see Moore (1987), pp. 515–45.

101. Mozart (1962), vol. 1, p. 407 (1770).

102. Weinstock (1963), pp. 298–301.

103. Rosselli (2000), pp. 2–5; and Verdi (1971), p. 90.

104. Weinstock (1968), pp. 60–69.

105. Weinstock (1968), p. 60.

106. Brown (1978), p. 284. Schubert wanted to include his Symphony in C Major (the *Great*) on the program, but the Musikverein musicians concluded after rehearsals that it was too difficult.

107. Warrack (1968), p. 342.

108. See Moore (1987), p. 292.

109. Braunbehrens (1989), p. 67.

110. Braunbehrens (1989), p. 93, and Mozart (1962), vol. 1, p. 295. See also Einstein (1962), pp. 93 and 383–84.

111. See King (2001), p. 29.

112. Einstein (1972), p. 34. Einstein quotes a 1781 letter by Gluck asserting that "how much soever of talent a composer may have, he will never produce any but mediocre music, if the poet does not awaken in him that enthusiasm without which the productions of all the arts are but feeble and drooping" (p. 67).

113. Beethoven (1969), vol. 1, pp. 221–22.

114. Weinstock (1963), pp. 37–38. See also Weinstock (1968), p. 120; and Kimbell (1981), p. 137.

115. Rosselli (1996), p. 45.

116. Fantel (1971), p. 175; and Vallas (1951), p. 246.

117. Braunbehrens (1989), pp. 197–200.

118. Moore (1987), pp. 305–7; and Braunbehrens (1989), p. 256.

119. See Moore (1987), pp. 287, 297, and 307–11.

120. Courcy (1977), vol. 2, pp. 3–15.

121. For a discussion of Viennese pension practices, see Moore (1987), pp. 546–48.

122. Haydn (1959), pp. 240 and 249.

123. David and Mendel (1966), pp. 189–90.

124. Mozart (1962), vol. 4, p. 175; and Einstein (1962), p. 60.

125. Warrack (1968), p. 346.

126. McVeigh (1993), pp. 37, 180 (on a Handel Festival that raised £6,000), and 201.

127. Haydn (1959), p. 234.

128. Robbins Landon (1988), pp. 183–84. In her original petition to Emperor Leopold seeking a pension, Constanze Mozart explained that Wolfgang had not joined the Sozietät because he could not conceive that he would die and leave his family impoverished. He expected among other things a post-1791 improvement in his finances. Mozart (1962), vol. 4, p. 176. A second petition emphasizing the birth certificate problem may have been a tactical invention, although earlier Mozart letters to his father do contain requests for a birth certificate.

129. See Baumol and Baumol (1994b); and McVeigh (1993), p. 197.

130. Reproduced in Robbins Landon (1991), especially pp. 62–117.

131. David and Mendel (1966), p. 193.

132. Hill, Hill, and Hill (1963), pp. 252 note and 266.

133. Moore (1987), p. 452. Beethoven's estate included (p. 398) a value for "printed music and manuscripts" of £33.

134. Courcy (1977), various.

135. Moore (1987), especially pp. 503–4.

136. The data are from Phelps Brown and Hopkins (1955). To illustrate, 1790 average annual earnings (with linear interpolation for grouped years), assuming a 300-day working year, were £38.88. In 1850, the average income was £62.50, so nominal estate values for 1850 are divided by (62.50 / 38.88) = 1.608. Note that the estate of Wolfgang Amadeus Mozart, who died in 1791, very close to our benchmark year, is altered by indexing because Moore adjusted the values for Vienna composers to a 1795 purchasing-power base.

137. Moore (1987), especially pp. 413–17 and 463–65.

138. Moore (1987) also tallies data (not analyzed here) for opera singers and actors.

139. See Scherer (2001c); Scherer, Harhoff, and Kukies (2000); Caves (2000), p. 83; and Towse (1999), pp. 385–86.

140. Author's calculations, from Kennickell et al. (2000).

141. See DeVany and Walls (1996); and DeVany and Walls (2001).

142. Scherer, Harhoff, and Kukies (2000), p. 198.

143. The variable to be explained is WEALTH, defined as the value of a composer's estate, adjusted for changes in the value of building craftsmen's earnings in southern England. Because the variable is highly skew, logarithms (to base 10) were taken. Since logarithms do not exist for negative numbers, negative values were treated as 10 divided by the absolute value of the negative estate value. Explanatory variables were YEAR, the year of a composer's birth; LIFE, the number of years a composer lived; a dummy variable FREE with value of 1 if the composer engaged in substantial freelance composing and / or performance and zero otherwise; and SCHWANN, the length (in centimeters) of Fall 1996 *Schwann* catalogue listings. Because of skewness, logarithms were also taken of SCHWANN.

With 23 usable observations, the fitted regression equation was:

$$\text{Log}_{10}\ \text{WEALTH} = -15.79 + \underset{[1.30]}{0.0083}\ \text{YEAR} + \underset{[1.23]}{0.058}\ \text{LIFE} + \underset{[3.17]}{0.907}\ \text{FREE}$$
$$-\ \underset{[0.51]}{0.201}\ \text{log}_{10}\ \text{SCHWANN};\ R^2 = 0.442.$$

144. Mozart (1962), vol. 2, p. 274. See also chapter 1, notes 13 and 14. Needless to say, Papa Mozart did not anticipate the invention of phonographs and broadcasting.

145. The results are sensitive to the inclusion of Schubert and Mozart in the sample. If they are deleted, so that $N = 21$, the years-of-life variable remains positive but fades to statistical insignificance, with t = 1.14. The *t*-ratio for FREE rises to 1.81 and the sign for SCHWANN turns positive, with $t = 0.26$. Reverse causality cannot be ruled out: composers who achieved greater economic success may have lived longer.

146. Mozart (1962), vol. 3, p. 124.

147. Mozart (1962), vol. 3, p. 60.

148. Mozart (1962), vol. 3, pp. 345–46.

149. McVeigh (1993), p. 225.

150. Benyovszky (1934), p. 32. See also DeNora (1991), p. 113.

151. David and Mendel (1966), p. 52 (1706). Bach's early biographer Johann Nicolaus Forkel attributed to Bach the belief of Schiller, "If you cannot please all by your art or your work, satisfy the few: to please many is bad." David and Mendel (1966).

152. Petzoldt (1974), p. 17.

153. Forbes (1967), p. 804.

154. Forbes (1967), p. 801.

155. Vallas (1951), p. 211.

156. McVeigh (1993), passim.

157. See, e.g., Einstein (1962), pp. 149–51.

158. Robbins Landon and Jones (1988), p. 225.

159. Robbins Landon and Jones (1988), p. 309.

160. Reich (1985), pp. 262 and 271.

161. Beethoven (1969), vol. 1, p. 106.

162. Heller (1997), pp. 110–17 and 259.

163. Girdlestone (1957), p. 497.

164. Weinstock (1968), pp. 167 and 180.

165. Verdi (1971), p. 197 (1876).

166. Schumann (1971), vol. 2, p. 114.

167. Lang (1966), pp. 441–48.

168. Forbes (1967), p. 567.

169. Forbes (1967), p 566.

170. Moore (1987), pp. 311 and 392. Carl Maria von Weber's similarly motivated cantata, *Kampf und Sieg* (Struggle and Victory), was poorly attended because of a snowstorm, but was praised by Austrian General Nostitz, "In Beethoven's music boys play at soldiers; in yours, sir, we have heard the voices of nations." Warrack (1968), p. 295.

171. Robbins Landon and Jones (1988), p. 247.

172. Brown (1978), pp. 174 and 264. See also pp. 127 and 137.

173. Samson (1996), p. 29; and Wierzynski (1949), p. 198.

174. Chopin (1984), p. 143 (1833).

175. Weinstock (1968), p. 273.

176. Rees (1999), pp. 17–18.

177. Berlioz (1966), p. 481; and Holoman (1989), pp. 194, 333, 429, 557, and 568. On a more mixed reaction from the Leipzig press, see p. 453 of Holoman.

178. Vallas (1951), pp. 42–45, 66–69, 72–73, and 75–76.

179. Avins (1997), p. 168.

180. Avins (1997), p. 284.

181. Avins (1997), p. 728 (1895).

182. Verdi (1971), pp. 57 (1848) and 184 (1871).

183. On the advertising of operas and concerts in eighteenth-century London, see McVeigh (1993), pp. 73–79.

184. Scherer (2001c), pp. 15–19.

185. Schumpeter (1942), pp. 73–74.

186. From Johann Pezzl's account, gambling on the Viennese lottery between 1750 and 1786 amounted to 41 million florins, of which, as in modern American lotteries, less than half was paid out to the winners. Robbins Landon (1991), p. 122; and Clotfelter and Cook (1989).

CHAPTER 5

1. Parts of this chapter are adapted with permission from Scherer (2001d).

2. See, e.g., Forbes (1967), p. 4 (derived from work by Alexander Wheelock Thayer a century earlier); Blum (1978), pp. 160–61; and Raynor (1972), pp. 290–305 ff.

3. Elias (1969); Elias (1991); and Baumol and Baumol (1994a).

4. On conflicting estimates of the number of separate courts, see King (2001), p. 31. A conservative estimate, attributed by King to Geoffrey Barraclough, is 234 individual noble courts.

5. This is the emphasis of Elias's earlier (1969) book.

6. Elias (1993) (translated from the 1991 original), p. 26.

7. Baumol and Baumol (1994a), p. 73. See also Baumol and Baumol (1994b). Baumol and Baumol were influenced by the earlier work of Moore (1987). Moore, whose research was remarkably exhaustive, does not cite the work of Elias in her bibliography.

8. See chapter 2, section on "The Reform of Feudal Institutions." See also Moore (1987), especially pp. 91–101.

9. The territorial definitions were chosen to mesh, after consolidation of the two Germanies, with population data from McEvedy and Jones (1978).

10. The source was McEvedy and Jones (1978).

11. Clapham (1979), p. 9. See also Gradenwitz (1984), vol. 1, pp. 70–71.

12. Berlioz (1966), p. 414. An early musicologist, Charles Burney, observed in 1773 that the Bohemians were "the most musical people of Germany, or, perhaps, of all Europe." See Burney (1959), pp. 131–32. Like Clapham, Burney attributes the Bohemians' musicality to extensive musical training in the primary schools.

13. The births per million ratio is computed by averaging the population counts across all composers for whom matched birth data and population data were available and dividing that average into the count of composers for which matches were effected.

14. To repeat a statistic from chapter 1, the average age at death for the 646 composers was 64.5 years. In obtaining the figure 5.4 statistics, equivalent working lives were summed for a nation, and that sum was divided by the average across composers of the lagged population counts.

15. See Raynor (1972), p. 301; and Theophil Antonicek, "Vienna," in Sadie (1980), vol. 19, pp. 717–18.

16. The source is Chandler and Fox (1974). A somewhat more wide-ranging source that differs only marginally for most jointly covered cities is Bairoch, Batou, and Chèvre (1988).

17. Weinstock (1968), pp. 135–40.

18. Kimbell (1981), p. 203.

19. Chopin (1984), p. 317. See also p. 290.

20. Cooper (1935), pp. 160–202.

21. Cooper (1935), p. 236. See also Einstein (1972), p. 151.

22. Mozart (1962), vol. 2, p. 162.

23. Mozart (1962), vol. 2, p. 277 (February 1778).

24. Presumably, Leopold is referring to British attacks on Dutch merchant ships during the American war of independence.

25. Schumann (1971), vol. 2, pp. 445–46.

26. Schumann (1971), vol. 2, p. 206.

27. Marek (1972), p. 327.

28. Sitwell (1967), p. 290.

29. Tchaikowsky (1945), p. 310; and Clapham (1979), p. 107. At p. 315 in his translated diaries, Tchaikovsky muses on the favorable reviews he received in the press, "Is it possible that I really conduct so well? Or do the Americans exaggerate?"

30. Maddison (2001), p. 264; supplemented (especially for 1850) using Maddison (1995), pp. 194–200. Missing observations have been estimated through interpolation or, in the case of Czechoslovakia for 1700, by extrapolation assuming the growth rate for Austria.

31. The dependent variable is WORKLIVES, that is, the measure of equivalent working lives per million population plotted in figure 5.6. Three of the explanatory variables are 1–0 dummy variables. They include COURT1, for the strong form of the competing courts hypothesis, with Germany alone having values of 1 for the first three 50-year periods and all other COURT1 values being zero; COURT2, with Germany, Austria, Czechoslovakia, and Italy all having values of 1 for the first three periods; and MAGNET, with values of 1 for England, France, and Austria in all four 50-year periods, and Russia having values of 1 only for the 1750–1799 and 1800–1849 birth cohorts. GDP measures (crudely) estimated gross domestic product per capita, adjusted to constant 1990 purchasing power.

The regression equation, assuming Germany to be the only nation in which the competing noble courts hypothesis applied, is as follows, with t-ratios in subscripted brackets:

$$\text{WORKLIVES} = \underset{[1.71]}{1.51} - \underset{[0.18]}{0.0001} \text{ GDP} + \underset{[1.81]}{1.042} \text{ MAGNET}$$
$$+ \underset{[0.59]}{0.610} \text{ COURT1}; R^2 = 0.086, N = 40.$$

The regression equation has only meager ability to explain differences in composer employment, and none of the explanatory variables is statistically significant by conventional standards.

32. The computed regression equation was:

$$\text{WORKLIVES} = \underset{[0.41]}{-0.29} + \underset{[1.41]}{0.00080} \text{ GDP} + \underset{[2.70]}{1.127} \text{ MAGNET}$$
$$+ \underset{[5.58]}{2.497} \text{ COURT2}; R^2 = 0.505, N = 40.$$

From the R^2 value, we find that the regression equation explains half the variance in FTE composers per million population.

33. See this chapter's notes 10 and 11.

34. I am indebted to seminar participants at the Technische Universität Freiberg for this suggestion.

35. See, e.g., Raynor (1972), p. 57 and 88. Raynor argues at p. 120 that before the Thirty Years War and the definitive breakup of the Holy Roman Empire, the center of gravity in German music-making was in the commercial cities rather than the courts.

36. Petzoldt (1974), p. 30. See also the section on "Servility and Dependence" in chapter 4.

37. Mendelssohn-Bartholdy (1986), p. 172.

38. Avins (1997), p. 392. Another Brahms biographer, Jan Swafford (1997, p. 11), observes that by the time of Brahms's birth in 1833, Hamburg had lapsed into being what some called "the unmusical city."

39. Wolff (2000), p. 349.

40. Wolff (2000), p. 442.

41. Hase (1968), vol. 1, p. 231.

42. MacDonogh (1999), p. 229–30.

43. Chandler and Fox (1974), pp. 143–52.

44. Good (1984), p. 46.

45. The data are from U.S. Bureau of the Census (1960), p. 72; and Bowden, Karpovich, and Usher (1937), pp. 6–9.

46. After this adjustment, the combined population of the free cities is found to be 12.6 percent of total German population (assuming 1992 boundaries) for 1650 and 11.85 percent for 1850.

47. On the complex changes during this period, see Blum (1978).

48. Monte Carlo simulation methods were used to estimate the standard errors needed to draw this statistical inference, since one expects unobserved random errors in both the numerator of the calculated ratio (the number of composers born) and the denominator (population, which varies, depending upon the date of the composer's birth). The t-ratio in a test of mean differences is 3.27.

49. Sixteen additional German-born composers spent none of their working years from age twenty in Germany; another German-born composer was dropped because of insufficient data on work locations.

50. Again, Monte Carlo methods were used to derive standard error estimates. In a test of mean ratio differences, the relevant t-ratio was 2.81.

51. The counts per million population are not comparable across subperiods because the subperiods are of differing length. When they are converted to comparable counts per decade per million population, the results are as follows:

	1650–1785	*1786–1849*
Births		
Free cities	0.48	0.77
Rest of Germany	0.52	0.28
Equivalent work lives		
Free cities	0.45	0.30
Rest of Germany	0.34	0.19

52. The dependent variable is a dummy variable with a value of 1 if a composer had primary or secondary employment in a particular occupational category (FREE for freelance composition and/or performance, COURT, and CHURCH) and zero otherwise. The explanatory variables are BIRTH, which is defined as the year of the composer's birth minus the all-sample mean birth year 1756; and indices characterizing the fraction of a composer's working life (assumed to begin at age twenty) in each of six nations — Germany, France, Italy,

Austria, England, and what in 1992 was Czechoslovakia. The estimated regression coefficients for these nations show differences in the probability of earning a living by some specified means associated with working one's whole adult life, as compared to not working at all, in a particular nation. These effects additively augment a base case (the intercept coefficient) that encompasses all other sample nations, including Scandinavia, Iberia, the Benelux countries, Russia, all other European nations, and the Americas.

In principle, the regressions should be estimated using probit methods. This was done, but the estimated probit coefficients were in several cases outside the 0–1 range, and so more plausible (even if statistically inefficient) ordinary least squares coefficients are reported here. The results with the two methods are qualitatively identical. Subtracting the all-sample mean birth year 1756 from the actual birth year permitted the "intercept" variable to have more meaningful values.

The resulting occupational-choice regression equations, with t-ratios in brackets [ ], were as follows:

Explanatory *Variable*	*Dependent Variable*		
	FREE	COURT	CHURCH
BIRTH	0.0037 [12.02]	−0.0028 [8.66]	−0.0027 [8.10]
Germany	0.165 [2.74]	0.293 [4.69]	−0.176 [2.80]
France	0.181 [3.13]	0.006 [0.11]	−0.138 [2.29]
Italy	0.423 [6.18]	−0.008 [0.11]	0.021 [0.30]
Austria	0.121 [1.67]	0.267 [3.58]	−0.118 [1.57]
England	0.374 [5.23]	−0.071 [0.96]	−0.094 [1.26]
Czechoslovakia	0.190 [1.51]	0.049 [0.38]	−0.130 [0.99]
Intercept	0.408 [10.06]	0.366 [8.69]	0.471 [11.13]
N	646	646	646
R^2	0.205	0.165	0.119

CHAPTER 6

1. Clough and Cole (1941), p. 442.

2. Massie (1980), p. 384.

3. Mozart (1962), vol. 2, pp. 490–91. See also pp. 301 and 326, where Mozart reports to his father that his somewhat (about ten percent) longer journey from Mannheim to Paris via Metz required nine and one-half days, with no indication of how many overnight stops there were.

4. Mozart (1962), vol. 4, pp. 112–13. Mozart was so pleased with the speed and amenities of the trip that, on reaching Frankfurt, he wanted to "kiss the coach."

5. Wolff (2000), pp. 95–97.

6. Mozart (1962), vol. 3, pp. 12–13. Now, absent peak holidays traffic, driving sensibly by car (that is, slower than the speeds chosen by many German drivers), one can make the trip from Salzburg to the outskirts of Munich in an hour and a quarter.

7. Berlioz (1966), p. 424.

8. Mozart (1962), vol. 2, pp. 344–45. See also pp. 355 and 427.

9. Rosselli (1996), p. 126.

10. Duchen (2000), pp. 69–73.

11. Forbes (1967), p. 38.

12. Clapham (1951), p. 109.

13. Mendelssohn-Bartholdy (1986), pp. 61–64.

14. Berlioz (1966), pp. 118–19; and Holoman (1989), p. 112.

15. Schumann (1971), vol. 2, p. 372.

16. Mendelssohn-Bartholdy (1986), p. 73.

17. Clough and Cole (1941), p. 448.

18. Chopin (1984), p. 335.

19. The source is Mitchell (1998), pp. 673–74.

20. The one-way fare in 1842 was 2.25 thaler, or about 6.5 English shillings. Schumann (1971), vol. 3, Part 1, p. 221; and vol. 2, pp. 235 and 244.

21. Schumann (1971), vol. 2, pp. 272–73.

22. Monrad-Johansen (1938), pp. 247–49.

23. Monrad-Johansen (1938), p. 260.

24. Garden (1973), passim.

25. See Rees (1999).

26. Weinstock (1968), p. 192.

27. Fantel (1971), p. 122.

28. Rosselli (2000), pp. 124 ff.

29. Ostwald (1985), p. 69.

30. Ostwald (1985), p. 242.

31. See Adelman (1969).

32. The dependent variables are DIEOTHER, with a value of 1 if a composer died in a nation other than the one in which he was born and zero otherwise; and NUMBERS, the numbers-equivalent index whose averages are plotted in figure 6.3. Explanatory variables include three 1–0 dummy variables, one (D1700–49) identifying composers born in the 1700–1749 interval, another for 1750–1799 births, and another for 1800–1849 births. With controls for three 50-year intervals, the intercept case covers composers born between 1650 and 1699. The three half-century-cohort coefficients in effect modify base-case (1650–1699) predictions. Other explanatory variables include FREECOMP, with a value of 1 if a sample member engaged in substantial freelance composing activity and zero otherwise; and FREEPERF, with a value of 1 if a composer engaged in substantial freelance performance activity and zero otherwise. Regressions (3) and (4) add two dummy variables FREECOMP* and FREEPERF*, allowing the freelance composition and performance variables for composers born in the nineteenth century to have coefficients different from those estimated for composers born between 1650 and 1799. The total effect of an occupational category in this instance is the algebraic sum of the starred and unstarred variable coefficients, for example, the coefficients on FREECOMP plus FREECOMP*.

Least-squares regression equations using these variables and 646 observations, first without and then with the FREECOMP* and FREEPERF* shift variables, are as follows, with t-ratios reported in brackets [ ]:

Explanatory Variable	(1)	(2)	(3)	(4)
	Dependent Variables			
	DIEOTHER	NUMBERS	DIEOTHER	NUMBERS
D1700–49	0.086 [1.64]	0.054 [0.99]	0.085 [1.61]	0.050 [0.92]
D1750–99	0.068 [1.30]	0.007 [0.12]	0.063 [1.19]	−0.009 [0.17]
D1800–49	−0.080 [1.52]	−0.102 [1.89]	−0.044 [0.60]	−0.004 [0.05]
FREECOMP	0.098 [2.63]	0.142 [3.71]	0.110 [2.47]	0.163 [3.58]
FREEPERF	0.195 [4.91]	0.273 [6.68]	0.205 [4.18]	0.322 [6.38]
FREECOMP*	———	———	−0.046 [0.56]	−0.095 [1.13]
FREEPERF*	———	———	−0.036 [0.43]	−0.156 [1.80]
Intercept	0.186 [4.75]	1.158 [28.71]	0.181 [4.56]	1.145 [28.01]
R^2	0.062	0.089	0.063	0.095

33. Mozart (1962), vol. 3, pp. 124 and 220.
34. Warrack (1968), p. 133.
35. Mendelssohn-Bartholdy (1986), p. 150.
36. See Rosen (1981), pp. 845–57.
37. See Table 4.1.
38. Sitwell (1967), pp. 182, 224, 250, and 305.
39. Avins (1997), p. 641.
40. Courcy (1977), vol. 1, pp. 235 and 303.
41. Schumann (1971), vol. 2, foreword by editor Gerd Nauhaus, p. 13.
42. Mozart (1962), vol. 1, pp. 66, 105, and 113.
43. Mozart (1962), vol. 2, pp. 288, 318, and 321–23.
44. Mozart (1962), vol. 2, p. 509.
45. See this chapter's note 4. His cousin-in-law Carl Maria von Weber bought a carriage for his trip from Dresden to London in 1826 — a trip that ended in Weber's death but little financial gain. Warrack (1968), pp. 306–38.
46. Mozart (1962), vol. 4, pp. 118 and 114–15.
47. Robbins Landon and Jones (1988), p. 247.
48. See Forbes (1967), pp. 675 and 737; and Beethoven (1969), vol. 2, p. 65.
49. Berlioz (1966), pp. 255 and 302 note.

CHAPTER 7

1. See Audretsch and Klepper (2000).
2. Donald W. Krummel, "Publishing," in Sadie (1980), vol. 15, pp. 260–72.
3. Benton (1990), p. x.
4. Courcy (1977), vol. 2, p. 105.
5. The other primary and secondary publishers besides Pleyel, Clementi, and Franz Anton Hoffmeister, were Johann Baptist Cramer (1771–1858), Leopold Kozeluch (1747–1818), Joseph Elsner (1769–1854), Anton Diabelli (1781–1858), Christian Horneman (1840–1906), Henry Litolff (1818–1891), François Couperin (1668–1773), and Carlo Tessarini (1690–1766).
6. Samuel F. Pogue, "Estienne Roger," in Sadie (1980), vol. 16, pp. 99–100.
7. Allsop (1999), p. 24.

8. Hase (1968) (company history originally published in 1917), vol. 1, p. 198.

9. Hase (1968), vol. 1, p. 198.

10. The source is Chandler and Fox (1974).

11. With SALES reflecting 1816–1818 sales of B&H agents by city, POPULATION the population within the agents' urban locations, and DISTANCE the distance from Leipzig to the sales location, the preferred gravity model regression equation was:

$$Log_{10} \text{ SALES} = \underset{[3.93]}{1.70} + \underset{[4.28]}{0.54} \text{ log POPULATION} + \underset{[0.03]}{0.004} \text{ log DISTANCE};$$

with $N = 26$, $R^2 = 0.467$, and with t-ratios indicated in subscripted brackets. A variable measuring gross domestic product per capita during 1820 for the nations in which the sample cities were located had an unexpected negative sign, undoubtedly because the average income of St. Petersburg or Warsaw residents was vastly different from the income of peasants comprising a majority of the Russian or Polish population. It is therefore omitted from the regression equation reported here. Its inclusion did not appreciably change the indicated population and distance relationships. A dummy variable differentiating German-speaking cities from other cities was positive but statistically insignificant, consistent with the universality of the language of music.

12. For more extensive treatments of the material in this section, see H. Edmund Poole, "Printing," in Sadie (1980), vol. 15, pp. 232–60; and Krummel and Sadie (1990). The latter volume includes histories of several hundred music publishing houses founded in the seventeenth through nineteenth centuries. The author has also benefited greatly from conversations with and demonstrations by members of the Gutenberg Museum staff in Mainz.

13. Hübel (1995), p. 41.

14. The count is from an inventory taken during the early 1800s, which listed 232 different musical elements and 138 alphabetical elements. Hase (1968), vol. 1, p. 216. Other companies later developed variants with as many as 452 different elements.

15. Hase (1968), vol. 1, p. 183.

16. See Warrack (1968).

17. Hase (1968), vol. 1, pp. 219–21. If one can believe a Weber letter of October 1800, a diligent worker could prepare 2 to 3 plates during short winter days and 3 to 4 during long summer days. The period from sunup to sundown in southern Germany was roughly 8 hours in December and 16 hours in June. Assuming a shorter period of usable daylight or (in summer) work time, it would appear that the inscribing time for lithography plates was one-third to one-half that for engraved plates. Even in the 1880s, the length of the sunlit day continued to constrain the amount of work music inscribers could do. See Altmann (1911), vol. 2, p. 235.

18. Raynor (1972), p. 333.

19. Altmann (1912), vol. 1, p. 41.

20. Altmann (1912), vol. 1, pp. 41 and 154–55.

21. Avins (1997), p. 523.

22. The estimates are found in Hase (1968), vol. 1, p. 225.

23. An exchange rate to Louis d'or is given in Hase (1968), vol. 1, at p. 194. It is consistent with other data contained in our wider-ranging table of exchange rates and implies that £1 = 4.1 thaler. As always, it is subject to some uncertainty.

24. This section is adapted from Scherer (2001a).

25. Similar estimates quoted in Holoman (1989), p. 230, probably shift some of what should correctly be considered fixed costs, such as press setup, into marginal costs.

26. A Schott calculation, apparently carried out later, when the originals for lithographed music could be inscribed on paper, showed the cost per sheet using lithography to be one-fourth to one-fifth the cost of engraved music. The volume at which this comparison was made is not stated. Hübel (1995), p. 21.

27. Hase (1968), vol. 2, part 1, p. 398.

28. This was the "most sad condition," for example, of Fridolin Weber, the father of Mozart's eventual wife Constanze and uncle of Carl Maria von Weber. Père Weber was attempting to support his wife and six children at an annual salary of 200 florins (£20) as musician and copyist in the ducal court at Mannheim. Mozart (1962), vol. 2, pp. 227, 447, and 428. Similarly, Ferdinand Ries (1784–1838), student and later benefactor of Beethoven, is described by Thayer as having before he joined Beethoven "very slender prospects . . . [and] was at last reduced to copy music at three-pence per sheet." Forbes (1967), p. 293.

29. Haydn (1959), pp. xx and 81; and Robbins Landon (1988), pp. 43–44.

30. Page counts were found in such sources as Kinsky (1955); Hoboken (1957–1978); and manuscripts in the excellent collection of the Loeb Music Library at Harvard University.

31. Moore (1987), p. 291, quoting Anton Schindler's biography of Beethoven.

32. See the editors' note in the King's Music edition of Handel's *Oratorio per la Resurrezione di Nostro Signor Gesù Christo*, written in 1708 while Handel was in Rome (Huntington, Cambridgeshire, UK: 1933).

33. I am indebted to Dr. Andreas Sopart, archivist of Breitkopf & Härtel, for clarification on this important point.

34. Hase (1968), vol. 1, p. 226.

35. Hübel (1995), p. 31. To be sure, there were exceptions. In England during the last three decades of the eighteenth century, more than 10,000 copies were sold of various popular songs by Charles Dibdin (1745–1814). See Hunter (1986), pp. 274–75.

36. Robbins Landon (1988), p. 44 and note 8. Unfortunately, Robbins Landon provides no clues as to the source from which his figures were gleaned.

37. The data are from Kinsky (1955). When data were available, all handwritten manuscripts were adjusted to a common basis of 12 staves per page.

38. Holoman (1989), p. 230.

39. In economics, this is known as "limit pricing." See Scherer and Ross (1990), pp. 374–96.

40. Like B&H, copyists also had to incur transaction costs to bring their products into the hands of would-be purchasers. No evidence on the magnitude

of those selling costs is known to exist. Except on local sales to a network of known customers, they could scarcely have been lower than those of well-established publishers.

41. Jensen (1989), pp. 34 and 90.

42. Hogwood (1984), p. 64.

43. Girdlestone (1957), p. 10.

44. Robbins Landon and Jones (1988), p. 104.

45. Mozart (1962), vol. 3, p. 236.

46. Mendelssohn-Bartholdy (1986), p. 107.

47. Pohlmann (1962), p. 173.

48. Pohlmann (1962), pp. 48–49.

49. The situation is not fundamentally different when modern-day scientists and engineers agree in their employment contracts to assign all work-related invention patents to the employer.

50. See generally Rosselli (1984).

51. Mozart (1962), vol. 1, p. 408. See also Caves (2000), p. 359, who quotes composer William Schuman's remark that twentieth century copyists often made more money than the composer.

52. Mozart (1962), vol. 1, pp. 416 and 421.

53. Hunter (1986), pp. 280–81.

54. Weinstock (1963), p. 14.

55. Weinstock (1968), p. 106.

56. Surian (1998), p. 299.

57. See Jensen (1989), pp. 14–32.

58. Translated and quoted in Surian (1998), p. 298. On Carl Eugen's budgetary problems, see Alt (2000), vol. 1, pp. 33–50. One reason why Jommelli's works were available for copying elsewhere is that the noble courts of Europe regularly exchanged musical manuscripts with their peers in order to broaden the repertoires available to each. Once a manuscript was available elsewhere, controlling unauthorized publication became difficult. Henry Raynor (1972), p. 334, states that Jommelli mentioned, to no avail, Johann Hasse's ability to retain scores written during his tenure with the king of Saxony in Dresden.

59. Pohlmann (1962), p. 129 (reproducing the text of Haydn's 1761 contract); and Gieseke (1995), p. 113.

60. The relevant text is found in Green (1997), p. 163.

61. Robbins Landon and Jones (1988), pp. 36 and 118–19.

62. Haydn (1959), p. 71.

63. Mozart (1962), vol. 3, p. 313.

64. Robbins Landon (1989), p. 120.

65. Mozart (1962), vol. 4, p. 259.

66. Robbins Landon (1989), p. 85.

67. Forbes (1967), p. 939 note.

68. Forbes (1967), pp. 302 and 339. Ignaz Pleyel did the same. See Benton (1990), p. xiii.

69. Noonan (1987), p. 107 (from the remembrances of Ferdinand Ries).

70. Forbes (1967), p. 163; and Beethoven (1969), vol. 1, p. 9.

71. Lang (1966), pp. 278–79.

72. Hunter (1986), p. 272.

73. See Lang (1966), p. 238, who asserts that Walsh "mercilessly plundered Handel" before their coming to terms; and Deutsch (1955), 488–89, printing the text of the privilege.

74. For a more detailed history, see Garnett, James, and Davies (1999), pp. 33–36.

75. These names, all in the sample of 646 composers, are drawn from a longer list in Hunter (1986), p. 277 note 51. For the text of Handel's privileges, see Deutsch (1955), pp. 105–6 and 488–89.

76. Lang (1966), pp. 278 and 460.

77. *Darcy* v. *Allein* (the so-called Case of Monopolies), 11 Coke 84b–88b (1603).

78. These and several others were uncovered through the biographical research on our sample of 646 composers.

79. See Petzoldt (1974), p. 61.

80. This account is drawn from Pohlmann (1962), pp. 238–42.

81. Haberstumpf (1996), p. 15.

82. Kaufer (1989), pp. 3–5.

83. For extended analyses, see Pohlmann (1962); Gieseke (1995); and Haberstumpf (1996).

84. Gieseke (1995), p. 59.

85. Pohlmann (1962), pp. 186 ff. For contrary arguments, see Gieseke (1995), pp. 67–69.

86. 8 Anne, c. 19 (1709).

87. Hunter (1986), p. 278.

88. Gärtner (1994), p. 299.

89. *Bach* v. *Longman* et al., 2 Cowper 623 (1777).

90. Hunter (1986), p. 281, drawing upon compilations by Donald W. Krummel.

91. Gärtner (1994), p. 331.

92. Earlier, in 1783, the Continental Congress recommended to the states that they enact copyright laws.

93. The U.S. law came to be interpreted quite differently than the British law: foreigners were ruled eligible to obtain British copyrights. See Nowell-Smith (1968), pp. 18 and 33.

94. Nowell-Smith (1968), p. 19; and Gieseke (1995), p. 143.

95. Hase (1968), vol. 1, p. 242–43.

96. Hase (1968), vol. 1, p. 176.

97. Hase (1968), vol. 2, part 1, pp. 1–2; Hübel (1995), p. 37; and Benyovszky (1934), pp. 134–37.

98. Benyovszky (1934), p. 137.

99. Benton (1990), p. xii. Henry Raynor (1972, p. 337) dates such arrangements back to the 1780s without providing evidence.

100. It is reproduced in Benyovszky (1934), pp. 131–33.

101. See Haberstumpf (1996), pp 19–20; and Gieseke (1995), pp. 235–43.

102. Hase (1968), vol. 2, part 1, pp. 14–15. Even after the new law was passed, enforcement difficulties remained. See Altmann (1911) vol. 2, p. 225.

103. There were as always loopholes. Giuseppe Verdi's letters include a discussion in 1855 of an English judicial decision stating that operas written by foreigners could not receive copyright unless the composer personally supervised the first English production. This was presumably an interpretation of the requirement that first publication be in England for printed matter to receive copyright. Verdi (1971), pp. 99–100.

104. On Richard Wagner's failure to secure English copyright after it was available and his concession of rights in Italy without being informed that a treaty with Prussia would be signed in 1869, see Altmann (1911), vol. 2, pp. 48 note, 133–34, and 238–44.

105. See Beethoven (1969), vol. 1, pp. 45, 102–3, 107, 120, 185, 386, 393, 400–401, 423, and 430; vol. 2, pp. 46, 134, 172, and 244; and Raynor (1972), pp. 346–47.

106. Nowell-Smith (1968, p. 35) remarks that "the need for first publication [in Great Britain] was never in doubt," but does not explain how that requirement became part of the law. The original Statute of Anne dated the issue of copyright on new works "from the day of the *first* publishing the same." "First" here could be interpreted to mean that publication must take place first in Great Britain, but that seems in context an inferior construction.

107. Benyovszky (1934), p. 71.

108. Raynor (1972), p. 237. Gaetano Donizetti's arrangements with the Paris Opéra were more generous: for *Les Martyrs*, written in 1840, he received 250 francs (£9.75) for each performance up to 40 and then 100 francs for every performance thereafter. Weinstock (1963), pp. 145–59.

109. Weinstock (1968), p. 343.

110. Rosselli (1996), p. 75. In the precopyright era, Beethoven received modest fees for the performance of *Fidelio* in diverse cities, for instance, 12 ducats (£6) each for performances in Stuttgart, Darmstadt, and Karlsruhe and 15 ducats for Hamburg. Forbes (1967), p. 588.

111. See also the section on "The Costs of Alternative Publication Methods" in this chapter.

112. Jensen (1989), p. 60.

113. See, e.g., Scherer and Ross (1990), p. 490.

114. Jensen (1989), p. 151.

115. Rosselli (2000), p. 119.

116. Weinstock (1963), p. 159.

117. For an itemized list with prices, see Jensen (1989), pp. 421–36.

118. Jensen (1989), p. 180.

119. See, for example, Altmann (1912), vol. 1, p. 133; and (1911), vol. 2, pp. 182 and 237.

120. Vallas (1951), p. 249.

121. Avins (1997), p. 648.

122. Avins (1997), p. 675 (December 1890). See also p. 654.

123. Hogwood (1984), p. 130.

124. Verdi (1971), p. 101.

125. Schubert (1974), p. 97.

126. Wierzynski (1949), p. 274; and Samson (1996), p. 72.

127. Avins (1997), p. 152.

128. Avins (1997), p. 523.

129. Avins (1997), p. 584.

130. Brown (1978), p. 128.

131. Schubert (1974), p. 69.

132. Altmann (1911), vol. 2, p. 5.

133. Altmann (1911), vol. 2, pp. 30–41.

134. Altmann (1911), vol. 2, p. 51.

135. Altmann (1911), vol. 2, pp. 57–58.

136. Rothschild (1965), pp. 104, 127.

137. Samson (1996), p. 72.

138. Rosselli (2000), p. 169.

139. Beethoven (1969), vol. 1, p. 334; vol. 2, pp. 28, 150, 197 and 246.

140. In economics, this problem is discussed under the rubric "asymmetric information." See A. Postelwaite, "Asymmetric Information," *The New Palgrave Dictionary of Economics* (London: Macmillan, 1987), vol. 1, pp. 133–35; and Towse (1999), p. 552.

141. Schubert (1974), p. 122. A similar letter was dispatched to the Probst firm in Leipzig, with equally negative results. See also chapter 4, section on "Extremes."

142. Hase (1968), vol. 1, p. 191.

143. For a composer to take copies in compensation was not an unusual practice. When Estienne Roger of Amsterdam printed Arcangelo Corelli's Concerti Grossi op. 6, for example, Corelli received 150 copies, which he planned to sell in Rome. Carl Czerny told Beethoven that he normally took sheet music as payment from publishers. Presumably, he could give or sell it to his many piano students. Forbes (1967), p. 956.

144. Raynor (1972), p. 339.

145. Clapham (1979), pp. 45–47.

146. On twentieth-century composers' preference for royalties (following a partial advance) and publishers' preference for front-end honoraria, see Towse (1999), pp. 373–75.

147. Altmann (1912), vol. 1, pp. 94–106.

148. Hase (1968), vol. 1, p. 225.

149. Hase (1968), vol. 1, p. 155.

150. Hase (1968), vol. 1, 161–78.

151. More exactly, the winner's curse reflects the tendency for the winning bid in competitive auctions to exceed the auctioned object's true value, revealed only after subsequent experience dispels valuation uncertainties. For a comprehensive survey, see Kagel and Levin (2002). On the winner's curse in book-publication advances, see Caves (2000), pp. 142–43.

152. Avins (1997), p. 328.

153. Samson (1996), p. 146.

154. Haydn (1959), pp. xxi, 53–55, and 76; and Raynor (1972), pp. 341–42.

155. Haydn (1959), p. 123.

156. Hase (1968), vol. 1, pp. 170–71.

157. Beethoven (1969), vol. 1, p. 30 (to Franz Wegeler in 1800).

158. See Moore (1987), pp. 40 and 337–43.

159. Altmann (1911), vol. 2, pp. 196–97.

160. Altmann (1911), vol. 2, p. 189.

161. Wolff (2000), pp. 375–79 and 430.

162. Newbould (1997), p. 175; and Hase (1968), vol. 1, p. 190.

163. The subscription list is reprinted in Robbins Landon (1977), vol. 4, pp. 622–32.

164. Hase (1968), vol. 1, p. 158.

165. Raynor (1972), pp. 343–44.

166. Forbes (1967), pp. 821–33.

167. Mozart (1962), vol. 3, p. 302.

168. Mozart (1962), vol. 2, p. 444.

169. Rothschild (1965), pp. 66–67.

170. Hase (1968), vol. 1, p. 162.

171. Hase (1968), vol. 1, p. 187.

172. Hase (1968), vol. 1, p. 191.

173. Beethoven (1969), vol. 1, p. 39.

174. Clapham (1979), p. 101.

175. Hase (1968), vol. 1, pp. 200–201.

176. The data, complete for 92 compositions with opus numbers listed, are from Schumann (1971), vol. 3, Part 2 (*Haushaltbücher*), pp. 669–83.

177. Moore (1987), pp. 331–33.

178. The dependent variable FEE is the amount received for a work or package of works. Explanatory variables include OPUS, the opus number; NRSONAT, the number of sonatas in a bundle; NRLIED, the number of songs in a lieder cycle; SONAT, a dummy variable with value of 1 if the composition was a sonata or equivalent and zero otherwise; OPERA, a dummy variable distinguishing *Peri* and *Genoveva*; a dummy variable CHORAL for other choral works; a dummy variable SYMPH identifying the four symphonies; a dummy variable ORCH identifying other major orchestral works (such as concertos and overtures); and a dummy variable LIED identifying song cycles. The base case, impounded in the equation intercept, measures an average fee for chamber works such as trios, quartets, and quintets. The least-squares regression equation analyzing 90 honorarium observations, with *t*-ratios in subscripted brackets, was as follows:

$$
\begin{aligned}
\text{FEE} = 51.12 &+ 0.57 \text{ OPUS} + 3.71 \text{ NRSONAT} + 3.73 \text{ NRLIED} \\
&\ [2.37]\quad [3.30]\qquad\quad [2.67]\qquad\qquad\quad\ [2.57] \\
&- 20.22 \text{ SONAT} - 55.08 \text{ LIED} + 27.63 \text{ ORCH} + 72.24 \text{ SYMPH} \\
&\ \ [0.90]\qquad\quad\ [2.69]\qquad\quad\ [1.12]\qquad\qquad [2.25] \\
&+ 567.95 \text{ OPERA} + 85.07 \text{ CHORAL}; R^2 = 0.756. \\
&\ \ [13.33]\qquad\qquad\ [3.03]
\end{aligned}
$$

The R^2 value tells the fraction of the FEE variable's variance explained by the various explanatory variables. Roughly three-fourths of the variance is explained, which is quite a lot for a cross-section analysis.

To interpret, for example, the coefficient for symphonies, we add the 72.24 value specially attributable to publishing a symphony to the intercept or base case value of 51.12 (which was what the average chamber work yielded), finding the total average compensation for a symphony to be 51.12 + 72.24 = 123.36 thaler, other things (such as the OPUS reputation effect) being held constant. Interpreting the data for lieder and sonatas is a bit more complicated. For sonatas, we add to the intercept value of 51.12 the −20.22 coefficient on SONATA, estimating that a single sonata brought 30.90 thalers. The coefficient on NRSONAT then tells us that each additional sonata in a bundle brought on average 3.71 thaler, or about a half week's wages for an English building craftsman. For songs, a similar procedure informs us that a single song brought 51.12 − 55.08 = −3.96 thaler, which is impossible and reveals statistical estimation error; but from NRLIED, we find plausibly that each additional song yielded 3.73 thaler.

179. In addition to averaging between exchange rates for different time periods, various methodological problems have to be surmounted. Notably, any statistical analysis can be strongly influenced by extreme observations or "outliers." The most extreme values in the combined sample are the 773 thaler Schumann received for his opera *Genoveva* and the 550 thaler for his oratorio *Peri*. Data on Beethoven's *Fidelio* honoraria, at least in full-score form, were not available. The only comparable piece by Beethoven was his oratorio *Christus am Ölberg* (Christ on the Mount of Olives), which was part of a three-work package (including a Mass and a piano arrangement of *Fidelio*) with a total value of 55 ducats, or 18.33 ducats (= 48.4 thaler) per item. The implied *Ölberg* fee is nowhere near the honoraria Schumann received for his two major operalike works. Should they be included in the same category, or should *Ölberg* be considered a work for choir, soloists, and orchestra, which would put it in the CHORAL category? Schumann wanted to write an opera for *Peri* and struggled with the issue for eighteen months before spending four months of hard work composing it as an oratorio, which he hoped at the time would be his "biggest and hopefully also best work." Beethoven composed *Ölberg* in two or three weeks. A contemporary review referred to it as a cantata. On modern CD performances, *Peri* runs nearly twice as long as *Ölberg*—95 minutes vs. 52 minutes on average from CDs in Harvard's Loeb music library. The decision was made to treat the two differently, classifying *Ölberg* as a choral work.

Given this assumption, the following regression equation was obtained for the pooled Schumann and Beethoven observations:

$$\text{FEE} = 32.74 + 0.75 \text{ OPUS} + 3.67 \text{ NRSONAT} + 3.73 \text{ NRLIED}$$
$$[1.93] \quad [4.70] \qquad [2.49] \qquad\qquad [2.14]$$
$$- 11.77 \text{ SONAT} - 48.68 \text{ LIED} + 23.37 \text{ ORCH} + 67.42 \text{ SYMPH}$$
$$[1.13] \qquad\quad [2.58] \qquad\quad [1.27] \qquad\qquad [2.93]$$
$$+ 575.00 \text{ OPERA} + 96.41 \text{ CHORAL} - 0.86 \text{ COMPOSER}; R^2 = 0.597.$$
$$[11.65] \qquad\qquad [3.82] \qquad\qquad [0.07]$$

The added dummy variable COMPOSER, with a value of 1 for Schumann works and zero for Beethoven works, is tiny and far from statistically significant, suggesting no systematic difference in the fees received by the two composers and that the thaler / ducat conversion ratio of 2.64 adequately accounted for differences in exchange rates. The homogeneity conclusion suggested by the

COMPOSER coefficient and a more general Chow test for coefficient homogeneity no longer holds if Beethoven's *Ölberg* is classified as an operalike work. Then the two composers' compensation schemes are found to be statistically heterogeneous, the main reason being the low fee received for *Ölberg* as compared to the very high honoraria received for *Peri* and *Genoveva*.

180. Julia Moore (1987), p. 330, expressly rejects the inflation hypothesis, but she did not control for the multiplicity of effects analyzed here.

181. Clara Schumann, ed., *Robert Schumann's Werke* (originally published in 13 series by Breitkopf & Härtel; republished by the Gregg Press: Farnborough, U.K., 1967).

182. For the opera *Genoveva*, performance fees were excluded from the computation; they were included in the previous analysis.

183. In a regression equation that controlled also for opus number, the differences in compensation per page for lieder, sonatas and similar works, and chamber compositions, as compared to large-scale works, were statistically significant at high confidence levels.

184. See also chapter 4, section on "Insights from Economic Theory."

185. See the concluding section in chapter 4.

CHAPTER 8

1. Haydn (1959), p. 118.

2. See "PolyGram Classics," Harvard Business School case study 9-588-074 (November 1997), p. 5, where it is estimated that classical recordings generated 5.2 percent of total world record sales in 1996—down from 9.0 percent in 1987.

3. Ibid.; and *In the Matter of Polygram Holding, Inc., et al.*, U.S. Federal Trade Commission Docket No. 9298, initial decision of the administrative law judge, June 2002, para. 58.

4. See Baumol and Bowen (1965); and Caves (2000), pp. 229–30, 265–67, and 356–59.

5. To be sure, there may be slight productivity gains if musicians of the twenty-first century are better trained than their nineteenth-century counterparts and hence can perform at a given quality level with less rehearsal time. But the differences here are almost surely small.

6. Government plays an indirect role, since donations to cultural activities are almost always deductible under income tax rules.

APPENDIX, CHAPTER 1

1. Mozart (1962), vol. 1, p. 103, and vol. 5, p. 86. At the time, northwestern Europe was experiencing a wave of bank failures, leading inter alia to florin devaluations about which Leopold was accurately informed. See Mozart (1962), vol. 1, pp. 86–87.

The twenty-one-year-old Felix Mendelssohn (1984, p. 129) wrote in the same vein to his brother from Linz, Austria, in 1830, "Oh Paul? Do you know how to get around with gold florins, heavy florins, light florins, Viennese florins, standard florins, and the devil and his grandmother's florins? I don't."

2. Maddison (2001), p. 264.

3. See Frey and Stutzer (2002) for confirmation through comparative evidence from surveys.

4. They are Mitchell (1988), pp. 700–703; McCusker (1978), especially tables 2.16, 2.23, and 2.25; Waschinski (1952), pp. 199–225; and Felloni (1968), tables 67 and 69. The author is indebted to Stefano Fenoaltea for calling attention to the fourth source.

5. The conversion rate of 21 shillings per guinea became firmly established only in 1717. See Sargent and Velde (2002), pp. 293–98.

6. The word "thaler," sometimes spelled "taler," originated from coins minted in the Joachimsthal (Valley of Joachim) of Bohemia. Many German coins were later minted from prolific silver mines in the vicinity of Freiberg, where Gottfried Silbermann established his organ-building business. The family name almost surely stems from the silver-mining operations that dominated the Freiberg economy for centuries.

7. The sharp devaluation of French currency in 1720 was attributable to the unconstrained issue of paper money by the Banque Royal and then the bursting of the Mississippi Bubble. See Kindleberger (1985), pp. 96–98.

8. For excellent analyses of the estimation problems, see McCusker (1978), pp. 18–25; and Shaw (1899).

Among the most severe market imperfections were absolute refusals to accept "foreign" currencies, as in the case of a transfer student to the University of Berlin in 1766 whose 400 thaler were confiscated by the Prussian customs police because they were in the form of Nürnberg Batzen, not accepted as legal tender. The student was more than fully reimbursed after a face-to-face meeting with Frederick the Great. MacDonogh (1999), pp. 344–45.

9. A monetary union adopted among most German states in 1838 supposedly stabilized the silver content of the diverse circulating thaler and gulden. See Sargent and Velde (2002), pp. 306–8.

10. See, e.g., Mozart (1962), vol. 1, pp. 155–57 (from the Mozarts' visit in 1764). The cost of living in London and environs was also higher than in northern and southwestern England and Scotland. See Hunt (1986).

APPENDIX, CHAPTER 4

1. The expenditure data are recorded in Schumann (1971), specifically, in vol. 3, *Haushaltbücher* (Household Books), pp. 171–203.

2. Schumann (1971), vol. 3, p. 242.

REFERENCES

Abel, Wilhelm (1978). *Agricultural Fluctuations In Europe from the Thirteenth to the Twentieth Centuries*, 3rd ed. Translated by Olive Ordish. New York: St. Martin's.

Adelman, M. A. (1969). "Comment on the 'H' Concentration Measure as a Numbers Equivalent," *Review of Economics and Statistics*, vol. 51, pp. 99–101.

Aldingen, Richard, ed. and trans. (1927). *Letters of Voltaire and Frederick the Great*. New York: Brentano's.

Allen, Robert (1994). "Agriculture during the Industrial Revolution." In Roderick Floud and Donald McCloskey, eds., *The Economic History of Britain Since 1700*, 2nd ed., pp. 96–122. Cambridge, U.K.: Cambridge University Press.

Allsop, Peter (1999). *Arcangelo Corelli: New Orpheus of Our Times*. Oxford: Oxford University Press.

Alt, Peter-André (2000). *Schiller: Leben-Werk-Zeit*. Munich: Beck.

Altmann, Wilhelm, ed. (1911). *Richard Wagners Briefwechsel mit B. Schotts Söhne* (Richard Wagner's Exchange of Letters with B. Schott's Sons). Vol. 2 of 2. Mainz: Schott.

——— (1912). *Richard Wagner: Briefwechsel mit seinen Verlegern* (Richard Wagner: Exchange of Letters with His Publishers). Vol. 1 of 2. Leipzig: Breitkopf & Härtel.

Asch, Ronald G. (1997). *The Thirty Years War*. New York: St. Martin's.

Audretsch, David, and Steven Klepper (2000). *Innovation, Evolution of Industry and Economic Growth*. Cheltenham, U.K.: Edward Elgar.

Avins, Styra, ed. (1997). *Johannes Brahms: Life and Letters*. Oxford: Oxford University Press.

Bairoch, Paul, Jean Batou, and Pierre Chèvre (1988). *La Population des Villes Européenes, 800–1850*. Geneva: Librairie Droz.

Barbier, Patrick (1996). *The World of the Castrati*. London: Souvenir Press.

Baumol, Hilda, and William J. Baumol (2002). "Maledizione! Or the Perilous Prospects of Beethoven's Patrons." *Journal of Cultural Economics*, vol. 26, no. 3, pp. 167–84.

Baumol, William J., and Hilda Baumol (1994a). "On the Economics of Musical Composition in Mozart's Vienna." In James M. Morris, ed., *On Mozart*, pp. 72–101. Cambridge, U.K.: Woodrow Wilson Center Press and Cambridge University Press.

——— (1994b). "On the Economics of Musical Composition in Mozart's Vienna." *Journal of Cultural Economics*, vol. 18, no. 3, pp. 171–98.

Baumol, William J., and William J. Bowen (1965). "On the Performing Arts: The Anatomy of Their Economic Problems." *American Economic Review*, vol. 55 supplement, pp. 495–502.

Beer, Samuel H., ed. (1955). *The Communist Manifesto*. New York: Appleton-Century-Crofts.

Beethoven, Ludwig van (1969). *Beethoven's Letters*. 2 vols. Edited by Alf C. Kalischer. Translated by J. S. Shedlock. Freeport, N.Y.: Books for Libraries Press.

Benton, Rita (1990). *Pleyel as Music Publisher*. Annotated Reference Tools in Music No. 3. Stuyvesant, N.Y.: Pendragon.

Benyovszky, Karl (1934). *J. N. Hummel: Der Mensch und Künstler* (J. N. Hummel: The Person and Artist). Bratislava: Eos.

Berlin, Isaiah, ed. (1956). *The Age of Enlightenment: The Eighteenth Century Philosophers*. Boston: Houghton Mifflin.

Berlioz, Hector (1966). *Memoirs of Hector Berlioz from 1803 to 1865*. Edited by Ernest Newmann. Translated by Rachel Holmes and Eleanor Holmes. New York: Dover.

Bianconi, Lorenzo, and Giorgio Pestelli, eds. (1998). *Opera Production and Its Resources*. Chicago: University of Chicago Press.

Blum, Jerome (1978). *The End of the Old Order in Rural Europe*. Princeton: Princeton University Press.

Boorstein, Daniel J. (1983). *The Discoverers*. New York: Random House.

Boulding, Kenneth (1962). *Conflict and Defense: A General Theory*. New York: Harper.

Bowden, Witt, Michael Karpovich, and Abbott P. Usher (1937). *An Economic History of Europe Since 1750*. New York: American Book Company.

Boyd, Malcolm (1986). *Domenico Scarlatti — Master of Music*. New York: Schirmer.

Braunbehrens, Volkmar (1989). *Salieri: Ein Musiker im Schatten Mozarts* (Salieri: A Musician in the Shadow of Mozart). Munich: Piper.

Brown, Maurice J. E. (1978). *Schubert: A Critical Biography*. London: Macmillan.

Burney, Charles (1959). *The Present State of Music in Germany, the Netherlands, and United Provinces*. Originally published in 1773–1775. Republished as vol. 2 of Percy A. Scholes, ed., *Dr. Burney's Musical Tours in Europe* (London: Oxford University Press).

Carhart, Thad (2001). *The Piano Shop on the Left Bank*. New York: Random House.

Caves, Richard E. (2000). *Creative Industries: Contracts between Art and Commerce*. Cambridge, Mass.: Harvard University Press.

Chandler, Tertius, and Gerald Fox (1974). *3000 Years of Urban Growth*. New York: Penguin.

Chopin, Frédéric (1984). *Frédéric Chopin Briefe* (Frédéric Chopin's Letters). Edited by Krystyna Kobylanska. Translated by Caesar Rymarowicz. Frankfurt: S. Fischer Verlag.

Clapham, J. H. (1951) *The Economic Development of France and Germany*, 4th ed. Cambridge, U.K.: Cambridge University Press.

Clapham, John (1979). *Dvořák*. New York: Norton.

Clotfelter, C. T., and Philip Cook (1989). *Selling Hope: State Lotteries in America*. Cambridge, Mass.: Harvard University Press.

Clough, Shepard Bancroft, and Charles Woolsey Cole (1941). *Economic History of Europe*. Boston: Heath.

Coase, Ronald (1937). "The Nature of the Firm." *Economica*, vol. 4, pp. 386–405.

Cooper, Martin (1935). *Gluck*. London: Chatto & Windus.

Courcy, G.I.C. de (1977). *Paganini: The Genoese*. New York: Da Capo Press.

Cowen, Tyler (1998). *In Praise of Commercial Culture*. Cambridge: Harvard University Press.

Crafts, Nicholas F. R. (1996). "The First Industrial Revolution: A Guided Tour for Growth Economists." *American Economic Review*, vol. 86, no. 2, pp. 197–201.

Crocker, Lester G., ed. (1969). *The Age of Enlightenment*. New York: Harper Torchbooks.

Croll, Gerhard, and Kurt Vössing (1987). *Johann Michael Haydn: Sein Leben, Sein Schaffen, Seine Zeit* (Johann Michael Haydn: His Life, His Works, His Era). Salzburg: Neff.

Czerny, Carl (1968). *Carl Czerny: Erinerungen aus meinem Leben*. Edited by Walter Kolneder. Baden-Baden: Valentin Koerner.

David, Hans T., and Arthur Mendel, eds. (1966). *The Bach Reader*, 1st rev. ed. New York: Norton.

Deathridge, John, and Carl Dahlhaus (1984). *The New Grove Wagner*. New York: Norton.

Delon, Michel, ed. (2001). *Encyclopedia of the Enlightenment*. Chicago: Fitzroy Dearborn.

Demetz, Peter (1997). *Prague in Black and Gold*. New York: Hill and Wang.

DeNora, Tia (1991). "Musical Patronage and Social Change in Beethoven's Vienna." *American Journal of Sociology*, vol. 97, pp. 310–46.

Deutsch, Otto Erich, ed. (1955). *Handel: A Documentary Biography*. New York: Norton.

DeVany, Arthur, and W. D. Walls (1996). "Bose-Einstein Dynamics and Adaptive Contracting in the Motion Picture Industry," *Economic Journal*, vol. 106, pp. 1493–1514.

——— (2001). "Momentum, Motion Picture Profit, and the Curse of the Superstars." Working paper, University of California, Irvine.

Dewitz, Margarethe von (1933). *Jean Baptiste Vanhal: Leben und Klavierwerke* (Jean Baptiste Vanhal: Life and Piano Works). Munich: Salesianische Officin.

Duchin, Jessica (2000). *Gabriel Fauré*. London: Phaedon.

Ehrlich, Cyril (1990). *The Piano: A History*, rev. ed. Oxford: Clarendon Press.

Einstein, Alfred (1962). *Mozart: His Character, His Work*. Translated by Arthur Mendel and Nathan Broder. Oxford: Oxford University Press.

——— (1972). *Gluck*. Translated by Eric Blom. New York: McGraw-Hill.

Elias, Norbert (1969). *Die höfische Gesellschaft* (The Court Society). Darmstadt: Luchterhand.

——— (1991). *Mozart: Zur Soziologie eines Genies*. Frankfurt: Suhrkamp Verlag.

——— (1993). *Mozart: Portrait of a Genius*. Translated by Edmund Jephcott. Berkeley: University of California Press.

Fantel, Hans (1971). *Johann Strauss: Father and Son and Their Era.* Newton Abbott, U.K.: David & Charles.

Feinstein, Charles H. (1988). "The Rise and Fall of the Williamson Curve." *Journal of Economic History*, vol. 48, pp. 699–729.

——— (1998). "Pessimism Perpetuated: Real Wages and the Standard of Living in Britain during and after the Industrial Revolution." *Journal of Economic History*, vol. 58, pp. 625–55.

Felloni, Giuseppe (1968). *Il Mercato Monetario in Piemonte nel Secolo XVIII* (The Piedmont Money Market in the Eighteenth Century). Milan: Banca Commerciale Italiana.

Forbes, Elliot, ed. (1967). *Thayer's Life of Beethoven*, rev. ed. Princeton: Princeton University Press.

Frey, Bruno S., and Alois Stutzer (2002). "What Can Economists Learn from Happiness Research?" *Journal of Economic Literature*, vol. 40, pp. 402–35.

Garden, Edward (1973). *Tchaikovsky.* London: Dent.

Garden, Edward, and Nigel Gotteri, eds. (1993). *To My Best Friend: Correspondence between Tchaikowski and Nadezhda von Meck.* Translated by Galina von Meck. New York: Oxford University Press.

Gardner, Howard (1994). "How Extraordinary Was Mozart?" In James M. Morris, ed., *On Mozart*, pp. 36–51. Cambridge, U.K.: Woodrow Wilson Center Press and Cambridge University Press.

Garnett, Kevin, Jonathan James, and Gillian Davies (1999). *Copinger and Skone James on Copyright*, 14th ed. London: Sweet & Maxwell.

Gärtner, Heinz (1994). *John Christian Bach: Mozart's Friend and Mentor.* Translated by Reinhard G. Pauly. Portland, Ore.: Amadeus Press.

Gieseke, Ludwig (1995). *Vom Privileg zum Urheberrecht* (From Privileges to Copyright). Göttingen: Otto Schwartz.

Girdlestone, Cuthbert (1957). *Jean-Philippe Rameau: His Life and Work.* London: Cassell.

Good, David (1984). *The Economic Rise of the Habsburg Empire, 1750–1914.* Berkeley: University of California Press.

Gotwals, Vernon, ed. and trans. (1963). *Joseph Haydn: Eighteenth-Century Gentleman and Genius,* collecting accounts by Georg August Griesinger published serially in the *Allgemeine Musikalische Zeitung* (1809); and Albert C. Dies, *Biographische Nachrichten von Joseph Haydn* (Biographical Accounts on Joseph Haydn), Vienna (1810). Madison: University of Wisconsin Press.

Gradenwitz, Peter (1984). *Johann Stamitz: Leben, Umwelt, Werke* (Johann Stamitz: Life, Environment, Works). Wilhelmshaven: Heinrichshofen.

Green, Rebecca (1997). "Representing the Aristocracy: The Operatic Haydn and *Le pescatrici.*" In Elaine Susman, ed., *Haydn and His World*, pp. 154–200. Princeton: Princeton University Press.

Haberstumpf, Helmut (1996). *Handbuch des Urheberrechts* (Copyright Handbook). Berlin: Luchterhand.

Hammermesh, Daniel S., and Albert Rees (1984). *The Economics of Work and Pay*, 3rd ed. New York: Harper & Row.

Hase, Oskar von (1968). *Breitkopf & Härtel.* 5th printing of original 1917 version. 3 vols. (vol. 3 by Hellmuth von Hase). Wiesbaden: Breitkopf & Härtel.

Haslip, Joan (1977). *Catherine the Great*. New York: Putnam.

Haydn, Franz Joseph (1959). *The Collected Correspondence and London Notebooks of Joseph Haydn*. Edited by H. C. Robbins Landon. Fair Lawn, N.J.: Essential Books.

Heller, Karl (1997). *Antonio Vivaldi: The Red Priest of Venice*. Translated by David Marinelli. Portland, Ore: Amadeus Press.

Helm, Ernest Eugene (1960). *Music in the Court of Frederick the Great*. Norman: University of Oklahoma Press.

Hildesheimer, Wolfgang (1982). *Mozart*. Translated by Marion Faber. New York: Farrar Straus Giroux.

Hill, W. Henry, Arthur Hill, and Alfred Hill (1963). *Antonio Stradivari: His Life and Work*. New York: Dover.

Hoboken, Anthony van (1957–1978). *Joseph Haydn: Thematisch-bibliographisches Werkverzeichnis*. 3 vols. Mainz: Schott.

Hogwood, Christopher (1984). *Handel*. London: Thames and Hudson.

Holland, A. K. (1932). *Henry Purcell: The English Musical Tradition*. London: Bell.

Holoman, D. Kern (1989). *Berlioz: A Musical Biography of the Creative Genius of the Romantic Age*. Cambridge, Mass.: Harvard University Press.

Hübel, Marlene (1995). *Gedruckte Music: 225 Jahre Musikverlag Schott in Mainz* (Printed Music: 225 Years of the Schott Music House in Mainz). Mainz: Gutenberg-Museum.

Hunt, E. H. (1986). "Industrialization and Regional Inequality: Wages in Britain, 1760–1914." *Journal of Economic History*, vol. 46, pp. 935–66.

Hunter, David (1986). "Music Copyright in Britain to 1800," *Music & Letters*, vol. 67, pp. 269–82.

Jensen, Luke (1989). *Giuseppe Verdi and Giovanni Ricordi with Notes on Francesco Lucca*. New York: Garland.

Kagel, John H., and Dan Levin (2002). *Common Value Auctions and the Winner's Curse*. Princeton: Princeton University Press.

Kaufer, Erich (1989). *The Economics of the Patent System*. Chur, Switzerland: Harwood.

Keates, Jonathan (1996). *Purcell: A Biography*. London: Pimlico.

Kelly, Thomas F. (2000). *First Nights: Five Musical Premieres*. New Haven: Yale University Press.

Kennedy, Michael, ed. (1994). *The Oxford Dictionary of Music*, rev. ed. Oxford: Oxford University Press.

Kennedy, Paul (1987). *The Rise and Fall of the Great Powers*. New York: Random House.

Kennickell, Arthur B., Martha Starr-McCluer, and Brian Surette (2000). "Recent Changes in U.S. Family Finances: Results from the 1998 Survey of Consumer Finances." *Federal Reserve Bulletin*, vol. 86, no. 1, pp. 1–29.

Kimbell, David R. B. (1981). *Verdi in the Age of Italian Romanticism*. Cambridge, U.K.: Cambridge University Press.

Kindleberger, Charles F. (1985). *A Financial History of Western Europe*. London: George Allen & Unwin.

King, Timothy (2001). "Patronage and Market in the Creation of Opera Before the Institution of Intellectual Property." *Journal of Cultural Economics*, vol. 25, pp. 21–45.

Kinsky, Georg (1955). *Das Werk Beethovens: Thematisch-bibliographisches Verzeichnis seiner sämtlichen vollendeten Kompositionen* (The Work of Beethoven: Thematic and Bibliographic Index of His Entire Completed Compositions). Edited by Hans Halm. Munich: Henle.

Krummel, D. W., and Stanley Sadie, eds. (1990). *Music Printing and Publishing*. New York: Norton.

Landes, David (1969). *The Unbound Prometheus: Technology and Industrial Development in Western Europe from 1750 to the Present*. Cambridge, U.K.: Cambridge University Press.

——— (1998). *The Wealth and Poverty of Nations*. New York: Norton.

Lang, Paul Henry (1966, 1977). *George Frideric Handel*. New York: Norton.

Large, Brian (1970). *Smetana*. New York: Praeger.

Leitner, Thea (1994). *Habsburgs verkaufte Töchter* (Habsburg's Sold Daughters). Munich: Piper.

Lindert, Peter H. (1986). "Unequal English Wealth since 1670." *Journal of Political Economy*, vol. 94, pp. 1127–62.

MacDonogh, Giles (1999). *Frederick the Great: A Life in Deed and Letters*. New York: St. Martin's.

Maddison, Angus (1995). *Monitoring the World Economy: 1820–1992*. Paris: OECD.

——— (2001). *The World Economy: A Millennial Perspective*. Paris: OECD.

Mantoux, Paul (1961). *The Industrial Revolution in the Eighteenth Century*. New York: Harper.

Marek, George R. (1972). *Gentle Genius: The Story of Felix Mendelssohn*. New York: Funk & Wagnalls.

Massie, Robert K. (1980). *Peter the Great: His Life and World*. New York: Ballantine.

McCusker, John J. (1978). *Money and Exchange in Europe and America, 1600–1775*. Chapel Hill: University of North Carolina Press.

McEvedy, Colin, and Richard Jones (1978). *Atlas of World Population History*. London: Penguin.

McVeigh, Simon (1993). *Concert Life in London from Mozart to Haydn*. Cambridge, U.K.: Cambridge University Press.

Medoff, Marshall (1996). "A Citation-Based Analysis of Economists and Economics Programs." *The American Economist*, vol. 40, pp. 46–59.

Mendelssohn-Bartholdy, Felix (1986). *Felix Mendelssohn: A Life in Letters*. Edited by Rudolf Elvers. Translated from the 1984 German original by Craig Tomlinson. New York: Fromm.

Merton, Robert K. (1962). "Puritanismn, Pietism, and Science." In Bernard Barber and Walter Hirsch, eds., *The Sociology of Science*, pp. 33–66. Glencoe, Illinois: Free Press.

Mitchell, B. R., ed. (1988). *British Historical Statistics*. Cambridge, U.K.: Cambridge University Press.

——— (1998). *International Historical Statistics: Europe 1750–1993*. London: Macmillan.

Mokyr, Joel (1988). "Is There Still Life in the Pessimist Case?" *Journal of Economic History*, vol. 48, pp. 69–92.

—— (1990). *The Lever of Riches.* Oxford: Oxford University Press.

—— (2002). *The Gifts of Athena: Historical Origins of the Knowledge Economy.* Princeton: Princeton University Press.

Mokyr, Joel, ed. (1999). *The Economics of the Industrial Revolution*, 2nd ed. Boulder, Colo.: Westview.

Monrad-Johansen, David (1938). *Edvard Grieg.* Translated by Madge Robertson. Princeton: Princeton University Press.

Moore, Julia V. (1987). "Beethoven and Musical Economics." Ph.D. dissertation, University of Illinois at Urbana-Champaign.

Mozart, Wolfgang Amadeus (1962 et seq.). *Mozart: Briefe und Aufzeichnungen* (Mozart: Letters and Notes). Edited by Wilhelm A. Bauer and Otto Erich Deutsch. 7 vols. Kassel: Bärenreiter.

Müller, Werner (1972). *Auf den Spuren von Gottfried Silbermann* (Following the Clues to Gottfried Silbermann). Berlin: Evangelische Verlagsanstalt.

Newbould, Brian (1997). *Schubert: The Music and the Man.* Berkeley: University of California Press.

Newman, Ernest (1933). *The Life of Richard Wagner.* 4 vols. New York: Knopf.

Niemann, Walter (1937). *Brahms.* Translated by Catherine A. Phillips. New York: Tudor.

Noonan, Frederick, trans. (1987). *Beethoven Remembered.* Translation of F. G. Wegeler and Ferdinand Ries, *Biographische Notizen über Ludwig van Beethoven* (1835, 1845). Arlington, Va.: Great Ocean.

Nowell-Smith, Simon (1968). *International Copyright Law and the Publisher in the Reign of Queen Victoria.* Oxford: Clarendon Press.

Ostwald, Peter (1985). *Schumann: The Inner Voices of a Musical Genius.* Boston: Northeastern University Press.

Petzoldt, Richard (1974). *Georg Philipp Telemann.* Translated by Horace Fitzpatrick. Oxford: Oxford University Press.

Phelps Brown, E. H., and S. V. Hopkins (1955). "Seven Centuries of Building Wages." *Economica*, New Series vol. 22, pp. 195–205.

—— (1956). "Seven Centuries of the Prices of Consumables, Compared with Builders' Wage Rates." *Economica*, New Series vol. 23, pp. 296–314.

Piperno, Franco (1998). "Opera Production to 1780." In Bianconi and Pestelli, eds. *Opera Production and Its Resources*, pp. 1–80. Chicago: University of Chicago Press.

Plantinga, Leon (1977). *Clementi: His Life and Music.* Oxford: Oxford University Press.

Pohlmann, Hansjörg (1962). *Die Frühgeschichte des musikalischen Urheberrechts* (The Early History of Musical Copyright). Kassel: Bärenreiter.

Raynor, Henry (1972). *A Social History of Music from the Middle Ages to Beethoven.* New York: Schocken.

Rees, Brian (1999). *Camille Saint-Saëns: A Life.* London: Chatto & Windus.

Reich, Nancy B. (1985). *Clara Schumann: The Artist and the Woman.* Ithaca: Cornell University Press.

Richardson, Lewis F. (1960). *Arms and Insecurity*. Chicago: Quadrangle.

Riesemann, Oskar von (1926). *Moussorgsky*. Translated by Paul England. New York: Knopf.

Robbins Landon, H. C. (1977). *Haydn: Chronicle and Works*. Bloomington: Indiana University Press.

—— (1988). *1791: Mozart's Last Year*. New York: Schirmer.

—— (1989). *Mozart: The Golden Years*. New York: Schirmer.

—— (1991). *Mozart and Vienna*. New York: Schirmer.

Robbins Landon, H. C., and David Wyn Jones (1988). *Haydn: His Life and Music*. Bloomington: Indiana University Press.

Romer, Paul M. (1990). "Endogenous Technological Change," *Journal of Political Economy*, vol. 98 supplement, pp. S71–102.

Rosen, Sherwin (1981). "The Economics of Superstars," *Journal of Political Economy*, vol. 71, pp. 845–57.

Rosselli, John (1984). *The Opera Industry in Italy from Cimarosa to Verdi: The Role of the Impresario*. Cambridge, U.K.: Cambridge University Press.

—— (1996). *The Life of Bellini*. Cambridge, U.K.: Cambridge University Press.

—— (1998). "Opera Production, 1780–1880." In Bianconi and Pestelli, eds. *Opera Production and Its Resources*, pp. 81–164.

—— (2000). *The Life of Verdi*. Cambridge, U.K.: Cambridge University Press.

Rothschild, Germaine de (1965). *Luigi Boccherini: His Life and Work*. Translated by Andreas Mayor. Oxford: Oxford University Press.

Sadie, Stanley, ed. (1980). *The New Grove Dictionary of Music & Musicians*. 20 vols. New York: Macmillan.

—— (1996). *The New Grove Book of Operas*. New York: St. Martin's Press.

Salmen, Walter (1988). *Das Konzert: Eine Kulturgeschichte*. Munich: C. H. Beck.

Samson, Jim (1996). *Chopin*. New York: Schirmer.

Sargent, Thomas J., and François R. Velde (2002). *The Big Problem of Small Change*. Princeton: Princeton University Press.

Scherer, F. M. (1999). *New Perspectives on Economic Growth and Technological Innovation*. Washington: Brookings Institution.

—— (2001a). "An Early Application of the Average Total Cost Concept," *Journal of Economic Literature*, vol. 39, pp. 897–901.

—— (2001b). "The Evolution of Free-Lance Music Composition, 1650–1900," *Journal of Cultural Economics*, vol. 25, pp. 307–19.

—— (2001c). "The Innovation Lottery." In Rochelle Dreyfuss, Diane Zimmerman, and Harry First, eds. *Expanding the Boundaries of Intellectual Property*, pp. 4–15. Oxford: Oxford University Press.

—— (2001d). "Servility, Opportunity, and Freedom in the Choice of Music Composition as a Profession," *The Musical Quarterly*, vol. 85, no. 4, pp. 718–34.

—— (forthcoming). "The Economics of Innovation and Technological Change." In *Encyclopedia of the Social Sciences*. New York: Oxford University Press.

Scherer, F. M., and David Ross (1990). *Industrial Market Structure and Economic Performance*, 3rd ed. Boston: Houghton-Mifflin.

Scherer, F. M., Dietmar Harhoff, and Jörg Kukies (2000). "Uncertainty and the Size Distribution of Rewards from Innovation." *Journal of Evolutionary Economics*, vol. 10, pp. 175–200.

Scherer, F. M., Dietmar Harhoff, Francis Narin, and Katrin Vopel (1999). "Citation Frequency and the Value of Patented Inventions." *Review of Economics and Statistics*, vol. 81, pp. 511–15.

Schmookler, Jacob (1966). *Invention and Economic Growth*. Cambridge, Mass.: Harvard University Press.

Schubert, Franz (1974). *Franz Schubert's Letters and Other Writings*. Edited by Otto Erich Deutsch. Translated by Venetia Savile. New York: Vienna House.

Schumann, Robert and Clara (1971 et seq.). *Robert Schumann: Tagebücher* (Robert Schumann's Diaries). Edited by Georg Eismann and Gerd Nauhaus. 3 vols. Parts 1 and 2 of vol. 3 are titled *Haushaltsbücher*. Leipzig: VEB deutscher Verlag für Musik.

Schumpeter, Joseph A. (1942). *Capitalism, Socialism, and Democracy*. New York: Harper.

Schwann Opus Reference Guide to Classical Music (1996), vol. 7, no. 4. Santa Fe, N.M.: Schwann Publications.

Shaw, W. A. (1899). *The History of Currency: 1252 to 1894*. New York: Putnam's.

Sitwell, Sacheverell (1967). *Liszt*. New York: Dover.

Smith, Adam (1937). *An Inquiry into the Nature and Causes of the Wealth of Nations*. Edited by Edwin Cannan. New York: Modern Library Edition (originally published in 1776).

Smith, Douglas (1999). *Working the Rough Stone: Freemasonry and Society in Eighteenth-Century Russia*. DeKalb: Northern Illinois University Press.

Spence, Michael, and Bruce Owen (1977). "Television Programming, Monopolistic Competition and Welfare." *Quarterly Journal of Economics*, vol. 91, pp. 103–26.

Steinberg, Sigfrid H. (1966). *The Thirty Years War and the Conflict for European Hegemony, 1600–1660*. London: Edward Arnold.

Surian, Elvidio (1998). "The Opera Composer." In Bianconi and Pestelli, eds., *Opera Production and Its Resources*, pp. 291–344.

Swafford, Jan (1997). *Johannes Brahms*. New York: Knopf.

Tchaikovsky, Pyotr Ilyich (1945). *The Diaries of Tchaikovsky*. Edited and translated by Wladimir Lakond. New York: Norton.

Towse, Ruth (1993). *Singers in the Marketplace*. Oxford: Oxford University Press.

———— (1999). "Copyrights and Economic Incentives: An Application to Performers' Rights in the Music Industry." *Kyklos*, vol. 52, no. 3, pp. 369–90.

U.S. Bureau of the Census (1960). *Historical Statistics of the United States: Colonial Times to 1957*. Washington: USGPO.

Vallas, Leon (1951). *César Franck*. Translated by Hubert Foss. Oxford: Oxford University Press.

Verdi, Giuseppe (1971). *Letters of Giuseppe Verdi.* Edited and translated by Charles Osborne. New York: Holt Rinehart & Winston.

Walker, Alan (1983). *Franz Liszt.* 3 vols. New York: Knopf.

Warrack, John (1968). *Carl Maria von Weber.* New York: Macmillan.

Waschinski, Emil (1952). *Während, Preisentwicklung und Kaufkraft des Geldes in Schleswig-Holstein von 1226–1864* (Exchange Rates, Price Developments, and the Purchasing Power of Money in Schleswig-Holstein from 1226 to 1864). Neumünster: Karl Wachholtz.

Wehmeyer, Grete (1983). *Carl Czerny und die Einzelhaft am Klavier* (Carl Czerny and His Engrossment with the Piano). Kassel: Bärenreiter.

Weinstock, Herbert (1963). *Donizetti and the World of Opera in Italy, Paris, and Vienna in the First Half of the Nineteenth Century.* New York: Pantheon.

——— (1968). *Rossini.* Oxford: Oxford University Press.

Welter, Kathryn Jane (1998). "Johann Pachelbel: Organist, Teacher, Composer." Ph.D. dissertation, Harvard University.

Westernhagen, Curt von (1956). *Wagner: Sein Werk, Sein Wesen, Seine Welt* (Wagner: His Work, His Nature, His World). Zurich: Atlantis Verlag.

Wierzynski, Casimir (1949). *The Life and Death of Chopin.* Translated by Norbert Guterman. New York: Simon & Schuster.

Williamson, Jeffrey G. (1985). *Did British Capitalism Breed Inequality?* Boston: Allen & Unwin.

Wolff, Christoph (1991). *Bach: Essays on His Life and Music.* Cambridge, Mass.: Harvard University Press.

——— (2000). *Johann Sebastian Bach: The Learned Musician.* New York: Norton.

INDEX

Abel, Karl Friedrich, 43, 50, 59–60, 175
Academie Royale de Musique, 15, 41
Academie Royale des Sciences, 15, 21
Adalid y Gurréa, Marcial del, 77
Agricola, Johann Friedrich, 95
Albinoni, Tomaso, 66, 77, 80, 157
Ancient Music, concert of, 110, 167
Arco, Graf Karl Josef, 94, 227n.74
arms race, cultural, 39–40, 118, 136–41, 232n.4
Arne, Thomas, 172
Arrau, Claudio, 225n.12
Arriaga, Juan, 8
Artaria, 170, 176, 186, 187
Augarten (Vienna), 45, 49

Bach, Anna Magdalena, 101
Bach, Carl Philipp Emanuel, 83, 85, 94, 95, 173
Bach, Johann Christian, 43, 50, 59–60, 85, 108–9, 172, 175
Bach, Johann Sebastian, 3, 5, 9, 39, 54, 75, 143, 152, 230n.151; and Collegium Musicum, 44, 59; compositions, 38, 55, 94, 109; finances, 88, 98, 103; relations with employers, 94, 134, 135; self-publication, 187
Bach, Wilhelm Friedemann, 77
Bacon, Francis, 21
Ballard. See LeRoy & Ballard
Barnum, P. T., 98, 130
Barsanti, Francesco, 73
Baumol, William and Hilda, 8, 117–8, 131
Baumol's cost disease, 199–201
Beaumarchais, Pierre Augustin, 25
Beethoven, Ludwig van, 6, 9, 65, 153, 180, 216n.5, 225n.11; compositions, 16, 100, 109, 111, 112; concerts, 60, 99, 101; deafness, 58, 153; liberal views, 95–96, 216n.7; and money matters, 1, 55, 56, 85; publication of works, 164, 165, 170–71, 176, 177–78, 180–81, 183, 185, 186–88, 189, 191–92, 242n.110

Bellini, Vincenzo, 100, 144, 179
Berlioz, Hector, 51, 56, 60–61, 76, 85, 86, 103, 113–14, 143, 144, 153, 223 nn. 35 and 36
Berne Convention, 17, 177, 199
Berwald, Franz, 77
Blow, John, 43
Boccherini, Luigi, 58, 183, 185
Boehm, Theobald, 77
Boismortier, Joseph de, 73
Boito, Arrigo, 77
Bonaparte, Napoleon, 19, 95, 142
Bononcini, Giovanni, 167–68
Bonporti, Francesco, 69
Borodin, Alexander, 76, 77
Boston Peace Festival, 17, 47, 221n.103
Boyce, William, 172
Brahms, Johannes, 17, 58, 59, 90–91, 95, 96, 114, 134, 151, 152, 161, 181–82, 183, 185
Breitkopf, Johann Gottlob Immanuel, 159–60
Breitkopf & Härtel, 135, 156, 157–58, 160, 161–66, 182, 184, 187, 189–90, 238n.11
Broschi, Carlo. See Farinelli
Bull, Ole, 89
Burgmüller, Norbert, 77
Burney, Charles, 232n.12
Buxtehude, Dietrich, 143

Caffarelli (Gaetano Majorano), 97
Carl Eugen, Duke of Württemberg, 169, 220n. 72, 240n.58
Carnegie, Andrew, 130
Catherine II (the Great), 16, 24, 130, 132
censorship, 26–27
Cervetto, Giacobbe, 8
Chabrier, Emmanuel, 77
Charles II, King of England, 43
Charles II, King of Spain, 15, 18
Cherubini, Luigi, 95
Chopin, Frédéric, 4, 45, 47, 59, 64, 65, 96, 100, 113, 129, 145, 181, 186
church music, 37–38, 53–54

class origins, 80, 225n.5
Clementi, Muzio, 58, 64, 77, 104, 157, 189
Collegium Musicum, 3, 15, 44, 59
Colloredo, Hieronymus Joseph, 55, 93, 94
competing courts. See arms race, cultural
concerts: attendance, 45–52; organization, 57–62; venues, 38–41, 43–45
Concert Spirituel, 15, 45
conservatories, 45, 66–67, 75, 83, 84
Copernicus, Nicholaus, 20
copyists, 163–66, 168, 170, 239n.40, 240 nn. 51 and 58
copyright, 194–96, 240n.49; law, 15, 16, 17, 174–78, 242 nn. 103 and 106; utilization, 178–80, 194
Corelli, Arcangelo, 39, 157, 243n.143
Couperin, François, 39, 57, 172, 187
Cramer, Johann Baptist, 77
criticism, music, 61, 76–77, 113–15
Croft, William, 172
Cromwell, Oliver, 15, 38
Csermák, Antal György, 77
Cui, César, 76
currency values, 10, 104, 203–8
Czerny, Carl, 58–59, 64, 76, 80, 176, 180, 243n.143

Dargomyzhsky, Alexander, 77
David, King of Israel, 37
demand: derived, 33; for musical performance, 33, 131–32, 141; for pianos, 34–37, 218n.58
Diabelli, Anton, 77, 182
Dibdin, Charles, 239n.35
Diderot, Denis, 16
Donizetti, Gaetano, 80, 90, 99, 100, 168–69, 180, 242n.108
Dvořák, Antonin, 130, 184, 189

education: of composers, 81–84
Elias, Norbert, 2, 117–18, 131
Elizabeth I, Queen of England, 38
Elsner, Joseph, 77
emancipation of peasants, 17, 24, 25–26, 217n.29
employment: church, 53–54, 69; locus of, 1–2, 140–41, 234n.52; in noble courts, 54–56, 68–69, 92, 97–98; security of, 93–95
Enlightenment, 20–27

Esterházy, Johann, 68, 87
Esterházy, Nikolaus I, 40, 54, 95, 170
Esterházy, Nikolaus II, 40, 95, 101
Esterházy, Paul Anton, 54, 170, 220n.74

family influences, 79–81
Farinelli (Carlo Broschi), 55, 77, 97
fashion. See Taste
Fauré, Gabriel, 144
Ferdinand, Archduke, 92
Ferdinand I, Holy Roman Emperor, 38
Ferdinand II, Holy Roman Emperor, 14
Ferdinand VI, King of Spain, 55
feudalism, 16, 22–26, 127, 131, 136
Field, John, 58, 130
Fischer, J. C., 172
Forqueray, Jean-Baptiste, 172
Forster, William, 186
Franck, César, 100, 109–10, 114, 181
Franklin, Benjamin, 77
Franz II, Emperor of Austria, 25, 26, 123
Frederick I, king in Prussia, 94
Frederick II (the Great), 15, 18–19, 24, 25, 26, 39, 55, 77, 93, 95, 135, 217n.23, 227n.68, 247n.8
free cities, 133–39, 141, 233n.35, 234 nn. 46 and 51
freelance activity, 2, 56–63, 70–75, 107, 150, 197; in composition, 70–74; in performance, 71
Friedrich Augustus II, King of Saxony, 38
Friedrich Wilhelm, King in Prussia, 51

Galilei, Galileo, 15, 20
Galilei, Vincenzo, 220n.75
Garcia, Manuel, 148
Garibaldi, Giuseppe, 17
Gay, John, 46, 73, 199
George II, King of England, 111, 171
George III, King of England, 187
George IV, King of England, 55
Gewandhaus (Leipzig), 44
Glinka, Mikhail, 130
Glorious Revolution, 15, 23
Gluck, Christoph Willibald, 16, 80, 89, 100, 129, 229n.112
Gonzaga family, 41
grand tour, 58
Graun, Karl Heinrich, 93, 95
gravity model, 157–58, 238n.11
Gregory I, Pope, 37

Grieg, Edvard, 65, 78, 146
Gustavus III, King of Sweden, 27
Gutenberg, Johannes, 155

Handel, George Frideric, 5, 10, 39, 41,
    46–47, 50, 57, 85, 128, 172, 181;
    adaptability, 110–12; economic for-
    tunes, 4, 99; as impresario, 4, 62, 75;
    relations with publishers, 167, 171,
    181; royal support, 55, 94
Hanslick, Eduard, 114
Härtel, Gottfried Christoph, 161–62, 176,
    184, 185, 189
Hartmann, Johan, 77
Hasse, Johann, 152
Haydn, Franz Joseph, 6, 47, 54, 58, 89,
    96, 110, 128, 157, 163, 167, 186, 197–
    98, 216n.5; compensation, 98; composi-
    tions, 16, 112, 187; London visits, 43,
    55, 153; relations with employers, 93,
    95, 101, 170
Haydn, Johann Michael, 55, 93, 216n.5
Heidegger, John Jacob, 62
Heinichen, Johann David, 98, 152
Heise, Peter, 77
Heller, Stephen, 84
Hensel, Fanny Mendelssohn, 77
Herschel, William, 77
Hickford, Thomas, 43
Hildesheimer, Wolfgang, ix, 2
Hoffmann, E.T.A., 77
Hoffmann, Leopold, 54
Hoffmeister, Franz Anton, 77, 156
Holy Roman Empire, 6, 12, 14, 117–19,
    126, 131, 133, 141, 173–74, 176–77,
    198, 233 nn. 31 and 32
honoraria. See Publication: fees
Hume, David, 15
Hummel, Johann Nepomuk, 58, 64, 84,
    96, 112, 176, 226n.37
Hus, Jan, 14

impresarios, 62–63, 74–75
income: composers', 94–95, 97–98,
    222n.1; national averages, 28–30, 131,
    233 nn. 31 and 32
Industrial revolution, 28–32, 127, 142

James II, King of England, 23, 43
Jesuits, 38, 83, 217n.34
Joachim, Joseph, 58

Jommelli, Niccolò, 93, 169–70, 240n.58
Joseph II, Emperor of Austria, 24–25, 38,
    40, 45, 54, 217n.24

Kalkbrenner, Friedrich, 176
Karl Friedrich, Duke of Baden, 25
Keiser, Reinhard, 75, 215n.8
Keyserlingk, Hermann von, 55
Kozeluch, Leopold, 77
Krause, Martin, 225n. 12
Kuhnau, Johann, 44, 75, 77
Kühnel, Ambrosius, 156
Kusser, Johann, 75

LaBarre, Michel de, 172
Lanner, Joseph, 47, 75
LaScala (Milan), 51–52
Leclair, Jean-Marie, 57
Leopold I, Duke of Lorraine, 25
Leopold I, Emperor of Austria, 39, 126
Leopold II, Emperor of Austria, 153
LeRoy & Ballard, 155, 172
Lichnowsky, Prince Karl von, 56
Lind, Jenny, 98, 130
Liszt, Franz, 5, 58, 65, 69, 84, 87, 96,
    130, 152, 226 nn. 25 and 27
lithography. See Publication: technology
Lobkowitz, Prince Joseph Franz, 40
Locatelli, Pietro, 72
Locke, John, 15, 21
Loeillet, Jean Baptiste, 75
London, as center of music, 43, 128–29;
    Philharmonic Society, 57
longevity, 8
Longman, James, 175
lotteries, 97, 99, 115–16, 231n.186
Lotti, Antonio, 98, 167
Louis XIV, King of France, 15, 18, 21, 123
Louis XVI, King of France, 25
Louis Ferdinand, Prince of Prussia, 19, 77
Ludwig II, King of Bavaria, 56, 86
Lully, Jean-Baptiste, 41
Luther, Martin, 14, 37, 167

magnet cities, 128–30, 132, 141, 233 nn.
    31 and 32
Manfredini, Vincenzo, 58
Marais, Marin, 39
Marcello, Benedetto, 77
Maria Theresia, Empress of Austria, 15,
    18, 24, 40, 92

Marie Antoinette, 25, 129
Marsh, John, 77
Martínez, Marianne, 77
Martini, Padre Giovanni Battista, 152
Marx, Karl, 216n.8
Mattheson, Johann, 77
Mayr, Simon, 168
Meck, Nadezhda von, 56, 89
Mendelssohn-Bartholdy, Felix, 51, 77, 80, 91, 96, 130, 134, 144, 151, 167, 246n.1
Metropolitan Opera (New York), 17, 37
Metternich, Klemens von, 123
Meyerbeer, Giacomo, 91, 112
mobility, geographic, 124, 132, 139, 147–50, 236n.32
Montesquieu, Charles Louis de, 15, 21
Monteverdi, Claudio, 15, 41, 92
Moscheles, Ignaz, 111, 176, 180
Mouret, Jean Joseph, 172
Mozart, Constanze, 101–2, 103, 185, 229n.128
Mozart, Leopold, 7, 76, 107, 168, 203, 217n.24, 221n.96
Mozart, Nannerl, 43
Mozart, Wolfgang Amadeus, ix, 6, 8, 9, 16, 45, 55, 78, 83, 88–89, 92, 93, 94, 104, 126, 167, 188; composing to tastes, 108, 109, 188–89; concert series, 49–50, 60, 100, 221n.112; as freelance artist, 57; operas, 8, 16, 24–25, 89, 99, 100, 168, 180; reasons for poverty, 54, 100–101, 153, 170; as teacher, 64–65, 84; travel, 43, 58, 129, 143–44, 151, 152–53, 235 nn. 3 and 4
Mussorgsky, Modest, 77, 92, 217n.29

Napoleon. See Bonaparte, Napoleon
Napoleonic wars, 16, 19, 24, 40, 60, 119, 127, 136, 208
Naudot, Jacques-Christophe, 72, 73
Newton, Isaac, 15, 21
New York Philharmonic, 17, 130

Offenbach, Jacques, 47, 75
opera: choice of libretti, 100; composition, 71–79, 99, 100, 108–9; fees, 57, 98–99, 178–81, 191–93, 242n.108, 245n.179; of the Nobility, 62, 99; organization, 41–43, 50, 62; repertory, 46; score reductions, 180

Opéra (Paris), 99, 129, 178
Ospedali (Venice), 66, 75
Ottoboni, Pietro Cardinal, 4, 151

Pachelbel, Johann, 94
Padua, 51
Paganini, Niccolò, 5, 17, 56, 58, 98, 101, 103–4, 115–16, 152, 157
Paine, John Knowles, 76
Palestrina, Giovanni da, 37
Pareto distribution, 9
Paris: Conservatoire, 45, 54, 60–61; as music center, 45, 128–29
Parry, Charles Hubert, 76
patriotic anthems, 111–12, 231n.170
patronage, 1, 55–56, 92
pensions, 101–2, 229 nn. 121 and 128
performance of music: fees, 57–59, 168, 178–80, 242 nn. 108 and 110
Peter I (the Great), Czar of Russia, 15, 45
Peter III, Czar of Russia, 19
Peters, Carl Friedrich, 156
Petrucci, Ottaviano dei, 158–59
Philidor, A. D., 15
Philip V, King of Spain, 18, 55
phonograph, 35–37, 198–99, 219n.59, 246n.2
piano: ownership, 48–49; prices, 36, 218n.57; production, 34–37, 198–99, 218n.58
Piccinni, Niccolò, 129
piracy, 167, 171, 176, 183
Pixis, Johann, 176
Playford, John, 171
Pleyel, Ignaz, 45, 77, 156–57, 176, 183, 189, 221n.90
population: growth of, 27–28, 123; national, 121, 195–96, 217n.32, 221n.90; urban vs. rural, 22, 27, 135–36
privileges, exclusive, 171–74, 175, 187
productivity: economic, 28–29, 200, 203–4, 217n.38; musical compositions, 8, 74, 198, 224n.70, 225n.13
publication: costs, 161–66, 238n.17, 239 nn. 25 and 26; fees, 57, 185–88, 190–94, 243 nn. 143 and 146, 244n.178, 245 nn. 179–83; freedom to engage in, 93, 95, 168–70; leading firms, 155–57, 238n.12; technology, 155, 158–61, 238n.14

public relations and promotion, 112–15, 218n.51, 231n.183
Purcell, Henry, 38, 39, 41, 43

Quantz, Johann, 39, 95

radio, 35–37, 198–99, 219n.59
Radziwill, Prince Walenty, 113
Rahier, Peter von, 93
railroads, 16, 17, 145–47
Rameau, Jean-Philippe, 66, 76, 94, 167, 172
reductions, opera, 180
reformation, Protestant, 37–38, 155
Ricordi, Casa, 156
Ricordi, Giovanni, 115, 156, 166, 169, 179
Ricordi, Tito, 115, 179, 181, 183
Ries, Ferdinand, 176, 239n.28
Risks, 96–102, 183, 243n.143
Roger, Estienne, 157, 243n.143
Romani, Felice, 100
Rossini, Gioachino, 16, 85–86, 90, 99, 100, 104, 109, 113, 147, 169
Rothschild, James de, 113
Rousseau, Jean-Jacques, 16, 21–22, 77
Royal Academy of Music (conservatory), 67; (London opera), 4, 15, 41, 50–51, 62
Royal Society, 15, 21
Rudolph, Archduke of Austria, 65, 69, 77, 96
Russia, as music locale, 45, 130

Salieri, Antonio, 8, 64–65, 100, 101, 112, 152
Salomon, Johann Peter, 57–58
salons, as music venue, 44–45, 92, 96, 113
San Cassiano, Teatro (Venice), 15, 41, 42
Scarlatti, Domenico, 3, 39, 157
Schikaneder, Emanuel, 47
Schirmer Inc., 156
schools: music, 38, 66–67, 75–76, 83; primary and secondary, 122, 232n.12
Schott, Bernhard, 156
Schott, Franz, 86–87, 182
Schott Musikverlag, 156, 165, 185, 187
Schubert, Franz, 63, 68, 77, 87–88, 95, 99, 104, 112–13, 181, 182, 183–84, 187, 228n.106

Schumann, Clara Wieck, 4, 58, 65, 83, 91, 98, 110, 146, 227n.53
Schumann, Robert, 4–5, 76, 85, 152, 190–94, 226n.18; spending patterns, 208, 210–13; travel, 129–30, 144–45, 147, 152
Schwarzenberg, Prince, 40
Senefelder, Aloys, 160
Senesino (Francesco Bernardi), 97
servility vs. freedom, 92–96, 119, 134, 141, 197–98, 201
Seven Years War, 16, 19, 40
Silbermann, Andreas, 17
Silbermann, Gottfried, 17
Simrock, Fritz, 152, 161, 181, 183
Simrock, Nicolaus, 156, 189
skew distribution, 9, 106–7, 115, 215n.19, 224n.70
Smetana, Bedrich, 63, 66, 75, 85
Spohr, Ludwig, 176, 184
Stamitz, Johann, 54
Stanley, John, 77
stationers, Company of, 171, 174
status, social, 91–92
Steffani, Agostino, 77
Steiner, Sigmund Anton, 183
Stradivari, Antonio, 15
Strauss, Eduard, 75
Strauss, Johann, Jr., 17, 20, 48, 75, 100, 199
Strauss, Johann, Sr., 47, 75
St. Saëns, Camille, 54, 113, 147
subsidies, 55–56, 69, 200–201
superstars, 97–98, 151, 199
Swieten, Gottfried van, 26, 60, 110, 152, 153

Tallis, Thomas, 171
taste: changes in, 108–11; prevailing, 6, 121–22, 188–90, 199
Tchaikovsky, Pyotr, 17, 56, 89, 130, 146–47, 233n.29
teaching music, 63–67; fees, 64–65, 84, 225n.11, 226n.27; specialized schools, 66–67; trade-offs, 65
Telemann, Georg Philipp, 39, 44, 57, 59, 75, 94, 134, 172–73, 215n.8
Thirty Years War, 14, 15, 17–18, 117
Thomasschule (Leipzig), 44, 66, 75, 80
Three Tenors, 199
Tonkünstler-Sozietät, 44–45, 102

Torricella, Christoph, 180
Toscanini, Arturo, 37
travel: cost, 146–47, 150–53, 236n.20;
  modes, 142–46
Treaty of Utrecht, 15, 18
Treaty of Vienna, 16, 19
Treaty of Westphalia, 15, 18, 118, 173

Vanhal, Johann Baptist, 80
Vauxhall Gardens, 46, 47–48, 221n.97
Verdi, Giuseppe, 18, 90, 100, 103, 181,
  194; censorship, 27; and public taste, 7,
  111, 114–15; relations with publishers,
  166, 169, 179–80, 183; success of
  operas, 17, 52, 99
Viardot, Pauline, 152
Vienna, 44–45; Congress of, 47, 101; as
  magnet city, 47, 130, 134;   standards
  of living, 102–3
Viotti, Giovanni, 58, 77
Vittorio Emanuele II, King of Italy, 17, 18
Vivaldi, Antonio, 63, 69, 75, 111
Vogler, Abbé Georg Joseph, 69
Voltaire, François Marie Arouet, 15, 24,
  135, 217n.23

wages, English craftsmen, 12, 31, 104,
  208–9, 229n.136
Wagner, Cosima, ix
Wagner, Richard, ix, 17, 75; financial
  needs, 20, 56, 59, 63, 86–87, 180; rela-
  tions with publishers, 160–61, 182,
  184, 187, 188, 242n.104
Walsh, John, 167, 171, 172, 181,
  241n.73
wealth: composers', 103–6; distribution of
  31–32, 105–7, 230n.143
Weber, Carl Maria von, 92, 99, 102, 151,
  176, 189, 226n.37, 237n.45
Weber, Franz Anton von, 160
Weber, Fridolin, 239n.28
Wesley, Samuel, 77
White Mountain, battle of, 17
Widor, Charles-Marie, 76–77
William of Orange, 23
Winner's curse, 185

Zeller, Carl Friedrich, 77
Zimmermann's Coffee House (Leipzig), 3,
  44, 59
Zwingli, Huldreich, 37